REINHOLD NIEBUHR AND
CONTEMPORARY POLITICS

Reinhold Niebuhr and Contemporary Politics

God and Power

Edited by

RICHARD HARRIES AND STEPHEN PLATTEN

OXFORD
UNIVERSITY PRESS

OXFORD
UNIVERSITY PRESS

Great Clarendon Street, Oxford OX2 6DP

Oxford University Press is a department of the University of Oxford.
It furthers the University's objective of excellence in research, scholarship,
and education by publishing worldwide in

Oxford New York

Auckland Cape Town Dar es Salaam Hong Kong Karachi
Kuala Lumpur Madrid Melbourne Mexico City Nairobi
New Delhi Shanghai Taipei Toronto

With offices in

Argentina Austria Brazil Chile Czech Republic France Greece
Guatemala Hungary Italy Japan Poland Portugal Singapore
South Korea Switzerland Thailand Turkey Ukraine Vietnam

Oxford is a registered trade mark of Oxford University Press
in the UK and in certain other countries

Published in the United States
by Oxford University Press Inc., New York

British Library Cataloguing in Publication Data

Data available

Library of Congress Cataloging in Publication Data
Library of Congress Control Number: 2010922494

Typeset by SPI Publisher Services, Pondicherry, India
Printed in Great Britain
on acid-free paper by
MPG Books Group, Bodmin and King's Lynn

ISBN 978–0–19–957183–3

1 3 5 7 9 10 8 6 4 2

For
BARACK OBAMA
As he faces the challenges of wielding power under God
and in thanksgiving for the work of
REINHOLD NIEBUHR

Contents

Notes on Contributors

Nigel Biggar is Regius Professor of Moral and Pastoral Theology at the University of Oxford. A former president of the Society for the Study of Christian Ethics, Professor Biggar is author of *The Hastening that Waits: Karl Barth's Ethics* and co-editor of *Religious Voices in Public Places*.

John D. Carlson is Assistant Professor of Religious Studies at Arizona State University where he is also Associate Director of the Center for the Study of Religion and Conflict. He is co-editor of, and contributor to, *The Sacred and the Sovereign: Religion and International Politics* and *Religion and the Death Penalty: A Call for Reckoning*.

Kevin Carnahan is Visiting Assistant Professor of Religion at Hendrix College in Conway, Arkansas. He has also held positions at Southwestern College in Kansas and at United Theological Seminary in Dayton, Ohio. His essay 'Which Niebuhr? Whose Realism? Reinhold Niebuhr and the Struggle against Islamic Radicalism' was published in the journal *Political Theology*.

Wendy Dackson is a research fellow of the Oxford Centre for Ecclesiology and Practical Theology at Ripon College Cuddesdon and of the Oxford Centre for Christianity and Contemporary Culture, Regent's Park College. Her doctoral dissertation on the ecclesiology of Archbishop William Temple was published by Edward Mellen Press.

Jean Bethke Elshtain is the Laura Spelman Rockefeller Professor of Social and Political Ethics at the University of Chicago. She also holds the Leavey Chair in the Foundations of American Freedom at Georgetown University. She is the author of many books, including *Just War Against Terror: The Burden of American Power in a Violent World* and *Sovereignty: God, State, and Self* (the 2005–6 Gifford Lectures).

Richard Harries was Bishop of Oxford from 1987 to 2006. On his retirement he was made a life peer (Lord Harries of Pentregarth) and he remains active in the House of Lords. He is Gresham Professor of Divinity and an honorary professor of theology at King's College, London. The author of some twenty-five books, most recently *The Re-enchantment of Morality: Wisdom for a Troubled World, Faith in Politics? Rediscovering the Christian Roots of our Political Values*, and *Questions of Life and Death*, he edited the 1986 collection *Reinhold Niebuhr and the Issues of our Time*.

Anatol Lieven is Chair of International Relations and Terrorism Studies at King's College London and a senior fellow of the New America Foundation in Washington, DC. He spent most of his career as a British journalist in South Asia and the former Soviet Union, and is author of several books on the latter region, including *Chechnya: Tombstone of Russian Power?* His latest book, co-authored with John Hulsman, is *Ethical Realism: A Vision for America's Role in the World*.

Robin W. Lovin is Cary Maguire University Professor of Ethics at Southern Methodist University in Dallas, Texas. He has also held positions at Drew University, Emory University, and the University of Chicago. His writings include *Christian Faith and Public Choices: The Social Ethics of Barth, Brunner, and Bonhoeffer, Reinhold Niebuhr and Christian Realism*, and *Christian Realism and the New Realities*.

Ian Markham is the Dean and President of Virginia Theological Seminary. He is also the Visiting Professor of Globalization, Ethics, and Islam at Leeds Metropolitan University. He is the author and editor of many books including *Plurality and Christian Ethics, Truth and the Reality of God*, and *Theology of Engagement*.

Wilfred M. McClay is SunTrust Bank Chair of Excellence in Humanities at the University of Tennessee at Chattanooga where he is also Professor of History. He is author of, among other works, *The Masterless: Self and Society in Modern America*, which won the Merle Curti Award of the Organization of American Historians. He spent the 2009–10 academic year in residence at the School of Public Policy, Pepperdine University, Malibu, California, as the Simon Distinguished Visiting Professor.

Mac McCorkle is President of McCorkle Policy Consulting in Chapel Hill, North Carolina. He has contributed to a number of scholarly publications. Most recently he co-authored with Congressman David Price the essay 'Wilson Carey McWilliams and Communitarianism' in Bathory and Schwartz (eds.), *Friends and Citizens: Essays in Honor of Wilson Carey McWilliams*.

Martyn Percy is Principal of Ripon College Cuddesdon. He is also Honorary Professor of Theological Education at King's College London and Canon Theologian of Sheffield Cathedral. He is a regular contributor to the *Guardian*, Radio 4, the World Service, and other media. His recent books include *Clergy: The Origin of Species* and *Engaging Contemporary Culture: Christianity and the Concrete Church*.

Stephen Platten is Bishop of Wakefield; Wakefield Diocese covers a significant part of West and South Yorkshire in England. He has taught theology for both college and other courses and is Chairman of the Church of England's Liturgical Commission. He has written a number of books including *Rebuilding Jerusalem, Vocation: Singing the Lord's Song* and, jointly with George Pattison, *Spirit and Tradition: An Essay on Change.*

Ben Quash is the first Professor of Christianity and the Arts to be appointed at King's College London. From 2004 to 2007 he was also Academic Convenor of the Cambridge Inter-Faith Programme in the University of Cambridge's Faculty of Divinity, developing research and public education programmes in Judaism, Christianity, and Islam, and their interrelations.

Samuel Wells is Dean of the Chapel at Duke University and Research Professor of Christian Ethics at Duke Divinity School. He has written several books on theological ethics, including *Transforming Fate into Destiny.* His book *Power and Passion: Six Characters in Search of Resurrection* was the Archbishop of Canterbury's 2007 Lent book.

Introduction

Richard Harries

Barack Obama, somewhat fatigued, was being interviewed yet again when out of the blue he was asked 'Have you ever read Reinhold Niebuhr?' Obama's tone changed. 'I love him. He's one of my favourite philosophers.' When asked what he took away from Niebuhr, he answered in a rush of words:

I take away the compelling idea that there's serious evil in the world, and hardship and pain. And we should be humble and modest in our belief we can eliminate those things. But we shouldn't use that as an excuse for cynicism and inaction. I take away... the sense we have to make these efforts knowing they are hard, and not swinging from naïve idealism to bitter realism.[1]

For a tired man moving rapidly from one event to another, that is a brilliant summary of the heart of Niebuhr's approach to politics.

Barak Obama is simply the latest in a long line of senior politicians and distinguished political theorists who have been influenced by Niebuhr. In Great Britain, to take just one example, Dennis Healey had in the 1930s been a member of the Communist Party. When he left he retained a strong moral vision and a desire to change society for the better without losing his grasp of the economic realities of life that Marxism had provided. He, and many others, found in Niebuhr an understanding of humanity and society and a structure of thought in which moral vision and a tough realism could be held together. As Healey has written:

The years I spent in the wartime army deepened my interest in the spiritual side of reality. After the war I was much impressed by Christian theologians such as Reinhold Niebuhr and Nicolas Berdjaev. They confirmed my belief in democratic socialism and rooted it firmly in realism about human nature and society—though they did not persuade me to believe in a personal God![2]

---

[1] David Brooks, *New York Times*, 27 Apr. 2007.
[2] Letter to Richard Harries, 14 Oct. 2006.

For obvious reasons the influence of Niebuhr in the United States has been even more pronounced. Jimmy Carter kept a collection of Niebuhr's writings by his bedside, calling it his 'political bible' and many other major political figures like Adlai Stevenson and Hubert Humphrey have acknowledged his influence. 'Niebuhr is the father of us all', said George Kennan whilst Hans Morgenthau, himself a respected political philosopher, wrote: 'I have always considered Reinhold Niebuhr the greatest living political philosopher in America.'

In the early stages of his ministry Niebuhr published *Leaves from the Notebook of a Tamed Cynic*,[3] reflecting his experience in the growing industrial city of Detroit from 1915 to 1928. The jottings in the notebook reveal an unblinkered awareness of the realities of life both in himself and in the people around him. This realism never left him and sometimes people found it difficult to reconcile with their understanding of the Christian faith. It is noteworthy that in the 1930s SCM Press (noted for their liberal publishing policy) refused to publish *Moral Man and Immoral Society*, on the grounds that they thought it was not a Christian book.

But this realism, if sometimes steely, was neither brutal nor cynical. The title says it all. Niebuhr saw himself as a *tamed* cynic, and one crucial element of his thinking was designed to stop people simply being content with realism or, worse, slipping over from realism into cynicism. It is not surprising therefore that with this deliberate tension in Niebuhr's thought he has been claimed by different groups for their own purposes. In the 1980s, for example, the New Right looked to him as a progenitor, ignoring the strong social vision that Niebuhr never repudiated or lost.[4] It is important to keep *An Interpretation of Christian Ethics* in view when interpreting Niebuhr, even though Niebuhr ostensibly set it aside, for, combined with his realism, it sets out Niebuhr's prophetic Christian vision.

In recent years in particular Niebuhr has been differently interpreted and Robin Lovin (Chapter 1) begins by setting him in historical perspective. Whilst very appreciative of his approach, he suggests that Niebuhr underestimated the power latent in the hopes and dreams of the oppressed, and therefore had a too limited view of what might be possible. The result was that he was too cautious at first both about the civil rights movement and about the folly of American involvement in Vietnam. However, he defends Niebuhr against the criticism of Hauerwas that he was totally blind to the way he shared the assumptions of his time and suggests that an ethic of responsibility

[3] Reinhold Niebuhr, *Leaves from the Notebook of a Tamed Cynic* (New York: Meridian, 1957).
[4] 'The new Right attitude is "unnuanced" ... in a way quite foreign to Niebuhr's thought' (Ronald Preston, 'Reinhold Niebuhr and the New Right', in Richard Harries (ed.), *Reinhold Niebuhr and the Issues of our Time* (London: Mowbray, 1986), 102).

can still serve us well. Mac McCorkle (Chapter 2) also looks at how Niebuhr has been variously interpreted and in his chapter shows up the falsity of a number of stereotypical readings.

A conference on Niebuhr was held in London in 1984, followed by a book of essays on him in relation to the issues of that time because it was felt that his theological insights into political realities were much needed and were not receiving proper attention. That was even more true at the height of the influence of the Christian right on the Bush administration and it provoked Arthur Schlesinger, one of the distinguished figures in America much influence by Niebuhr,[5] to write a major article for the *New York Times* which was headlined 'Forgetting Reinhold Niebuhr: Why has the supreme American theologian of the 20th century dropped out of our religious discourse?'[6] As well as setting out the main tenets of Niebuhr's thinking and its influence in America in his lifetime, he lamented the fact that not just the religious right, but Christian liberals at that time were ignoring Niebuhr, much to the detriment of their thought. Schlesinger wrote: 'Maybe Niebuhr has fallen out of fashion because 9/11 has revived the myth of our national innocence. . . . Niebuhr was a critic of national innocence, which he regarded as a delusion.'

In fact a Niebuhrian revival was just about beginning at that time, as McCorkle shows. It is in the conviction that this revival is very much needed, and that Niebuhr's thought is still applicable to a whole range of contemporary modern political dilemmas, that this present book has been written. It is both interesting and revealing that Niebuhr's *The Irony of American History*[7] has just been reprinted, with an introduction by Andrew J. Bacevich which calls it 'the most important book ever written on US foreign policy'.

Niebuhr's approach to political and economic issues was rooted in a carefully thought through Christian understanding of human beings in society. This foundational element in his thought is explored and evaluated by Jean Elsthain (Chapter 3). However, in recent years there has been some strong criticism of Niebuhr from people who believe this foundational position is deeply flawed, and who think that as a result Niebuhr has a wrong understanding of the relationship between the Christian community and the wider society in which it is set. Such criticisms are particularly associated with Stanley Hauerwas and John Milbank and we thought it important that they should be reflected in this book and evaluated. The essays by Ben Quash

---

[5] Arthur Schlesinger promised to write about the influence Niebuhr had on his own thought for this volume, but sadly he died before being able to do so.

[6] Arthur Schlesinger, *New York Times*, 18 Sept. 2005.

[7] Reinhold Niebuhr, *The Irony of American History* (Chicago: University of Chicago Press, 2008). Review by Brian Urquart in the *New York Review of Books*, 26 Mar. 2009.

(Chapter 4) and Samuel Wells (Chapter 5), who are in part sympathetic to such criticisms of Niebuhr, provide this element.

Other criticisms of Niebuhr include the fact that his ecclesiology is either non-existent or thin, and he has virtually nothing to say about Christian liturgy and its relationship to his political stance. The first subject is considered by Wendy Dackson (Chapter 6), who suggests that what Niebuhr had was an outsider's view of the church, and that this might be particularly useful for us today, if we can build on its implications by taking seriously the humility such a perspective presupposes. Stephen Platten (Chapter 7) argues that it is a mistake to understand liturgy as being enacted in a place of withdrawal from society. Liturgy is a public event with a relationship to public life. If this is understood it ought to be possible to have a much more integral relationship between the kind of political theology represented by Niebuhr and liturgy as performative and transformational for society as a whole.

One of the fundamental features of Niebuhr's political theology was the importance he placed on the concept of sin, not least in its corporate aspect. In our time, however, the concept of sin, at least in Europe, has virtually disappeared from discourse. Martyn Percy (Chapter 8) argues that the a concept of sin is still vital for a true understanding of human beings in society, and suggests a way in which sense can be made of it for our time.

The concept of Christian hope was also important for Niebuhr, but Ian Markham (Chapter 9) rightly distinguishes this from all forms of utopianism about which Niebuhr was highly critical. He argues that the neo-conservative years were driven by a utopian hope that the years of 'boom and bust' were ended for ever. This has now been exposed for the folly it was. At the same time we must beware of developing utopian hopes about what state action can achieve in this time of crisis. Christian hope urges us to work for a better world, but always with an awareness of our limitation and fallibility as human beings.

One of the major themes in this book is the relationship between the radical teaching of Jesus and the brutal political realities of the world in which we live. Nigel Biggar (Chapter 10) considers this in relation to the tension that is felt between the call to forgive and the demands of justice. Whilst appreciating Niebuhr he believes that by careful analysis of the nature of forgiveness, it is possible to go further than Niebuhr in bringing forgiveness and justice together.

Richard Harries (Chapter 11) considers Niebuhr's defense of liberal democracy and argues that he did not give a firm enough theological foundation to the first part of his famous aphorism, namely that 'Man's capacity for justice makes democracy possible.' He then considers the criticism of Oliver O'Donovan who, whilst regarding democracy as good for our own society rejects the idea that it is of universal validity and applicability. Harries suggests to the contrary, that whilst rejecting any hint of imperialism, there are elements within liberal democracy that are fundamental to a Christian view of every society.

Anatol Lieven (Chapter 12) considers the tension between realists and progressives in American policy and argues that Niebuhr's approach is still needed to avoid a triumphalist moralism on the one hand, and an inadequate realism on the other. John D. Carlson (Chapter 13) considers the issues in relation to humanitarian interventions, arguing that moral compassion without a sense of the political realities can be disastrous. He also looks at Niebuhr's ethical realism in relation to the Just War tradition as represented for example by Paul Ramsey.

During George W. Bush's administration the religious right was a dominant influence. At the same time, other evangelicals have been critical of this identification of evangelicalism with the Republican cause and have called for a stronger social message based on the Gospel. Kevin Carnahan (Chapter 14) considers this development and argues that to be effective this brand of evangelicalism must take on board both Niebuhr's criticism of the evangelicals of his time and some of his abiding insights about the application of the Christian faith to public affairs.

One of the most pressing challenges of our time is how different religions can live peacefully together. Wilfred M. McClay (Chapter 15) explores the contribution that Niebuhr's fundamental approach to conflict might make to this and identifies some insights which seem both illuminating and potentially helpful to the issue. However, as he shows, the basis of Niebuhr's approach to pluralism is in fact deeply rooted in assumptions that belong to the Western Christian tradition: one is the conviction about the universality of original sin; the other is the imperative towards progress, albeit on Niebuhr's highly qualified form of understanding of such progress. This poses, in an acute way, the question of whether Niebuhr's basis for a fruitful pluralism can in fact exist without those religious assumptions, and even more somberly, whether religious pluralism is even possible.

It seems appropriate that this note, in the final contribution, should be somber and salutary, forcing us, in true Niebuhrian mode, to think more critically about our own tradition and draw more deeply from the wells of Christian faith. It is the hope of the editors of this book that these chapters will help us do this.

Richard Harries
London, 2009

1

Reinhold Niebuhr in Historical Perspective

Robin W. Lovin

In 1932, Reinhold Niebuhr made his reputation as a fierce critic of American Protestant liberalism. In *Moral Man and Immoral Society*, he subjected the work of his immediate predecessors to withering social and economic analysis and dismissed the hopes cherished by a generation of Social Gospel reformers as sentimental illusions, unsupported either by social reality or by genuine theology.[1] Later, he came to a more moderate position, appreciative of the contributions of those who had gone before him, but still clear that they were so closely tied to a modern understanding of historical progress that they could not identify the points where biblical faith parts company with it. In a 1958 article titled 'Walter Rauschenbusch in Historical Perspective', he shows how the leading theologian of the Social Gospel accommodated the Christian doctrine of original sin to the historical materialist's notion that individual ideas and actions are the product of social structures. But he also acknowledges that it is difficult to transcend the assumptions of one's time, and he even recognizes that some of his own early criticisms were rooted in the same assumptions that shaped Rauschenbusch's work.[2] Rauschenbusch saw historical progress beyond the present social crisis. Niebuhr expected a social catastrophe that would be the necessary prelude to social reconstruction. But both of them shared the modern assumption that the meaning of history is available to those who live in it. There was more continuity between the

---

[1] Reinhold Niebuhr, *Moral Man and Immoral Society: A Study in Ethics and Politics* (Louisville: Westminster John Knox Press, 2001). See especially 68–72. *Moral Man and Immoral Society* was first published in 1932.

[2] Reinhold Niebuhr, 'Walter Rauschenbusch in Historical Perspective', in *Faith and Politics*, ed. Ronald Stone (New York: George Braziller, 1968), 40. This essay originally appeared in Reinhold Niebuhr, 'Walter Rauschenbusch in Historical Perspective', *Religion in Life*, 27 (Autumn 1958), 527–36.

liberals and their critics than the critics could see at the time, Niebuhr concludes.

Niebuhr might appreciate the irony that his own work was judged harshly by a younger generation that followed him in the pulpit, political activism, and the seminary classroom. Some of the criticism began in the late 1960s, when the rapid pace of change made Niebuhr's earlier caution about legal challenges to racial segregation seem like an apology for the status quo. Similar criticisms followed as feminist writers noted the conventional assumptions about gender roles in his writings and suggested that even his characteristic emphasis on the sin of pride assumed that the important moral failings and temptations are those faced by men in positions of power.[3] A second wave of criticisms pronounced Niebuhr's work theologically unsatisfactory. His willingness to compromise, to accept the lesser of two evils as measured by some secular, consequentialist standard reveals an indifference to the radical demand of the Gospel. As Stanley Hauerwas puts it, Christians are called to be faithful, not effective. 'Christians are engaged in politics, but it is a politics of the kingdom that reveals the insufficiency of all politics based on coercion and falsehood and finds the true source of power in servanthood rather than dominion.'[4]

The terms in which Niebuhr is criticized sound curiously like his own judgments on Protestant liberalism. Indeed, from this new perspective, Niebuhr tends to disappear into the liberal background. The decisive moment that signals the arrival of a newer and truer theology is shifted to some other time—the emergence of liberation movements in the 1970s. Renewal is found in some other place—the Barthian theology of the Word, rather than the residual liberalism of Niebuhrian realism. In the hands of these critics, Niebuhr's work is not so much discarded as it is rendered obsolete by its entanglements with secular values that no longer claim the attention of serious Christians. Stanley Hauerwas pronounces the judgment: 'Niebuhr's work now represents the worst of two worlds: most secular people do not find his arguments convincing; yet his theology is not sufficient to provide the

---

[3] On Niebuhr and the civil rights movement, see Herbert O. Edwards, 'Racism and Christian Ethics in America', *Katallagete* (Winter 1971), 15–24; and Charles Marsh, *The Beloved Community: How Faith Shapes Social Justice from the Civil Rights Movement to Today* (New York: Basic Books, 2005), 39–41. For the feminist critique, see Valerie Saiving Goldstein, 'The Human Situation: A Feminine View', *Journal of Religion* 40 (April 1960), 100–12; Daphne Hampson, 'Reinhold Niebuhr on Sin: A Critique', in Richard Harries (ed.), *Reinhold Niebuhr and the Issues of Our Time* (Grand Rapids: Eerdmans, 1986), 46–60.

[4] Stanley Hauerwas, *The Peaceable Kingdom* (Notre Dame, IN: University of Notre Dame Press, 1983), 102.

means for Christians to sustain their lives... Niebuhr's theology reflects the loss of truthful Christian speech and, hence, of faithful Christian practice.'[5]

It would be a mistake to count Niebuhr out, however, especially among 'secular people' who increasingly find his assessment of the limits of power and his arguments for self-restraint newly relevant to global politics in the post-Cold War era.[6] Even some of Niebuhr's theological critics now make use of his critique of the quasi-religious claims of imperial powers, and with the passage of time, we see his imprint more clearly on all the ways in which religious thinkers have understood the relations between faith and politics.[7]

Perhaps, then, it is time to put Reinhold Niebuhr in historical perspective, in the same way that Niebuhr himself arrived at a more balanced appreciation of Walter Rauschenbusch and the generation that brought American Protestantism through the years of 'social crisis' and the First World War. By this, I do not mean that we should seek some sort of neutral standpoint from which to locate Niebuhr objectively and permanently in relation to the flow of historical and theological change. I intend, rather, to treat Niebuhr's work with the same sort of Christian realism that he himself eventually applied to Rauschenbusch and the Social Gospel. What follows, then, is a Niebuhrian view of Niebuhr and his critics which seeks to recognize both continuity and difference and to further our own reflections on what it means to be realistic about our place in history.

HOPE

Feminist and liberation theologians questioned whether Niebuhr's 'Christian realism' could be realistic enough, given his entanglements with the centers of political and economic power in the Cold War years. Niebuhr's commitments to American democracy were never uncritical, but he tended to accept the social limitations placed on women and legalized discrimination against African Americans as lesser evils when compared to the general loss of freedom in totalitarian systems. Even when he opposed the more egregious

[5] Stanley Hauerwas, *With the Grain of the Universe* (Grand Rapids, MI: Brazos Press, 2001), 139–40.

[6] See especially Anatol Lieven and John Hulsman, *Ethical Realism* (New York: Pantheon Books, 2006); Andrew Bacevich, *The Limits of Power: The End of American Exceptionalism* (New York: Metropolitan Books, 2008). Bacevich has also provided a new introduction to Reinhold Niebuhr, *The Irony of American History* (Chicago: University of Chicago Press, 2008).

[7] Robin Lovin, *Christian Realism and the New Realities* (Cambridge: Cambridge University Press, 2008), 19–42.

forms of discrimination, his concern for order made him reluctant to move vigorously against them. His views on gender and the role of women remained grounded in the physical differences that structure relationships in heterosexual families.[8] His enthusiasm for the end of legalized racial segregation was tempered by a fear that massive resistance by white Southern culture would wipe out the incremental gains that could be made in Federal courts and the Congress, or that impatient African Americans and idealistic whites would demand too much, too fast, producing a reaction that would actually slow progress.[9]

Niebuhr's critics concluded that he lacked the capacity to see the world through the eyes of the oppressed. As a result, his realism about the possibilities and limits of change reinforced the existing structures of power. In historical perspective, we must acknowledge that these critics were right in important ways. Because they were involved in local, grass-roots movements where political identities are formed and new ideas gain strength, the critics saw something that Niebuhr did not see, even when it was happening in Harlem, a short distance from his home at Union Theological Seminary.[10] Niebuhr neglected such movements in his assessments of power, but they proved decisive in setting the pace of change, first in the Civil Rights Movement in the United States, then in ending apartheid in South Africa, and finally in toppling Communist regimes in Eastern Europe.

Today's Niebuhrian realists have to take this failure of Niebuhr's realism into account. We may hesitate to affirm a 'hermeneutical privilege of the oppressed' that accepts their view of reality uncritically, but in a realistic assessment of the possibilities for change, the hopes and aspirations of people in their local communities, churches, and cultures have to figure in the calculation. Barack Obama's rapid rise from community organizer to the presidency is one indication of why a new kind of Niebuhrian realism needs to take account of these resources. Established systems of power have an obvious role in shaping events, but shared hope is not a negligible force in social life, especially when that hope is articulated by someone who has shared direct experience with the people who hold it. Hope is not the naive optimism for which Niebuhr criticized his liberal Protestant contemporaries. Hope is closer to the 'essential freedom' that must be recognized by any lasting

[8] Reinhold Niebuhr, *Faith and History: A Comparison of Christian and Modern Views of History* (New York: Scribner's, 1949), 75.

[9] See, for example, Reinhold Niebuhr, 'The Effect of the Supreme Court Decision', *Christianity and Crisis* 17 (4 Feb. 1957), 3; 'Civil Rights and Democracy', *Christianity and Crisis* 17 (8 Jul. 1957), 88.

[10] See Traci C. West, *Disruptive Christian Ethics: When Racism and Women's Lives Matter* (Louisville: Westminster John Knox Press, 2006), 3–35.

political system.[11] The freedoms protected by law in a stable democracy are less the results of politics than its preconditions. Human beings are capable of imagining other possibilities, no matter how limited their actual choices may be. They dream of other things in songs and prayers, in the lives they want for their children, and in the words they want to say to their neighbors and to those in authority, long before the law tells them what they may or may not do.

Niebuhr's fully developed argument for democracy rests on the way that this freedom of consciousness requires political freedom.[12] It is one of the points at which his political thought recognizes constraints that are very much like requirements of natural law. No police power can repress all talk of change, just as no ideology can render a different order of things unthinkable. Over the long run, that is part of what makes democracy more stable and more adaptable than the totalitarian systems that seem at first to exercise a tighter control over people and events. Totalitarian politics flies in the face of the realities of human nature.

Niebuhr spoke of 'essential freedom'. He might also have spoken of 'hope', although he rarely did so.[13] Even people without knowledge or power know that the system that oppresses them is not as permanent as it pretends to be. No one can impose a direction on us and call it necessary, or demand that we accept it as inevitable. People do not arrive at hope by a careful calculation of their political chances. They maintain hope against the odds, even when totalitarian constraints seem for the moment to be successful. This irrepressible hope is unsettling for those who prefer the way that things happen to be going now, but it is empowering for those who seek conditions of life more suited to their sense of their own dignity and possibilities.

Niebuhr thus had the resources for an account of hope that affirms the aspirations of ordinary people and their ability to change their surroundings, despite the forces that give prevailing social arrangements a sense of permanence, even rightness, that is difficult to overcome. That is why community organizers and grassroots movements for change have drawn heavily on Niebuhr's thought in recent years,[14] although Niebuhr himself had doubts

---

[11] Reinhold Niebuhr, 'Freedom', in *Faith and Politics*, 81. See also Reinhold Niebuhr, *The Children of Light and the Children of Darkness: A Vindication of Democracy and a Critique of Its Traditional Defence* (New York: Scribner's, 1972), 3.

[12] See Robin W. Lovin, *Reinhold Niebuhr and Christian Realism* (Cambridge: Cambridge University Press, 1995), 123–8.

[13] A more extensive study of these possibilities is found in John K. Burk, 'The Foundation of Hope: An Examination of Christian Realism as the Basis for Hope in the Thought of Reinhold Niebuhr' (Ph.D. diss., University of Edinburgh, 2008), 151–87.

[14] See Mary Beth Rogers, *Cold Anger: A Story of Faith and Power Politics* (Denton, TX: University of North Texas Press, 1990), 69–78.

about the prospects for some movements for peace and racial justice that were active during the last two decades of his life.

His political realism perhaps made him hesitant to rely too much on this hope, for while freedom is essential, its triumph is not inevitable. Power cannot control the sources of hope, but hope cannot overcome oppression without acquiring some countervailing power. Niebuhr was clear about that point already in *Moral Man and Immoral Society*, and his insistence on it provided important guidance to Martin Luther King, Jr., as he began his non-violent campaign for civil rights in the American South.[15]

By the time King had studied and adapted *Moral Man and Immoral Society*, however, Niebuhr was less confident in the direction of historical change and more clear that the meaning of history lies in a judgment beyond history. Niebuhr continued to believe in the strategic value of his ideas about power, but he now set them in the context of a divine reality that transcends our strategies and evaluations. As Langdon Gilkey put it,

Unless the meaning of life in the midst of its passage is perfectly clear and fully secure—and [Niebuhr] has surely shown that it is not—then the presence of the power and mercy of God at the Beginning and at the End, to complete what we cannot complete and purge what we have corrupted, are the sole grounds for any real hope.[16]

Niebuhr's conviction that the judgment of God lies beyond history protects those who risk change from despair when their hopes are disappointed. But it makes a Christian realist more cautious about the calculation of political forces than a liberal Protestant who shares the modern conviction that the direction of history is determined and can be known. It was not just the conservatism of old age that made Niebuhr cautious. It was the wariness of one who knows that history can move backward as well as forward. A movement for change that sparks massive resistance may be crushed, and the hope that seemed within reach may then be lost for decades.

Niebuhr's caution at these points can seem like pure consequentialism, ready to acquiesce in injustice if that seems the lesser evil. This is particularly true when we know in hindsight that the risks run by Freedom Riders in Mississippi, Anti-Apartheid marchers in South Africa, and the citizens of Prague, Warsaw, and Leipzig produced changes out of all proportion to a political realist's reasonable expectations. The problem with consequentialism is that the results of a new strategy, applied on a large scale, are impossible to

---

[15] Martin Luther King, Jr., 'Letter from Birmingham City Jail', in *A Testament of Hope: The Essential Writings and Speeches of Martin Luther King, Jr.*, ed. James M. Washington (San Francisco: Harper San Francisco, 1991), 292.

[16] Langdon Gilkey, *On Niebuhr: A Theological Study* (Chicago: University of Chicago Press, 2001), 222.

predict. Niebuhr was no better at those predictions than anyone else. His realism was most effective in analyzing the constraints on decisions from the perspective of those who have to make them, avoiding temptations to claim too much mastery of events, with too much certainty about one's own virtue and too little imagination for how the situation looks to one's adversaries. He could think his way into the situation of politicians and diplomats after the Second World War, but age and ill health gave him too little time in church basements with civil rights leaders and community organizers, where he might have seen for himself the power of hope that today's Niebuhrian realists have to take more seriously.[17]

The first group of Niebuhr's critics thus leaves us with the suggestion that his ethical analysis is detached from the situation of the poor and marginalized, too distant to understand the power of hope in a concrete situation. This may have been partly the result of age and experience, but it owes something, too, to the development of his theological thinking, which comes to place more emphasis on God's judgment beyond history than on the ambiguous moral directions within the movements of history. This avoids despair, but Niebuhr's critics appropriately ask whether it is sufficient to sustain real hope.

JUDGMENT

By contrast, a second group of critics argues that Niebuhr is entirely too closely tied to his own time and place. Their complaint is the opposite of the feminist and liberation critics. They argue that Niebuhr lacks the theological distance required to proclaim an authentic word of judgment.

Stanley Hauerwas is perhaps the most prominent of these critics, and he has made the most extended effort to understand Niebuhr on Niebuhr's own terms before launching his critique.[18] For Hauerwas, the key to understanding Niebuhr is the pragmatic understanding of religion, which he first explored in a B.D. thesis on William James. According to Hauerwas, James' account of religious experience remained central to Niebuhr's thought for the rest of his career. In James' understanding of religion, God is limited by the bounds of experience that all persons share. There is no place for a Word that breaks into our experience and disrupts its unity and order. Niebuhr's

---

[17] See Reinhold Niebuhr, 'A View of Life from the Sidelines', in *The Essential Reinhold Niebuhr*, ed. Robert M. Brown (New Haven: Yale University Press, 1986), 250–7.
[18] Hauerwas, *With the Grain of the Universe*, 87–140.

theology, Hauerwas argues, is thus reduced to saying what everyone needs to believe to make sense of experience. 'It appears that for Niebuhr, God is nothing more than the name of our need to believe that life has an ultimate unity that transcends the world's chaos and makes possible what we can achieve in this life.'[19] A pragmatist's theology is necessarily confined to what everyone already believes, at least implicitly. By contrast, the central affirmations of Christian theology 'cannot help but appear a "confessional" assertion that is unintelligible to anyone who is not already a Christian.'[20] Niebuhr's work thus enjoys an immediate resonance with the culture to which it is first delivered, but it loses power and influence as that cultural context becomes more distant.

Because we are trying to understand Reinhold Niebuhr in historical perspective, it should give us pause that Hauerwas' criticism of Niebuhr is very similar to the one Niebuhr levels at Rauschenbusch, whose work, he says, 'proves how vulnerable we are to the illusions of our generation.'[21] In historical perspective, it seems, each generation seeks a theology that escapes the limits of history and culture, and their successors always say they failed to find it. But Niebuhr lived long enough to recognize this pattern, and he tried not simply to repeat it.

During the 1930s, Niebuhr moved rapidly through three ways of thinking about the meaning of historical events that carried him a considerable distance beyond the pragmatism that he had studied at Yale. First, at the beginning of the decade, he thought that the economic depression and political unrest that spread around the globe after the First World War were manifestations of deeper historical forces that were bringing bourgeois civilization to an end. The theologian's task was to face up to these hard realities and dispense with the sentimental illusions of liberalism. That was the message of *Moral Man and Immoral Society* and, even more, of *Reflections on the End of an Era.*[22]

His quest for understanding moved on quite quickly to a second, different objective. What was needed was not a way of understanding events from within, but a place to stand apart from them. So he turned with a new seriousness to theology, in search of 'an independent Christian ethic' that would provide a basis for choice and action uncompromised by Protestant liberalism and more relevant to modern life than Protestant orthodoxy.[23] *An*

---

[19] Ibid. 131.   [20] Ibid. 15.
[21] Niebuhr, 'Walter Rauschenbusch in Historical Perspective', 42.
[22] Reinhold Niebuhr, *Reflections on the End of an Era* (New York: Scribner's, 1934).
[23] Reinhold Niebuhr, *An Interpretation of Christian Ethics* (New York: Seabury Press, 1979), 1–3. *An Interpretation of Christian Ethics* was first published in 1935.

Interpretation of Christian Ethics worked this out in great detail, arguing that the ethics of Jesus transcends all ordinary moral choices and yet remains relevant as an 'impossible ideal'.[24] We are able to understand what justice is, and even in some measure to do it, by reference to a divine standard which transcends the world's chaos, in which competing interests are ultimately reconciled. Or, to put the matter more precisely, we are able to understand ethics only in light of Jesus' ability to see the world wholly in light of that ultimate judgment. The author of *An Interpretation of Christian Ethics*, who declares that 'obligation can be felt only to some system of coherence and some ordering will',[25] still sounds like the pragmatist Hauerwas criticizes in *With the Grain of the Universe*, but he is now seeking his coherences in a prophetic faith that supplies what human experience of the moral life cannot. In that, he also sounds like Hauerwas in his search for an independent Christian ethic.

That quixotic idealism did not last long. To understand Niebuhr's final assessment of Walter Rauschenbusch and of his own early writings, it is essential to see a third change, as his thinking developed from *An Interpretation of Christian Ethics* to the Gifford Lectures of 1939–40.[26] Niebuhr comes to see that the aspiration for an independent Christian ethic is theologically unsatisfactory when it leads us to think that we can participate in God's judgments on particular events, even by way of approximation. Human freedom gives us the capacity to make history, but not to escape from it. This duality of finitude and freedom, which Christianity understands better than any of the ancient or modern alternatives, preserves a meaningful moral life, but does not allow us to complete it. Indeed, it is our efforts at premature completion that fall most directly under divine judgment.

The Christian faith affirms that the same Christ who discloses the sovereignty of God over history is also the perfect norm of human nature... As the revelation of the paradoxical relation of the divine justice and mercy, He discloses the ultimate mystery of the relation of the divine to history. This revelation clarifies the meaning of history; for the judgment of God preserves the distinction of good and evil in history; and the mercy of God finally overcomes the sinful corruption in which man is involved at

[24] Reinhold Niebuhr, *An Interpretation of Christian Ethics* (New York: Seabury Press, 1979) 62–83.

[25] Ibid. 63.

[26] Much later, Niebuhr summarily dismissed *An Interpretation of Christian Ethics* as the product of an early period in his thinking about Christian ethics that he no longer wished to defend. See Reinhold Niebuhr, 'Reply to Interpretation and Criticism', in Charles W. Kegley and Robert W. Bretall (eds.), *Reinhold Niebuhr: His Religious, Social, and Political Thought* (New York: Macmillan, 1956), 434–5. The Gifford Lectures were first published in 1941 and 1943 as Reinhold Niebuhr, *The Nature and Destiny of Man*, 2 vols. (Louisville: Westminster John Knox Press, 1996).

every level of moral achievement by reason of his false and abortive efforts to complete his own life and history.[27]

The resolution of history's conflicts can only be known from a point which lies outside history and which is, to that extent, beyond reason as well. God's judgment stands beyond the inadequacies and contradictions in our judgments, and there is no formula by which the distance between them can be measured to calibrate our response. God's judgment is eschatological, not dialectical.[28]

It is important not to be misled at this point by criticisms of Niebuhr's earlier theology, which located God more clearly within the boundaries of human experience and the comprehension of human reason. Niebuhr is at one here with Karl Barth and other theological contemporaries, who sought to place God beyond the reach of political ideologies that would claim the right to remake history in their own image. Like Barth, Niebuhr will allow no appeal to our own reason or our own righteousness to justify our choices in ultimate terms. We are completely dependent on God's mercy to 'complete what we cannot complete and purge what we have corrupted', as Gilkey puts it.[29]

To summarize the development of Niebuhr's thinking, then, he continues to believe that the meaning of history lies beyond history, not within it. But he no longer thinks, as he did briefly around the time of *An Interpretation of Christian Ethics*, that the judgment that gives meaning to history provides us with the starting point for an independent Christian ethic. Indeed, he now questions whether such independence of our contemporaries, our circumstances, and the thinking of those who have gone before us is possible.

RESPONSIBILITY

It is at this point that Niebuhr returns to pragmatism, not as a way to locate God in human experience, but as a way to handle the specifically human choices that must not be confused with divine judgments. It is this return to politics that distinguishes Niebuhr from Barth, without diminishing the theological emphasis on divine judgment that the two share.

Pragmatism now takes the form of 'responsibility', an idea that became increasingly important to Niebuhr and to ecumenical social ethics in the years

[27] Niebuhr, *Nature and Destiny*, II.68.
[28] Ibid. 2. See Gilkey, *On Niebuhr*, 213–22.
[29] Gilkey, *On Niebuhr*, 222. See p. 1. See also Reinhold Niebuhr, *The Irony of American History* (Chicago: University of Chicago Press, 2008), 63.

after the Second World War.[30] Responsibility involves us in judgments that can only be made in light of particular circumstances and social relationships. Awareness of God's ultimate judgment keeps us from defining the scope of responsibility too narrowly or taking our accountability lightly, but theology does not make the choices for us. That is why, for Niebuhr, a 'critical attitude', which brings every course of action under God's judgment, must be paired with a 'responsible attitude, which will not pretend to be God nor refuse to make a decision between political answers to a problem because each answer is discovered to contain a moral ambiguity in God's sight'.[31]

It is no easy task to put Reinhold Niebuhr in historical perspective, especially if we think about history in his way. To make a responsible judgment about the way he related to his times, we have to understand our own. These conclusions can never be final, but we have enough distance to stand a little apart from the early critics who sometimes saw Niebuhr's realism as a defense of the existing order. We may also want to create more intellectual distance between ourselves and the contemporary critics who find Niebuhr insufficiently theological.

We view Reinhold Niebuhr in historical perspective from the other side of a remarkable period in history in which movements of people with little apparent power toppled systems of segregation and apartheid and finally undid the 'structure of nations and empires' that provided the terms in which Niebuhr thought about global politics.[32] Those developments were unprecedented, and they may over the longer run prove to have been unique. But no one who claims to be a realist about the forces of change can hedge the power of hope with as many constraints as Niebuhr placed on it when the civil rights movement in the United States was just beginning, when courts and legislatures were still trying to undo the structures of legalized segregation. A realist now may be more hopeful than Niebuhr was. Indeed, it would be unrealistic and irresponsible to repeat Niebuhr's caution in his own terms, as though nothing much had happened since then. The field for responsible politics is much larger today than it was in Niebuhr's time, both within the United States and on a global scale.

Niebuhr's theological critics, however, find this new reality irrelevant to Christian politics. The task of Christian politics remains what it has always been: It reveals 'the insufficiency of all politics based on coercion and

---

[30] See, for example, Study Department of the World Council of Churches, *The Responsible Society* (Geneva: World Council of Churches, 1949).

[31] Reinhold Niebuhr, 'Theology and Political Thought in the Western World', in *Faith and Politics*, 56.

[32] Reinhold Niebuhr, *The Structure of Nations and Empires* (New York: Charles Scribner's Sons, 1959).

falsehood', as Stanley Hauerwas puts it.[33] The problem that 'all politics based on coercion and falsehood' becomes for Hauerwas the field of politics generally. 'All social orders and institutions to a greater and lesser extent are built on the lie that we, not God, are the masters of our existence.'[34] The key point is the ubiquity of the lie. Questions of degree, the 'greater and lesser extent', do not figure in the subsequent moral evaluation.

Here, then, we come to the central difference between Niebuhr and his theological critics. Both sides share the theological judgment that political systems tempt leaders and people to think that they are more righteous and less vulnerable than they really are. All political systems do this, ancient and modern, democratic and totalitarian. Reinhold Niebuhr does not disagree on this point. In *The Nature and Destiny of Man*, he gives one of the most compelling modern expressions of it.[35] What he insists, however, is that responsible choices between relative goods and evils must still be made, 'even when our Christian faith, illuminating the human scene, makes it quite apparent that there is no pure good in history, and probably no pure evil either'.[36] Nothing about those responsible choices justifies them in the face of God's ultimate judgment on all politics, but that judgment does not relieve us of the burden of the proximate choices. 'The fate of civilizations may depend upon these choices between systems of which some are more, others less, just.'[37]

Niebuhr does not deny the ambiguity of history, the fragility of our best achievements, or the likelihood of ironic reversals in which freedom will yield new kinds of tyranny or deteriorate into new forms of meaningless consumer choices. The final meaning of history lies beyond the narratives of triumph, tragedy, and irony by which we make sense of it for ourselves. Christian faith tells us that, but it does not provide a theological alternative to deciding between the concrete possibilities available to us. In historical perspective, Reinhold Niebuhr appears to be someone who was increasingly aware of the dignity and misery of that distinctly human task. He did not always get it right, but he saw enough of the possibilities and limits to help us find our way through our own difficult and very different choices.

---

[33] Hauerwas, *The Peaceable Kingdom*, 102.
[34] Ibid. 142.
[35] See especially Niebuhr, *The Nature and Destiny of Man*, i. 186–207.
[36] Niebuhr, 'Theology and Political Thought in the Western World', 56.
[37] Ibid.

2

On Recent Political Uses
of Reinhold Niebuhr

Toward a New Appreciation of his Legacy

Mac McCorkle

'I'm amazed that Reinhold Niebuhr hasn't made a comeback since September 11', remarked neoconservative columnist David Brooks in the *Atlantic* monthly magazine one year after al-Qaeda's murder of almost 3,000 people on American soil. During The Second World War and the Cold War, according to Brooks, Niebuhr was 'one of America's most profound writers on war and international conflict'. Yet a Nexis search revealed only a handful of references to Niebuhr over the past year.[1]

Five years later in the *Atlantic*, however, Paul Elie—an editor at a New York publishing house with Reinhold's daughter Elizabeth Sifton—was appraising a 'Niebuhr revival underway...[i]n think tanks, on op-ed pages, and on divinity school quadrangles'. Even though Niebuhr's ideas had become 'more prominent than at any time since his death in 1971', Elie was still not that happy about the revival. While framing his complaint as opposed to the bewildering babel of voices claiming Niebuhr, Elie as a left-liberal was mainly irritated about what he saw as the gross misappropriation of Reinhold's name by such neoconservative hawks as Brooks.[2]

Actually, by the time of Elie's article, the Niebuhr revival was well on its way to becoming far more a liberal and leftist affair. In the immediate wake of

---

[1] Brooks, 'A Man on a Gray Horse', *The Atlantic Monthly*, Sept. 2002, 24–5. See also Brooks, 'How Niebuhr Helps Us Kick the Secularist Habit: A Six–Step Program', in E. J. Dionne Jr., et al. (eds.), *One Electorate under God? A Dialogue on Religious and American Politics* (Washington, DC: Brookings Institution, 2004), 67–71; 'The Age of Conflict: Politics and Culture after September 11', *The Weekly Standard*, 5 Nov. 2001, 19.

[2] Elie, 'A Man for All Reasons', *Atlantic*, November 2007, 83–96. For reflections on her father, see Elisabeth Sifton, *The Serenity Prayer: Faith and Politics in Times of Peace and War* (New York: Norton, 2003).

9/11, Brooks and others on the right had indeed seized upon Niebuhr's hawkishness during the Second World War and the Cold War to help make the case for military action against Islamic terrorism. Yet as the American invasion of Iraq turned into another quagmire, intellectual momentum swung leftward to those who point to Niebuhr's dovish reputation on Vietnam or his 1930s radicalism.

Shortly before the invasion of Iraq, William Kristol—Brooks' former boss at the *Weekly Standard* and godfather of today's neoconservatism—had even ruled Niebuhr out of the neoconservative canon. In *The War Over Iraq*, Kristol dismissed the Cold War Niebuhr as an amoral 'realist' who obsessed over maintaining 'the balance of power with the Soviet Union' and would never have been enough of a 'democratic idealist' to support the United States' military overthrow of Saddam Hussein.[3]

And after joining the *New York Times*, Brooks increasingly cited Niebuhr to gain critical distance from the neoconservative Iraq project.[4] During the 2008 presidential campaign, Brooks went so far as to highlight Barack Obama's praise of Niebuhr and take the dovish Democrat seriously as a Niebuhrian. In contrast, Republican presidential candidate John McCain's effort in his 2007 book *Hard Call* to enlist Niebuhr on behalf of his hard-line Iraq stance fell on deaf ears.[5]

* * * * *

[3] Lawrence Kaplan and William Kristol, *The War Over Iraq: Saddam's Tyranny and America's Mission* (San Francisco: Encounter Books, 2003), 213. See also Kagan, 'Neocon Nation: Neoconservatism, c. 1776', *World Affairs* (Spring 2008), 13–35, at p. 23. For a running critique covering the generational changes and coalition tensions in the neoconservative camp, see Gary Dorrien, *The Neoconservative Mind: Politics, Culture, and the War of Ideology* (Philadelphia: Temple Press, 1993); *Soul in Society: The Making and Renewal of Social Christianity* (Fortress Press, Minneapolis 1995); *Imperial Designs: Neoconservatives and The New Pax Americana* (New York: Routledge, 2004).

[4] Brooks, 'For Iraqis to Win, The U.S. Must Lose', *New York Times*, 11 May 2004, 23. Others previously associated with neoconservatism more defiantly deserted over Iraq. See Fukuyama, *America at the Crossroads: Democracy, Power, and the Neoconservative Legacy* (New Haven: Yale University Press, 2006). Even the otherwise stalwart 'theo-con' ally Father John Richard Neuhaus and his magazine *First Things* increasingly began to express some discomfort with Kristol-like unalloyed good versus evil rhetoric over Iraq—and used Niebuhr to make the point. See, e.g., Careese, 'The Ironies of American Power', Sept. 2003, 39–42 (criticizing neocon Kagan's *Of Paradise and Power* as 'the irony of American history...without the irony'); Neuhaus, 'Internationalisms, etc.', Dec. 2004, <http://www.firstthings.com/article.php3?id_article=405> (declaring that the fight against Islamic terrorism should not be presented as 'the children of light against the children of darkness'); McClay, 'The Continuing Irony of American History', Feb. 2002, 20–5.

[5] Brooks, 'Obama, Gospel, and Verse', *New York Times*, 26 Apr. 2007, 25. See John McCain, with Mark Salter, *Hard Calls: The Art of Great Decisions* (New York: Hachette Book Group, 2007) 319–39.

This turn in the latest Niebuhr revival should please someone like myself. I am a liberal Democratic political consultant and a born as well as bred Presbyterian with Reinhold's framed portrait (on the cover of *Time*'s 25th anniversary issue in 1948)[6] prominently displayed in my office. I have long believed that a better appreciation of Niebuhr's legacy could enrich American intellectual discourse generally and benefit the liberal-left side of the political spectrum in particular.

However, after surveying recent uses of the Niebuhr legacy from my political side, I walk away with mixed feelings. I focus here on two representative writers—former *New Republic* editor Peter Beinart[7] and historian David Chappell.[8] Their efforts range widely and impressively beyond a focus on Niebuhr. But both fit the mold of public intellectuals who desire to reconstruct a 'usable' Niebuhrian legacy for our times.

Their common flaw is to claim a more or less perfect Niebuhr from one stage of his intellectual career.[9] While Chappell celebrates the radical 1930s Niebuhr of *Moral Man and Immoral Society*, Beinart champions the Cold War Niebuhr found in such 1950s works as *The Irony of American History*. In effect, their accounts serve as critiques of each other's portraits.

Both have the virtue of identifying foundational elements in Niebuhr's legacy. While Chappell pursues the 'prophetic' mode in Niebuhr's 1930s writings, Beinart focuses on Niebuhr's counsel to statesmen in his Cold War writings. But like many others who have laid claim to the Niebuhr legacy, neither recognizes that a dynamic tension between these two poles—prophet and statesman—is discernible during the course of Niebuhr's thought. Even in his most radical 'prophetic' mode of the 1930s, appreciation of the insider statesman compounded Niebuhr's thought. And after going almost dormant in the Cold War 1950s, Niebuhr's prophetic mode belatedly re-emerged during the 1960s.

$$* \quad * \quad * \quad * \quad *$$

[6] Whittaker Chambers, 'Faith for a Lenten Age', *Time*, 8 Mar. 1948, 70. A copy of the Niebuhr *Time* cover is available at <http://www.time.com/time/covers/0,16641,19480308,00.html>.

[7] Peter Beinart, 'An Argument for a New Liberalism: A Fighting Faith', *The New Republic*, 13 Dec. 2004, 17, 24, 29; *The Good Fight: Why Liberals—and Only Liberals—Can Win the War on Terror and Make America Great Again* (New York: HarperCollins, 2006); 'The Rehabilitation of the Cold War Liberal', *New York Times Magazine*, 30 Apr. 2006, 41–5.

[8] David L. Chappell, *A Stone of Hope: Prophetic Religion and the Death of Jim Crow* (Chapel Hill: University of North Carolina Press, 2004); see also Chappell, 'Niebuhrianisms and Myrdaleries: The Intellectual Roots of the Civil Rights Movement Reconsidered', in Ted Ownby (ed.), *The Role of Ideas in the Civil Rights South* (Oxford, MS: University Press of Mississippi, 2002), 3–18.

[9] For an even more recent assertion of a perfect Niebuhr legacy, see Urquhart, 'What You Can Learn from Reinhold Niebuhr', *New York Review of Books*, 26 Mar. 2009, 22–4. Urquhart's main guides are the recent writings of Andrew Bacevich on Niebuhr mentioned in fn. 69.

On its face, Chappell's *A Stone of Hope: Prophetic Religion and the Death of Jim Crow* is not a 'post 9/11' book. Like Niebuhr's *Moral Man, A Stone of Hope* focuses on domestic political struggle. Yet in exploring Niebuhr's influence on Martin Luther King's thinking, Chappell's treatment implicitly slides into foreign affairs.

Chappell highlighted the connections that King made between his growing up in the South and Niebuhr's embrace of original sin as well as the Hebrew prophets. During his graduate theological studies in the 1950s, King explained his attraction to Niebuhrian realism about humanity's sinful nature as 'root[ing] back to certain experiences that I had in the south with a vicious race problem'. The lesson that King drew was the need to challenge the institutionalized oppression of the society in which he grew up. 'Niebuhr makes it quite clear that government . . . must never be looked upon as divine', declared King. The prophet Jeremiah had similarly seized upon a revolutionary truth' that religious faith 'should never sanction the status quo'.[10]

But King, according to Chappell, espoused not liberalism but the Southern and African American version of a prophetic religion with roots deep in Judeo-Christian history—a tradition which Niebuhr had also tapped in *Moral Man*. King was a great synthesizer who succeeded Niebuhr in this American prophetic tradition. And this faith motivated an African American army of 'non-violent soldiers' to break the back of Jim Crow segregation through mass non-violent action.[11]

Chappell's account has been criticized for drawing too tight an intellectual link between the Niebuhr of *Moral Man* and King. Commentators have particularly objected that *A Stone of Hope* downplays the independent influence of African American religious traditions in King's thought.[12] Chappell also denied the connections between King's thought and the Social Gospel tradition which Niebuhr rejected in *Moral Man*. In particular, Chappell tiptoed around the difference that King was a pacifist while *Moral Man* announced Niebuhr's break with this Social Gospel tenet.[13]

[10] Chappell, *A Stone of Hope*, 50, 52, 47.
[11] Ibid., 48, 39, 3, 76, 206 n. 7, 220 n. 9, 242 n. 40, 310.
[12] See Charles Marsh's review of *A Stone of Hope* in *Political Theology*, Apr. 2005, 266–71; Luker, 'On David Chappell's *A Stone of Hope*', History News Network <http://hnn.us/blogs/entries/57532.html>.
[13] Chappell's analysis is inspired by the treatment of Niebuhr and King's intellectual relationship in his historical mentor C. Lasch's work, *The One and Only True Heaven: Progress and Its Critics* (New York: Knopf, 1992), 386–93. See Chappell, *A Stone of Hope*, 206 n. 5, 213 n. 41, 236 n. 41, 310. Yet Lasch provided an ultimately divergent analysis of King as a 'post-Niebuhrian liberal' whose 'political sympathies lay with the social gospel' and made him 'regard Niebuhr not as a political ally but as a formidable adversary whose gravely realistic but intellectually compelling theology made it necessary to restate the case for pacifism in a more rigorous form.' *True Heaven*, 391, 388. For King on his 'realistic pacifism', see 'My Pilgrimage to

Moral Man certainly contained the prescient call for mass non-violent resistance among American blacks that King and his lieutenants found so inspiring. Yet in Niebuhr's view non-violence was a strategy only suited for special cases where hopelessly outgunned minorities could appeal to the moral creed of the dominant majority. Otherwise in *Moral Man* Niebuhr promoted the Marxian dream of revolution—including the prospect of pro-letarian violence—as the necessary mass faith in the struggle for social justice.[14]

Chappell ignored Niebuhr's Marxist overcoat in *Moral Man*. Yet *Moral Man* was full of discussion about Marxist thinkers, proletarians, and revolutionary 'fanatics' while barely mentioning any Hebrew or other 'prophets'.[15] As Niebuhr biographer Richard Fox has pointed out, many religious contemporaries on the left as well as right thought that in *Moral Man* 'the [d]octrine of Christ [was] totally buried' and 'the doctrine of Marx [was] excessively glorified'.[16]

In a footnote Chappell granted that Niebuhr's 'most thorough articulation' of his prophetic religious stance came three years later in *An Interpretation of*

Nonviolence', *Fellowship* (September 1958), 4–9. For a summary of Niebuhr's evolution on pacifism, see Thompson, 'An Exception to Exceptionalism: A Reflection on Reinhold Niebuhr's Vision of 'Prophetic' Christianity and the Problem of Religious and U.S. Foreign Policy', *American Quarterly* (September 2007), 833–55, 840–2. For a helpful guide to Niebuhr's debate with pacifism, see Harries, 'Reinhold Niebuhr's Critique of Pacifism and his Pacifist Critics', in Harries (ed.), *Reinhold Niebuhr and the Issues of Our Time* (London: Mowbray, 1986), 105–21.

[14] Niebuhr's chief discussion on the role of non-violence is in chapter 9, 'The Preservation of Moral Values in Politics.' See *Moral Man*, 231–56, esp. 252. On Niebuhr's advocacy of non-violent strategies for the African American minority as well as its influence on King and his group, see Richard Fox, *Reinhold Niebuhr: A Biography* (New York: Pantheon, 1985), 283; Chappell, 216 n. 5; Dorrien, *Soul in Society*, 202–16.

[15] *Moral Man's* index contains single references to Amos (66) and Isaiah (61) with no listing for 'prophets' or any derivative thereof. But at least one mention of 'prophetic' religion can be found on 64.

[16] Fox, 136. After reading *Moral Man*, Langdon Gilkey's liberal ministerial father burst out of his home study and yelled 'Reinie's gone crazy.' Gilkey, *On Niebuhr: A Theological Study* (Chicago: University of Chicago Press, 2001), 4. But *Moral Man* was hardly devoid of theological reflection. Niebuhr's longest chapter (chapter 3) was entitled 'The Religious Resources of the Individual for Social Living.' See *Moral Man*, 51–82. Niebuhr there spelled out his view regarding the 'weakness of the spirit of [Christian] love' as a social or political ethic. 'The cross is the symbol of love triumphant in its own integrity, but not triumphant in the world and society.' *Moral Man*, 74, 82. See also 'The Ethic of Jesus and the Social Problem', *Religion in Life* (Spring 1932), in Robertson (ed.), *Love and Justice: Selections from the Shorter Writings of Reinhold Niebuhr* (Philadelphia: Westminster Press, 1957), 30 ('[G]ospel of Jesus' has 'no social ethic in the ordinary sense of the word'). Larry Rasmussen attributes Niebuhr's belief in the weakness of Jesus' love ethic as a social ethic to the understated influence of Ernest Troeltsch—from whom Niebuhr took the phrase 'moral man and immoral society', Rasmussen (ed.), *Reinhold Niebuhr: Theologian of Public Life* (London: Collins, 1989), 25–6, 40, 290 n. 69; 'Was Reinhold Niebuhr Wrong About Socialism?' *Political Theology*, 6/4 (2005), 429–57, at 437–42.

Christian Ethics.[17] Yet in *An Interpretation* Niebuhr stripped out the Marxist framework that enveloped *Moral Man*. Although continuing to accept much of the Marxist critique of capitalist injustice, Niebuhr emphasized his 'prophetic religion' as amounting to an 'independent Christian ethic' based on the Hebrew prophetic judgment and Jesus' 'love ethic'.[18]

Furthermore, full development in Niebuhr's thought regarding humanity's sinful nature being at the root of social injustice—which was at the core of King's prophetic view—awaited such later works as *The Nature and Destiny of Man* and *The Children of Light and the Children of Darkness*. Indeed some scholars see Niebuhr as moving in this 'neo-orthodox' theological direction after theological criticism (most strongly from his brother Richard) challenged his contrast between 'moral man' versus 'immoral society' as betraying a naive liberal secularism containing no deep notion of original sin.[19]

*   *   *   *   *

Yet such questionable elements hardly prevent *A Stone of Hope* from amounting to a representative account of the 1930s Niebuhr as the prophetic outsider creatively mixing radical religion and radical politics. It is not the first or the last effort to read the more overtly religious thrusts elsewhere in Niebuhr's thought back into *Moral Man*.[20] And certainly other left-wing partisans of Niebuhr echo *A Stone of Hope's* insistence that the real Niebuhrian legacy has a far better torchbearer in Martin Luther King than such a 'vital center' liberal as Arthur Schlesinger, Jr.[21]

---

[17] Chappell, 218 n. 13, citing Reinhold Niebuhr, *An Interpretation of Christian Ethics* (New York: Harper, 1935), 31.

[18] In his first chapter, entitled 'An Independent Christian Ethic', Niebuhr explained: 'The social justice which Amos demanded represented a possible ideal for society. Jesus' conception of pure love is related to the idea of justice as the holiness of God is related to the goodness of man. It transcends the possible and historical' (*An Interpretation*, 31). Rasmussen sees *An Interpretation* as presenting only a slightly revised version of Troeltsch's view about the weakness of Jesus' love ethic as a social ethic. 'Was Niebuhr Wrong About Socialism?', 439.

[19] See, e.g., Fox, 144–7. But see the discussion 'Reinhold and H. Richard Niebuhr', in Dorrien, *Soul in Society*, 157 ('Reinhold was already sprinkling his books with Pauline quotes on sin') and Reinhold's critique of his brother Richard's pacifist position against an economic embargo or any other intervention in the Sino-Japanese conflict over Manchuria, which was entitled 'Must We Do Nothing?', *Christian Century*, 30 Mar. 1932, 416–17 ('A truly religious man . . . remains a sinner to the end. The sense of sin is more central to religion than is any other attitude'). For an accessible guide to the much-debated 'neo-orthodox' movement from a Niebuhr admirer, see Miller, 'The Rise of Neo-Orthodoxy' in Arthur Schlesinger Jr. and Morton White (eds.), *Paths of American Thought* (Boston: Houghton Mifflin, 1963), 326–44.

[20] Among others King and his lieutenants certainly engaged in such a creative misreading of Niebuhr's *Moral Man* on non-violence and its religious thrust. See also n. 14.

[21] For Chappell's lambasting of Schlesinger and his effort to separate the 'real' *Moral Man* Niebuhr, see *A Stone of Hope*, 26–38. Chappell also does not shy away from unloading on Niebuhr

A Stone of Hope also shares the characteristic problem in many prophetic-left accounts of *Moral Man* and the 1930s Niebuhr: it leaves out the essential other half of his viewpoint. In *Moral Man* and other works, Niebuhr's outlook began but did not end with the opposition of revolutionaries and prophets against the status quo. His outlook instead displayed a rough division of labor between such outsiders and statesmen insiders. 'The realistic wisdom of the statesman is reduced to foolishness if it is not under the influence of the moral seer', declared Niebuhr. 'The latter's idealism results in political futility and sometimes in moral confusion, if it is not brought into commerce and communication with the realities of man's collective life.'[22]

This split in Niebuhr's thought is reminiscent of Max Weber's division in 'Politics as a Vocation' between an ethic of ultimate ends and an ethic of responsibility. While recognizing the prophet and revolutionary as political types, Weber clearly favored the responsible statesman. In *Moral Man*, however, Niebuhr was far more even-handed.[23]

Within the specific Marxian context of *Moral Man*, Niebuhr was splitting the difference in the sectarian debate between 'evolutionary socialism' and more orthodox revolutionary socialism. Niebuhr criticized such conservative revisionists as the German thinker Eduard Bernstein for devaluing mass action and relying on parliamentary politics. At the same time, while appreciating the 'motive power' of Marxism against social injustice, Niebuhr

for his Cold War alliance with Schlesinger. *A Stone of Hope*, 28, 41, 85, 224 n. 44. Throughout his career Lasch held the same dim view of the Cold War Niebuhr. *True Heaven*, 383; *The New Radicalism in America: The Intellectual and Social Type* (New York: Knopf, 1965), 299–308.

[22] *Moral Man*, 258. The otherwise insightful works of Gary Dorrien and Dennis McCann are typical in emphasizing the 'revolutionary' side of *Moral Man* and not mentioning the role of the statesman. Dennis McCann, *Christian Realism and Liberal Theology: Practical Theologies in Creative Conflict* (Mayknoll, NY: Orbis Books, 1982), 87–93; Dorrien, *The Making of American Liberal Theology: Idealism, Realism, and Modernity, 1900–1950* (Louisville, KY: Westminster John Knox Press, 2003), 449–51; *Soul in Society*, 88–92. While identifying a prophet–statesman dynamic in such earlier writings as *Leaves from the Notebook of a Tamed Cynic* (Chicago: Willett, Clark and Colby, 1929), Arthur Schlesinger, Jr., argued that Niebuhr dropped the statesmanship element by the time of *Moral Man*. Schlesinger, 'Reinhold Niebuhr's Role in American Political Thought and Life', in Charles W. Kegley and Robert W. Bretall (eds.), *Reinhold Niebuhr: His Religious, Social, and Political Thought* (New York: Macmillan, 1956), 125–50, 132. See *Leaves*, xii–xiv.

[23] Fox, 102. H. H. Gerth and C. Wright Mills (eds.), *From Max Weber: Essays in Sociology* (New York: Oxford University Press, 1946), 77–128. I am here pointing only to a similarity rather than asserting the influence of Weber's 'Politics as a Vocation' on Niebuhr. But for general evidence of Weber's influence on Niebuhr, see Fox, 102 (Niebuhr 'introducing most [American] readers to the untranslated Weber' on the Protestant ethic and the spirit of capitalism). Other commentators have linked Niebuhr's thought to Weber's two ethics in his post-*Moral Man* writings where he celebrated the statesmanship-like 'ethics of responsibility.' See, e.g., Gustafson, 'Theology in the Service of Ethics', in Harries (ed.), *Reinhold Niebuhr*, 24–45, 30; Dorrien, *Soul in Society*, 155, 88–92.

viewed 'Western civilization' as probably 'not ripe for proletarian revolutions' and thus revolutionary socialism would be 'unable to press through its goal'.[24]

Thus despite his relatively even-handed approach, Niebuhr ultimately came down on the statesman side. In *Moral Man*, with a spirit akin to a modern artist, Niebuhr undeniably sought to 'épater les bourgeois' by headlining the need for Marxist revolutionary fervor and proletarian violence.[25] But the balancing role of parliamentary statesmen still constituted Niebuhr's bottom line in *Moral Man*. In the absence of a parliamentary shock absorber, Niebuhr acknowledged that the proletarian vision would engender 'a permanent state of civil war'. Assuming that he was forced to choose, Niebuhr found 'parliamentary socialism' to be 'clearly preferable' even though alone it would have 'no hope of final and complete triumph'.[26]

Moral Man's non-revolutionary leanings were particularly on display in Niebuhr's partiality to Britain rather than the Soviet Union. The development of welfare states in Britain and continental Europe, according to Niebuhr, had 'at least partially justified . . . the hope that socialism could be achieved progressively by parliamentary action'. English Fabian socialism had actually compiled a respectable record of progress as an extension of 'British liberalism' that was more dismissive of Marxist class conflict analysis than evolutionary socialists were on the European continent. Furthermore, despite its hypocrisy on India and other aspects of its traditional imperialism, the 'measure of genuine humanitarian interest' in British foreign policy was '[p]erhaps the best that can be expected of nations'.[27]

---

[24] *Moral Man*, 220–1. See Kenneth Durkin, *Reinhold Niebuhr* (Harrisburg, PA: Morehouse Publishing 1990), 50–3.

[25] 'At times, Niebuhr appears to be a modernist thinker (in the authentic sense of the term.)', Halliwell, 21. Gary Dorrien points out that Niebuhr demonstrated even more 'posturing' about the prospect of significant violence in a *Harper's* article published during the summer of 1932. Dorrien, *Soul in Society*, 92, citing Niebuhr, 'Catastrophe or Social Control?' *Harper's* 165, June 1932, 118. See also Niebuhr, 'After Capitalism—What?', *The World Tomorrow*, Mar. 1933, 203–5. While not providing a detailed textual analysis *of Moral Man*, Donald Meyer's *The Protestant Search for Political Realism* (Berkeley: University of California Press, 1961) remains the best guide to Niebuhr's politics and the immediate political context during the 1930s.

[26] *Moral Man*, 220. As *Moral Man* was being published in 1932, Niebuhr was making his own foray into electoral statesmanship as a New York congressional candidate on Norman Thomas' Socialist ticket. While Thomas received 2.2% of the presidential vote, Niebuhr received 4.4% of the vote in his New York City congressional district. Fox, 135–6.

[27] *Moral Man*, 206, 204–5, 108. See Rich, 'Reinhold Niebuhr and the Ethics of Realism in International Relations', *History of Political Thought*, Summer 1992, 281–98, 285. For an emphasis on Niebuhr's partiality to 'the British model' as part of an effort to downplay the revolutionary Marxist side of Niebuhr's equation, see Charles C. Brown, *Niebuhr and His Age: Reinhold Niebuhr's Prophetic Role and His Legacy* (Harrisburg: Trinity Press, 2002), 43. Other commentators have characterized Niebuhr as an Anglophile and noted his wife Ursula (whom he married in 1931) was an Englishwoman but do not apply that point to *Moral Man*. See Fox,

So in no way did Niebuhr exempt revolutionary or Bolshevik fervor from his concern about the immorality of collective action or 'immoral society'. On the other hand there was, as Niebuhr put it in *An Interpretation of Christian Ethics*, 'the inevitable opportunism of statesmanship'. Niebuhr explained in *Moral Man*: 'There is only one step from a rationally moderated idealism to opportunism, and only another step from opportunism to dishonest capitulation to the status quo.' Thus, according to Niebuhr: 'The absolutist and fanatic is no doubt dangerous; but he is also necessary.'[28]

Ironically, while moving to more of a prophetic religious position in *An Interpretation of Christian Ethics*, Niebuhr leaned further away from radicalism. Niebuhr still saw the Marxist critique of capitalist injustice as essentially correct and continued to embrace revolt among workers and the poor even if they insisted on the option of resorting to violence. Yet Niebuhr condemned the communist goals of proletarian dictatorship for generating 'an intransigence and dogmatism' in too many 'rebels against justice'. An *Interpretation* displayed Niebuhr's move to a defense of 'democratic institutions' and 'the statesmanship of . . . liberalism' that would fully bloom in such later works as *The Children of Light and the Children of Darkness*. The 'prophetic religion' position still stood in judgment over the political opportunism of statesmanship but did not really compete as a political alternative. Prophets moreover needed to recognize 'what kind of world we are living in' and give breathing room to statesmen's necessary compromises.[29]

Clearly this split between prophet and statesman in Niebuhr's 1930s work punches a big hole in one-dimensional leftist celebrations of *Moral Man*. The role of statesmen in Niebuhr's prophetic outlook also establishes an obvious line of continuity with his later and more 'conservative' writings. Moreover, since the Social Gospel tradition had already championed the prophetic side

124–34, 149–50, 173; Cornell West, *The American Evasion of Philosophy: A Genealogy of Pragmatism* (Madison: University of Wisconsin Press, 1989), 158.

[28] *Interpretation*, 197; *Moral Man*, 222. Such discussion demonstrated that Niebuhr's implicit definition was not limited to a narrow high-minded notion of 'statesman'. But in both works Niebuhr seemed to be focused on statesmen sympathetic to the left side of the political spectrum and whose opportunism or corruption involved ideological capitulation more than graft on the Tammany Hall model.

[29] *Interpretation*, 134, 184–5, 189, 190–1, 193, 197. Departing from *Moral Man's* strict dichotomy between radical action and parliamentary statesmanship, Niebuhr even called for 'wise statesmanship' among labor and other radical leaders to avoid violence and more generally reaction among petit-bourgeois elements in society. *An Interpretation*, 134, 193. Elsewhere Niebuhr more strongly emphasized 'the solitary prophet'. See *Beyond Tragedy: Essays on the Christian Interpretation of History* (New York: Scribner's, 1937), 76. For other references to the prophet–statesman dynamic, see also *Beyond Tragedy*, 65–8, 286. For a brief discussion of prophet and statesman in *Beyond Tragedy*, see Eyal Naveh, *Reinhold Niebuhr and Non-Utopian Liberalism* (Brighton: Sussex Academic Press, 2002), 38.

of the equation, it could even be said that the distinctly Niebuhrian element was recognition of a major role for statesmen.[30]

Critics from various perspectives may want to dismiss Niebuhr's prophet-statesman compound as little more than an under-defined sociological description and not near a prescriptive political theory. In *Moral Man* Niebuhr even acknowledged that he knew no systematic way to balance, synthesize, or prioritize between these two poles.[31] Yet from a less perfectionist standpoint, Niebuhr's hybrid outlook constituted an interesting heterodox political perspective—one that allowed him to appreciate the political virtue of prophets and even revolutionary fanatics on the left as well as electoral politicians while still holding all of them up to critical examination.

*   *   *   *   *

In late 2004, after Chappell's *A Stone of Hope* had already hit bookstores, *New Republic* editor Peter Beinart began his contribution to the Niebuhr revival. Although evolving somewhat over the next two years, Beinart's basic frame of reference represented quite a dramatic contrast. On its face, Beinart's effort was very much a response to 9/11. He never mentioned *Moral Man* or the prophetic Niebuhr. The intellectual alter ego for his Niebuhr was not Martin Luther King but the 'atheist for Niebuhr' and Kennedy confidant Arthur Schlesinger Jr. While Chappell barely made any references to JFK, LBJ, or 1960s civil rights legislation, Beinart's focus was on Washington's statesmen and the exemplary framework that the Cold War Niebuhr established for them.[32]

[30] On the Social Gospel's prophetic emphasis, see Niebuhr, 'Walter Rauschenbusch in Historical Perspective', in Ronald H. Stone (ed.), *Faith and Politics* (New York: Braziller, 1968), 33–46; *Man's Nature and His Communities* (New York: Scribner's, 1965), 17; 'Mission and Opportunity: Religion in a Pluralistic Culture', in Lewis Finkelstein (ed.), *Social Responsibility in an Age of Revolution* (New York Jewish Theological Press, 1971), 177, 211, 197. Nevertheless, on such issues as racial discrimination his Social Gospel predecessor Rauschenbusch was far more conservative than Niebuhr. See Dorrien, 'Social Ethics in the Making: Method, History, White Supremacism, Social Salvation', *Union Seminary Quarterly Review* (Fall 2007), 1–21.

[31] *Moral Man*, 230 ('no purely rational moral choice is possible between them'). See also Weber, 'Politics as a Vocation', 127 ('One cannot prescribe to anyone whether he should follow an ethic of absolute ends or an ethic of responsibility').

[32] See Arthur Schlesinger, Jr., *The Vital Center: The Politics of Freedom* (Cambridge, MA: Houghton Mifflin, 1949). On his 'atheist for Niebuhr' position, see Schlesinger's review of Niebuhr's *Faith and History* in *Christianity and Society* (Summer 1949), 26–7. See also Perry Miller, 'The Influence of Reinhold Niebuhr', *The Reporter* (1 May 1948), 40. For criticisms of atheists for Niebuhr, see the epilogue in the 1957 edition of Morton White, *Social Thought in America: The Revolt Against Formalism* (Boston: Beacon Press, 1947), 247–80.

One month after Senator John Kerry's dispiriting presidential defeat, Beinart rolled out Niebuhr in a *New Republic* cover story entitled 'A Fighting Faith: An Argument for a New Liberalism'. In a back-to-the-future vein, Beinart lifted 'fighting faith' from Arthur Schlesinger Jr.'s anti-communist manifesto *The Vital Center*. He identified the 'totalitarianism Islam' of Osama Bin Laden as today's equivalent of a Cold War foe. Along with some other liberal hawks, Beinart had acknowledged before the 2004 election that he was wrong to have supported the invasion of Iraq. In 'Fighting Faith' Beinart nonetheless declared that dovish liberals needed to get beyond their Vietnam-like 'alienation over Iraq'.[33]

Except for his Iraq caveat, Beinart could have been mistaken for making a neo-conservative call to global arms. Like William Kristol, Beinart argued that war against global terrorism was the key to restoring America's sense of moral purpose and national greatness.[34] Yet Beinart saw the fight for democracy across the globe as strengthening the liberal case for greater democracy at home. In particular, according to Beinart, Cold War liberals 'repeatedly argued that the denial of African American civil rights undermined America's anti-communist efforts in the Third World'.[35]

Even though Schlesinger was the main intellectual actor in Beinart's Cold War drama, knowledgeable readers had reason to suspect that the *eminence grise* in Beinart's tale was Schlesinger's intellectual mentor Niebuhr. Beinart did not cite any of Niebuhr's writings. Yet he named Niebuhr first in his list of distinguished liberal heroes who met at Washington's Willard Hotel on 4 January 1947 to form the anti-communist Americans for Democratic Action and thereby, in Beinart's words, 'save American liberalism'.[36]

Beinart bluntly explained that the Niebuhr Schlesinger and anti-communists essentially saved liberalism by ridding its ranks of the 'soft' isolationist attitudes toward the Soviet Union personified in former Vice President Henry Wallace. 'One of the lessons of the early cold war is scrupulousness about whom liberals let speak in their name', declared Beinart. Subsequent Democratic candidates should follow this example and abandon 'the unity-at-all costs ethos that governed American liberalism in 2004'. Beinart therefore called for marginalizing such 'heirs of Henry Wallace' as documentary

---

[33] Beinart, 'Fighting Faith', 23, 18, 24. See Beinart, 'Partisan Review', and Editors, 'Were We Wrong?', *New Republic,* 28 Jun. 2004, 6, 8–9.

[34] Beinart, 'Fighting Faith', 17–18, 23–4, 29. See, e.g., Kristol and Brooks, 'What Ails the Right', *Wall Street Journal,* 15 Sept. 1997, <http://www.opinionjournal.com/forms/printThis.html?id=95000513>. Brooks actually penned an initial longer version entitled 'A Return to National Greatness: A Manifesto for a Lost Creed', *The Weekly Standard,* 3 Mar. 1997, 16–21.

[35] 'Fighting Faith', 24.

[36] Ibid. 17.

filmmaker and author Michael Moore and the leadership of the 'net-roots' group MoveOn.org.[37]

Yet as the Iraqi misadventure continued to unravel and dominate the American political picture, Beinart moderated his rhetoric and discovered the usefulness of leaning on Niebuhr's dovish reputation regarding Vietnam. As Beinart acknowledged in his 2006 book *The Good Fight* and accompanying articles, Niebuhr took center stage as the intellectual hero who provided 'the theoretical heft' in 'defining Cold War liberalism'.[38] Yet Beinart did not portray Niebuhr as breaking with and becoming a critic of Cold War liberalism. He instead portrayed Niebuhr as *fulfilling its promise* by being the wise sage who could embrace its anti-communist creed 'and still oppose the [Vietnam] war' while exhibiting an exemplary progressive position on such crucial domestic issues as civil rights.[39]

*   *   *   *   *

Beinart obviously left himself open to charges that he was torturing reality to fit Niebuhr on Vietnam into his idealized Cold War liberal box. For if a Niebuhrian dovishness on Vietnam actually represented Cold War liberalism, how did the United States end up fighting there?

Beinart tried to answer that the right people 'were almost never in the room when key decisions were made'—specifically such first-string Cold War thinkers as Niebuhr and George Kennan. The real best and brightest, in other words, would have gotten Vietnam right from the beginning and the Cold War liberal consensus could have continued to make America great.[40] As reviewers have pointed out, Beinart in effect created a stark generational divide between the original Truman generation of Cold War statesmen at the helm and their epigones in the Kennedy and Johnson administrations.[41] The JFK–LBJ generation, according to Beinart, was full of 'arrogant, blinkered men ... who had forgotten their [Cold War liberalism's] emphasis on self-restraint'.[42]

---

[37] Ibid. 23, 22. For a treatment mainly critical of Niebuhr, see Mark Klarman, *A World of Hope, A World of Fear: Henry A. Wallace, Reinhold Niebuhr and American Liberalism* (Columbus, OH: Ohio State University Press, 2000).

[38] Beinart, *Good Fight*, 5, 16. See 'Rehabilitation of the Cold War Liberal', 41–5.

[39] Beinart, *Good Fight*, 42.

[40] Beinart specifically asserts that Senator Joe McCarthy's witch-hunt had purged the State Department experts on Asia who would have heeded the Niebuhr–Kennan wisdom. Ibid. 41, 16.

[41] See, e.g., Klein, 'The Truman Show', *New York Times Book Review*, 11 Jun. 2006, <http://www.nytimes.com/2006/06/11/books/review/llklein.thml>.

[42] *Good Fight*, 41.

Yet Beinart admitted that it was the Truman Doctrine's globalist rhetoric in aiding Greece and Turkey that set the precedent of 'pledging the United States to oppose virtually any communist movement'. Adding to the incoherence of his generational argument, Beinart in *The Good Fight* even claimed that JFK's hard line during the 1960 debates with Nixon 'echoed Schlesinger and Niebuhr' and that 'Kennedy's central theme was the one born at the Willard Hotel' where Niebuhr and Schlesinger inaugurated Cold War liberalism.[43] Indeed, as commentators have pointed out, Beinart's national greatness stance 'calls to mind nothing so much as the [Cold War] liberalism of John F. Kennedy' and his inaugural rhetoric about bearing any burden against world communism.[44]

Some pro-Niebuhr liberals to the left of Beinart try to place him at always a far greater critical or even adversarial distance from the Cold War establishment.[45] Yet the central reality obscured by all such accounts is simply this: during the 1950s Niebuhr failed to give decisive counsel about avoiding the Vietnam quagmire or the need to push on civil rights. The Niebuhr positions which Beinart and others want to claim as so prescient represented belated changes in his outlook during the 1960s.[46]

As Niebuhr scholar Dennis McCann has observed, 'the difficulty in establishing Niebuhr's superior perceptiveness' during the Cold War 'is apparent as soon as his thinking on Vietnam is discussed'.[47] For example, while containing misgivings about the prospect of military involvement in Asia, Niebuhr's 1952 work *The Irony of American History* emphasized the necessity of confronting Soviet communism's expansionist drive.[48] And through the early 1960s, as

[43] *Good Fight*, 40, 26, 25. On Niebuhr's support for the Truman Doctrine, see Mary Spelling McAuliffe, *Crisis on the Left: Cold War Politics and American Liberals, 1947–1994* (Amherst, MA: University of Massachusetts Press, 1978), 24, 31.

[44] Chartier, 'Niebuhr's Ghost', *Conversations in Religion and Theology*, May 2007, 91–115. at 99. See also Hitchins, 'Blood for No Oil', *The Atlantic Monthly*, 133–6, 134 (May 2006); Gaddis, 'The Gardener', *New Republic*, 16 Oct. 2006, 26–32, 26–7. For a neoconservative response characterizing Beinart's *Good Fight* as an incoherent ideological brew, see Emory, 'The Inconvenient Truth About Truman', *Weekly Standard*, 17 July 2006, available at <http://www.weeklystandard.com/Content/Public/Articles/000/000/012/407mnulof.asp>.

[45] See, e.g., the writings of historian Kevin Mattson: *When America Was Great: The Fighting Faith of Post-War Liberalism* (New York: Routledge, 2004); 'Why We Should Be Reading Reinhold Niebuhr Now More Than Ever', *The Good Society*, 14/3 (2005), 77–82; 'Age of Anxiety', *Boston Review*, 31/4 (2006), 23–24 (review of Beinart's *The Good Fight*).

[46] On the belatedness of Niebuhr's position against the Vietnam War, see, e.g., Marty, 'The Lost Worlds of Reinhold Niebuhr', *American Scholar*, Fall 1976, 566–72, 568. On civil rights, see Martin Halliwell, *The Constant Dialogue: Reinhold Niebuhr and American Intellectual Culture* (Lanham, MD: Rowman and Littlefield, 2005), 249.

[47] Dennis McCann, *Christian Realism and Liberation Theology: Practical Theologies in Creative Conflict* (New York: Orbis Books, 1981), 122.

[48] *The Irony of American History* (New York, Scribner's, 1952), 16, 41–2. See the comment of Niebuhr's long-time colleague and interpreter John Bennett in the forum entitled 'Christian

biographer Richard Fox has explained, 'Niebuhr was actually of two minds on Vietnam.'[49] Niebuhr was still declaring in 1963 that 'if we withdrew the communists will overrun the whole of Southeast Asia', concluding in 1964 that '[u]ndoubtedly we must continue our support of South Vietnam indefinitely', and hesitating in early 1965 to criticize the Johnson administration because Vietnam was an 'insoluble problem'.[50]

Niebuhr's lack of any decisive policy dissent on Vietnam is consistent with Kennan's observation that his friend provided 'unexceptional' policy advice when invited to State Department planning staff meetings during the Truman era.[51] Moreover, it should not be swept under the historical rug that Niebuhr's hesitations about United States involvement stemmed in large part from an 'Atlanticist' or 'Europeanist' perspective (shared with Kennan) that not only doubted the strategic importance of Vietnam but also denigrated 'Oriental' culture as incapable of democratic flowering.[52]

Niebuhr came even closer to an outright default on civil rights during the 1950s.[53] In striking contrast to *Moral Man* three decades before, Niebuhr's

Realism: Retrospect and Prospect', *Christianity and Crisis*, 5 Aug. 1968, 177: 'When Reinhold Niebuhr wrote *The Irony of American History* in 1952, his criticisms of the moral temptations that went with American power were overshadowed by his emphasis on American response to check Stalin's power.' Yet other figures recalibrated the balance to emphasize the cautionary critique regarding American power. See historian C. Vann Woodward's 'The Irony of Southern History' (1953), in *The Burden of Southern History*, 3rd edn. (Baton Rouge: Louisiana State University Press, 1993), 187–213.

[49] Fox, 283–4. For Niebuhr statements from the 1950s regarding Vietnam, see 'Editorial Notes', *Christianity and Crisis*, 31 May 1954, 66; 14 Jun. 1954, 74–5; and 'The Limits of Military Power', *New Leader*, 30 May 1955, 16–17. But in 1963 Niebuhr was a founding member of the Ministers' Vietnam Committee, which criticized the way that the United States was carrying out its Vietnam policy. Michael B. Friedland, *Lift Up Your Voice Like A Trumpet: White Clergy and the Civil Rights and Antiwar Movements, 1954–1973* (Chapel Hill: University of North Carolina Press), 142.

[50] Niebuhr, 'The Problem of South Vietnam', *Christianity and Crisis*, 5 Aug. 1963, 142–3; 'Johnson and the Myths of Democracy', *The New Leader*, 25 May 1964, 18–20; 'Vietnam: An Insoluble Problem', *Christianity and Crisis*, 8 Feb. 1965, 1–2; 'Pretense and Power', *The New Leader*, 1 Mar. 1965, 6–7. See Ribuffo, 'Moral Judgments and the Cold War: Reflections on Reinhold Niebuhr, William Appleman Williams, and John Lewis Gaddis', in Ellen Schrecker (ed.), *Cold War Triumphalism: The Misuse of History After the Fall of Communism* (New York: Norton, 2004), 27–70, 37, 303 n. 20.

[51] Fox, 238.

[52] *Irony*, 142, 115–29; Niebuhr, 'American Conservatism and the World Crisis: A Story in Vacillation', *Yale Review* 385 (1951), 394–95. Niebuhr held similar views regarding Islamic religion and Arab culture. *Irony*, 114, 128. See West, 162. Niebuhr similarly referred to African Americans as 'backward' in 'historical' and 'cultural' terms owing to slavery and segregation while also treating the white American South as a backward region. *Man's Nature*, 89–90; 'The States Rights Crisis', *The New Leader*, 29 Sept. 1958, 6–7; 'School, Church, and the Ordeals of Integration', *Christianity and Crisis*, 1 Oct. 1956, 121–2.

[53] See generally Carol Polsgrove, *Divided Minds: Intellectuals and the Civil Rights Movement* (New York: Norton, 2001), 42–8, 61.

The Irony of American History painted the United States as a unique middle-class country with no class conflict and failed to mention the plight of racial minorities.[54] In 1957, arguing that '*such pressure would do more harm than good*', Niebuhr refused Martin Luther King's request to sign an open letter to President Eisenhower requesting federal enforcement of Southern school desegregation. Niebuhr instead continued to defend Democratic presidential candidate Adlai Stevenson's stance against federal enforcement because 'prudence is as necessary as courage in the tasks of statesmanship.' After Eisenhower sent federal troops to Little Rock, Niebuhr actually castigated the President for being 'stupid' and making a 'hero out of the hillbilly' Governor (Faubus) who postured against the federal enforcement.[55]

But contrary to many accounts, the story of the post-Second World War Niebuhr does not end with the 1950s.[56] Increasingly during the 1960s 'the theologian for the establishment'[57] did indeed become more a voice of dissent. By 1967 former allies were scrambling to save the Niebuhrian Cold War legacy from Niebuhr. In Paul Ramsey's exasperated words, 'Niebuhr signs [anti-war] petitions and editorials as if Reinhold Niebuhr never existed.'[58] Although never celebrating the student New Left, Niebuhr grasped that its

---

[54] Niebuhr's view that 'America developed as a bourgeois society with only remnants of the older feudal culture to inform its ethos'—with the chief remnant being the slave South—was very similar to the interpretation more fully developed in Louis Hartz's influential work, *The Liberal Tradition in America* (New York: Harcourt Brace, 1955). See *Irony*, 3, 33, 102–3, 111. After reviewing galley drafts for *Irony*, Schlesinger recommended that Niebuhr address 'our treatment of the Negro.' See Ursula Niebuhr (ed.), *Remembering Reinhold Niebuhr: Letters of Reinhold and Ursula M. Niebuhr* (New York: HarperCollins, 1991), 371.

[55] Niebuhr to Justice Felix Frankfurter, 8 Feb. 1957 in *Remembering Niebuhr*, 311; 'Nullification', *The New Leader*, 5 Mar. 1956, 3–4; 'Stevenson, The Democrats, and Civil Rights', *The New Leader*, 9 Jul. 1956, 11; 'The States Rights Crisis', 6–7. A year earlier Niebuhr's critical tone was softer toward Eisenhower's use of federal force in 'Bad Days of Little Rock', *Christianity and Crisis*, 14 Oct. 1957, 131. Niebuhr was not alone among liberal intellectuals in arguing against federal enforcement in Little Rock. For another prominent example, see Hannah Arendt, 'Reflections on Little Rock', *Dissent*, Winter 1959, 47–58. See generally Polsgrove, *Divided Minds*.

[56] One of English scholar Martin Halliwell's central contributions is his challenge to 'the drift in Niebuhr scholarship' promoting the idea that his thought did not evolve and even significantly declined after his 'strokes of 1952.' *The Constant Dialogue*, 17. And although providing a muted assessment in his biography, Fox elsewhere emphasized Niebuhr's progressive moves in the 1960s. See Fox, 'Reinhold Niebuhr—The Living of Christian Realism', in Harries (ed.), *Reinhold Niebuhr*, 9, 23.

[57] Richard Rovere, *The American Establishment and Other Reports, Opinions, and Speculations* (New York: Harcourt Brace, 1962), 13.

[58] Fox, 284. In September 1965, a few months after the Johnson administration expanded the American military commitment to shore up the South Vietnamese regime, Niebuhr declared to his friend Will Searlett: 'For the first time I fear I am ashamed of our beloved nation' (Fox, 285, 324 n. 10). In 1966 he became a 'founding member of Clergy and Laymen Concerned about Vietnam (CALCAV), the foremost religious coalition against the war', Ribuffo, 37.

revolt over Vietnam indicted a status quo political culture lacking in 'moral integrity and humanness...most obvious in the failure to achieve racial justice and to eliminate the last remnants of the horrible traditions of the slave system'.[59]

In effect, the prophetic side of the Niebuhr equation re-emerged in the 1960s. And a chief influence on Niebuhr was none other than the prophetic example of Martin Luther King. During the early 1960s, Niebuhr began moving away from paternalistic counsel to African Americans calling for patience and toward support for non-violent direct action.[60] In 1960, Niebuhr highlighted the model set by King in explaining 'how my mind has changed'. In 1966 Niebuhr declared King to be 'the most creative Protestant, black or white'. On a number of occasions Niebuhr even praised King's anti-war position and downplayed any difference between them on the issue of pacifism.[61]

Niebuhr's 1960s evolution hardly represented a return to the 1930s radical posture of *Moral Man*.[62] Nevertheless, while Chappell and others have debated the influence of the 1930s radical Niebuhr on King, all sides of the Niebuhr debate need to appreciate the leftward push of King on the 1960s Niebuhr.[63]

Critics may want to emphasize that Niebuhr felt free to turn against the Vietnam War because it was Southerner LBJ not Eastern establishment JFK who initiated America's military build-up in the spring of 1965. Yet Niebuhr

[59] Halliwell, 189 and 255, quoting unpublished Niebuhr draft 'Our Two Youthful Rebellions: The Light They Throw On Our American Culture', c.1970, Niebuhr Papers, Library of Congress Box 44, 2–3 (copy in author's possession), which appeared in revised form as 'Indicting Two Generations', *New Leader*, 5 Oct. 1970, 13–14. See also Niebuhr, 'Toward New Intra-Christian Endeavors', *Christian Century*, 31 Dec. 1969, 1662–7, 1663 ('Perhaps there is not too much to choose between communist and anticommunist fanaticism, particularly when the latter, combined with our wealth, has caused us to stumble into the most pointless, costly and bloody war in our history').

[60] Halliwell, *The Constant Dialogue*, 315 n. 64; Mark Hulsether, *Building a Protestant Left: Christianity and Crisis Magazine, 1941–1993* (Knoxville: University of Tennessee Press, 1999), 49–55, 69–74. For a survey of the evolution in Niebuhr's thought, see De Lisio, 'Did Reinhold Niebuhr Care About Racism in America?' *Union Seminary Quarterly Review* (2008), 1–16. See, e.g., Niebuhr's introduction to *Mississippi Black Paper* (New York: Random House, 1965).

[61] Reinhold Niebuhr in Harold E. Fey (ed.), *How My Mind Has Changed* (Cleveland: Meridian Press, 1961), 116–32, 118, originally published as 'The Quality of Our Lives', *Christian Century*, 11 May 1960, 568–72; Niebuhr's Foreword to *Dr. Martin Luther King Jr. et al. Speak on the War in Vietnam* (New York: Clergy and Laymen Concerned About Vietnam, 1967), 3. Halliwell, 237; Fox, 283; 118.

[62] For Niebuhr on Marx in the 1960s, see his introduction to *Karl Marx and Friedrich Engels on Religion* (New York: Schocken Books, 1965) xii–xiv.

[63] See Halliwell, 236–40. Also pushing Niebuhr away from a Cold War paradigm was his growing concern about the threat of mutual annihilation from nuclear war. See Campbell Craig, *Glimmer of a New Leviathan: Total War in the Realism of Niebuhr, Morgenthau, and Waltz* (New York: Columbia University Press, 2003); Dorrien, *Soul in Society*, 134–6.

was actually slow to warm to JFK's presidency and emphasized that 'President Johnson was not the author of our gradual stumble into the quagmire.'[64] Niebuhr can also be seen as embracing King because he was a safe alternative to emerging Black Power and liberation theology proponents.[65] Yet the undeniable point is that unlike many contemporaries Niebuhr politically moved in the 1960s—contrary to the unregenerate Cold War stereotype of him as well as Beinart's claim that Niebuhr was opposing Vietnam and pushing for civil rights from within his 1950s Cold War framework.

Furthermore, reservoirs still existing in Niebuhr's thought made him relatively more open to the prophetic influence of a Martin Luther King. In *The Irony of American History* Niebuhr undeniably placed his political bets on statesmen— such as founding fathers James Madison and John Adams. Niebuhr even bemoaned the 'lack of a conscious philosophy' to justify 'policies of statesmanship' and filling this gap had become essential to his intellectual project.[66] He recognized no mass prophetic force in the working class, among minorities, or elsewhere in American society.[67] Yet in expressing his ambivalence about American power, Niebuhr did call upon *the memory* of the Hebrew prophets.[68] In particular, his last chapter invoked the Old Testament prophets who were 'never weary of warning both the powerful nations and Israel, the righteous nation, of the judgment which waits on human pretension.'[69]

---

[64] *Remembering Niebuhr*, 317–18; Niebuhr, 'A Question of Priorities', in Ronald H. Stone (ed.), *Faith and Politics* (New York: Braziller, 1968), 261–8, 268.

[65] 'By the mid-1960s Niebuhr was boosting King in his confrontation with 'black power' enthusiasts like Stokely Carmichael and H. Rap Brown' (Fox, 283). See also Hulsether, *Building a Protestant Left*, 73–4.

[66] *Irony*, 98, 21, 5. Niebuhr favorably contrasted the 'practical statesman' with intellectual and scholarly 'wise men' (*Irony*, 17–18). But Niebuhr could still criticize the occasional 'hysterical statesman' (*Irony*, 74). In a clear sign of a conservative shift, he also began to extol Winston Churchill as the 'greatest statesman of our age.' Niebuhr, 'Billy Graham's Christianity and the World Crisis', *Christianity and Society*, Spring 1985, 3; 'Winston Churchill and Great Britain' (1955), in Charles C. Brown (ed.), *A Reinhold Niebuhr Reader* (Philadelphia: Trinity Press, 1992), 90–2.

[67] *Irony*, 91 ('America . . . has achieved balances of power . . . and consequent justice which has robbed the Marxist challenge of its sting').

[68] For his further emphasis on memory, see Niebuhr, *Faith and History: A Comparison of Christian and Modern Views of History* (New York: Scribner's, 1949), 18–34. See also H. Richard Niebuhr, 'Reinhold Niebuhr's Interpretation of History', in William Stacy Johnson (ed.), *H. Richard Niebuhr: Theology, History, and Culture* (New Haven: Yale University Press, 1996), 91–107.

[69] *Irony*, 159. In his introduction to *Irony*'s 2008 re-issuance, Andrew Bacevich highlights such passages in arguing that Niebuhr provided a radical 'prophetic' critique of American foreign policy. *The Irony of American History* (Chicago: University of Chicago Press, 2008). See also Bacevich, 'The American Political Tradition', *Nation*, 17–24 Jul. 2006, 23–6 (review of Beinart); 'Prophets and Poseurs', *World Affairs*, Winter 2008, 24–37. For the more qualified suggestion that Niebuhr's writings during the Cold War period persisted in trying to address 'a prospective prophetic minority' in the liberal community who could grasp the perils of

Accordingly, while praising Kennan's writings on American diplomacy, Niebuhr in *Irony* still criticized the narrowness of his emphasis on national interest. And as he broke from Cold War orthodoxy on Vietnam, Niebuhr moved even closer to a prophetic mode in scolding the 'realist' foreign policy school for ignoring 'the possibility that even a residual loyalty to values, transcending national existence, may change radically the nation's conception of the breadth and quality of its "national interest."'[70] Even in the early 1960s, realist scholar Hans Morgenthau—who actually broke with Cold War orthodoxy over Vietnam sooner than Niebuhr—declared Niebuhr's central contribution to be the development of a theological perspective 'from the outside' that went beyond the world-view of 'a statesman who' takes 'America's political institutions for granted'.[71]

No book-length work from Niebuhr charted the re-emergence of his prophetic side during the 1960s.[72] Yet a prophet–statesman dynamic reminiscent of his earlier work was evident in such efforts as one of his last *Christianity and Crisis* articles in 1969. 'The King's Chapel and the King's Court' was a full-throated shot at President Nixon's hosting religious services in the White House and at Reverend Billy Graham for presiding over the first of the series. Niebuhr cast Graham as 'the king's chaplain' in the tradition of Old Testament priest Amaziah. In opposition to Graham was the prophetic tradition exemplified by Amaziah's nemesis Amos and most recently Martin Luther King, which featured criticism of 'the comfortable classes' and 'all religion' that fails to seek 'a just social policy'.

American power as well as the Soviet threat, see Michael Joseph Smith, *Realist Thought From Weber to Kissinger* (Baton Rouge: Louisiana State University Press, 1986), 118–19. See also Thomas Smith, 'The Uses of Tragedy: Reinhold Niebuhr's Theory of History and International Ethics', *Ethics and International Affairs*, 9 (1995), 171–91. But for a more critical view of Niebuhr's approach, see Aune, 'Reinhold Niebuhr and the Rhetoric of Christian Realism', in Beer and Hamman (eds.), *Post-Realism: The Rhetorical Turn in International Relations* (East Lansing: Michigan State University Press, 1996), 75–94; Riemer, 'Reinhold Niebuhr, Political Realism, and Prophetic Politics', in Neal Riemer (ed.), *Let Justice Roll* (Lanham, MD: Rowman and Littlefield, 1997), 155–68.

[70] *Irony*, 148; Niebuhr, *Man's Nature and His Communities* (New York: Scribner's, 1965), 77. See Rice, 'Reinhold Niebuhr and Hans Morgenthau: A Friendship with Contrast, Shades of Realism', *Journal of American Studies*, 42/2 (2008), 255–91; Good, 'The National Interest and Political Realism: Niebuhr's 'Debate' with Morgenthau and Kennan', *Journal of Politics*, Nov. 1960, 597–619.

[71] Morgenthau, 'The Influence of Reinhold Niebuhr in American Political Life and Thought', in Harold R. Landon (ed.), *Reinhold Niebuhr: A Prophetic Voice in Our Time* (Greenwich, CN: Seabury Press, 1962), 99–109, at 109. For Kennan's expression of a similar view, see Fox, 238. See also Jennifer See, 'A Prophet Without Honor: Hans Morgenthau and the War in Vietnam', *Pacific Historical Review*, Aug. 2001, 419–47.

[72] Halliwell finds communitarian overtones in Niebuhr's 1965 work *Man's Nature and His Communities* and speculates that they are due to King's influence. See *The Constant Dialogue*, 17, 158, 235, 262–3. In contrast to their invisibility in *Irony*, Niebuhr characterized African Americans as 'genuine proletarians in a bourgeois paradise' (*Communities*, 89).

At the same time Niebuhr praised the statesmanship of the Founding Fathers in constitutionalizing the principle of church–state separation that Nixon and Graham were mocking. The founders' wise move banning the establishment of religion, according to Niebuhr, had not just allowed but 'by implication encouraged the prophetic radical aspect of religious life, which insisted on criticizing any defective and unjust social order'.[73]

'The King's Chapel' hardly stands as a fully developed statement of political theory or theology for the Niebuhr of the 1960s. For example, as an easy hit against long-time conservative bêtes noires Nixon and Graham,[74] Niebuhr's critique hardly established the boundaries for a correct relationship between the Democratic regimes of Kennedys and the prophetic tradition of Martin Luther King. Although tilting back toward the prophetic religion of the Old Testament, Niebuhr was silent about the place of 'Jesus' love ethic' featured in his *Interpretation of Christian Ethics* during the 1930s.[75] And while Martin Halliwell has detected a drift toward King's 'beloved community' in contrast to his old pessimism about 'immoral society', Niebuhr in the 1960s showed only the faintest signs of incorporating the communitarian solidarity demanded by emerging feminist and radical-church critics.[76]

---

[73] Niebuhr, 'The King's Chapel and the King's Court', *Christianity and Crisis*, 4 Aug. 1969, 211–13. Niebuhr's last *Christianity and Crisis* article—'The Presidency and the Irony of American History', 13 Apr. 1970, 70–2—provided the more uncompromising critical tone that such Niebuhr admirers as Bacevich, see n. 69, strain to find in *The Irony of American History* almost two decades before. Niebuhr's 1970 'Irony' rhetorically asked '[A]re we not an imperial nation?' in light of our 'massive war with a little nation of Southeast Asia' and even argued with Lincoln's judgment that our electoral democracy provided a superior form of governmental accountability. See also Ronald A. Stone, 'Interview with Reinhold Niebuhr', *Christian Century*, 17 Mar. 1969, 48–52.

[74] See Finstuen, 'The Prophet and the Evangelist: The Public 'Conversation' of Reinhold Niebuhr and Billy Graham', *Books and Culture: A Christian Review*, Jul./Aug. 2006, <http://www.christiantoday.com/bc/2006/004/38thml>.

[75] In 1956, responding to questioning and criticism from Paul Ramsey about the role of Jesus' love ethic in *An Interpretation of Christian Ethics*, Niebuhr had declared: 'I am not . . . able to defend, or interested in defending, any position I took in *An Interpretation in Christian Ethics*', Niebuhr, 'Reply to Interpretation and Social Criticism', in Kegley and Bretall (eds.), *Reinhold Niebuhr*, 435. See also Ramsey, 'Love and Law', 79–124.

[76] Halliwell, 235. Niebuhr rather awkwardly recognized 'joint authorship' with his wife, Ursula: *Man's Nature*, 27. For Niebuhr and the women's movement, see generally Halliwell, 259–62, 323–4; Brown, *Niebuhr and His Age*, 196–7; Dorrien, *Soul in Society*, 155–6. For an assessment of the feminist critique sympathetic to Niebuhr, see Rebekah Miles, *The Bonds of Freedom: Feminist Theory and Christian Realism* (Oxford: Oxford University Press, 2001). For examples of Niebuhr's efforts to explore the social role of the church, see 'The Perils of American Power', *Messenger*, 22 May 1951, 6; 'Our Moral and Spiritual Resources for International Cooperation' *Social Action* 22 (Feb. 1956), 18–19. See also a number of essays in the Niebuhr collection edited by D. B. Robertson entitled *Essays in Applied Christianity* (New York: Meridian Books, 1959); and *Man's Nature*, 101–5.

The proliferation of such ambiguities confirms that Niebuhr's 1960s prophet–statesman dynamic was far more tentative and under-defined than even his 1930s version. But the re-emergence of his prophetic side certainly refutes the notion pushed by Beinart that Niebuhr had developed a paradigm of political thought at the dawn of the Cold War which neither needed nor received revision during the 1960s.[77]

*   *   *   *   *

I do not claim the tension between prophet and statesman to be the master key that unlocks the door to all of Niebuhr's political thought. But this double-edged framework is prominent enough throughout Niebuhr's work to undermine the one-dimensional ideological slices found in Chappell's 1930s radical and Beinart's post-Second World War portraits. Recognition of his dualistic outlook should also complicate any effort to distill the political essence of Niebuhr's 'Christian realism'.[78]

In this essay, however, I have implied something more: that the prophet–statesman dynamic in Niebuhr's thought should be useful for those on the progressive side of the spectrum in understanding, critiquing, and acting in American politics. Reinforcement for my belief comes from other respected intellectual figures—such as Richard Hofstadter, Garry Wills, and Michael Walzer—who have suggested that 'progressive change in America often rests upon a division of labor between dissenting leaders and democratic politicians.'[79] At the same time I know that this insight must be extensively refined to become a workable political praxis.[80]

[77] Beinart, 'Cold War Liberal', 42 ('[B]efore Vietnam, [Cold War] liberals had a clear story of their own' due to Niebuhr and Kennan).

[78] An influential re-articulation of Niebuhrian realism is Robin Lovin, *Reinhold Niebuhr and Christian Realism* (Cambridge: Cambridge University Press, 1995). See McCann, 'The Case for Christian Realism: Rethinking Reinhold Niebuhr', *Christian Century*, 7 Jun. 1995, 604–8 (praising the work but taking issue with its attempt to reject the presence of 'compromise' in the relationship between the ethics of Jesus and social ethics'). See also Ronald H. Stone, *Reinhold Niebuhr: Prophet to Politicians* (Nashville: Abingdon Press, 1972), 8 ('[N]o interpretation of his thought can neglect the chronology and remain accurate') and Rasmussen (ed.), 39.

[79] Bruce Miroff, *Icons of Democracy: American Leaders as Heroes, Aristocrats, Dissenters, and Democrats* (Lawrence: University of Kansas, 1993), 126. Miroff specifically cites Richard Hofstadter's chapter 'Wendell Phillips: The Patrician as Agitator' in his classic *The American Political Tradition and the Man Who Made It* (New York: Knopf, 1948), 119–74, and Garry Wills' *Confessions of a Conservative* (New York Penguin 1980), 159. I would add Michael Walzer. See, e.g., his *Interpretation and Social Criticism* (Boston: Harvard University Press, 1989), especially ch. 3 'The Prophet as Social Critic', 67–94; *The Company of Critics: Social Criticism and Political Commitment in the Twentieth Century* (New York: Basic Books, 1988); 'All God's Children Got Values', *Dissent*, Spring 2005, <http://www.dissentmagazine.org/menutest/articles/sp05/walzerhtm>.

[80] As Miroff points out, such a strict division of labor can assume artificially 'rigid and narrow' stereotypical roles in which prophets are completely beyond political pressure and

Even before such an effort is pursued, an objection to my view can be found within recent Niebuhr studies. In *The Constant Dialogue: Reinhold Niebuhr and American Intellectual Culture*, Martin Halliwell has suggested that throughout his career Niebuhr 'search[ed] for a leader who could combine elements of the poet, prophet, and statesman'. While acknowledging 'an untidy dialectic' between these poles in Niebuhr's work, Halliwell sees acceptance of a division of labor as a second-best position which Niebuhr desired to go beyond.[81]

The search in Niebuhr for a unified and unifying democratic hero cannot be denied. Such an urge may be endemic to intellectuals in democratic political culture. Even Max Weber at the end of 'Politics as a Vocation' rather incongruously concluded that 'an ethics of ultimate ends and an ethic of responsibility are not absolute contrasts but rather supplements which only in unison constitute a genuine man—a man who *can* have the "calling for politics"'.[82]

Niebuhr, however, never found such a complete democratic hero. As Halliwell indicates, President Abraham Lincoln was the historical figure who came closest to fulfilling his vision.[83] Yet Niebuhr went no further than

statesmen are so practical that they have no independent principle or vision (*Icons and Democracy*, 127). For example, under pressure from the LBJ White House and some allies, King the prophet actually agreed to a moratorium on civil rights activity in 1964 and muted his opposition to the Vietnam War until 1967. See Milkis, 'The President in the Vanguard: Lyndon Johnson and the Civil Rights Insurgency', in Stephen Skowroneck and Matthew Glassmann (eds.), *Formative Acts: American Politics in the Making* (Philadelphia: University of Pennsylvania Press, 2007), 280, 413, 45, 40; Fairclough, 'Martin Luther King, Jr., and the War in Vietnam', *Phylon*, 1st Qtr. 1984, 19–39. And Niebuhr's prophet–statesman dynamic leaves unarticulated any role(s) for 'followers' or 'citizens' or, in the religious context, the church body. But see the exploratory essays by Miroff, Milkis, and other contributors in Skowroneck (ed.), *Formative Acts* and Eric Gregory, *Politics and the Order of Love: An Augustinian Ethic of Democratic Citizenship* (Chicago: University of Chicago Press, 2008).

[81] Halliwell, 236, 182.

[82] *From Max Weber*, 127. See Davis, 'Max Weber on Religion and Political Responsibility', 29; *Religion*, 27–66, 41 (1999).

[83] Halliwell, 253. Niebuhr's admiration for Lincoln stands as the most consistent thread throughout the evolution of his thought. See, e.g., 'A Message from Reinhold Niebuhr' (1918), in William G. Chrystal (ed.), *Young Reinhold Niebuhr: His Early Writings, 1911–1931* (New York: Pilgrim Press, 1977), 98; *Leaves*, xii–xiv; *Beyond Tragedy*, 66–8; *Children of Light*, 181; *Irony*, 171–3; *Man's Nature and His Communities*, 113–15. As Richard Fox points out, Niebuhr favorably referred in an article the year before *Moral Man* to Gandhi as a combined prophet-statesman. Fox, *Niebuhr*, 130, citing Niebuhr, 'What Chance Has Gandhi?' *Christian Century*, 14 Oct. 1931, 1274–6. Yet Niebuhr hardly saw Gandhi as a political role model for the Western context. See, e.g., Niebuhr's review of Louis Fischer's *A Week With Gandhi* in *Christianity and Society*, Winter 1942, 43 (Gandhi as expressing 'an essentially Hindu anti-historical mysticism').

characterizing Lincoln as the model *statesman*. In a 1965 *Christian Century* article, Niebuhr did go so far as to claim that 'Lincoln's faith is closely akin to that of the Hebrew prophets' and was 'religiously superior to the pure moral idealism of the abolitionists'. Niebuhr nevertheless emphasized that 'Lincoln was primarily not a moral prophet but a responsible statesman.' He was also careful to cordon off Lincoln as 'a rare and unique human being' who stands 'alone among statesmen of the ancient and modern periods'.[84]

Yet the point is not just that division of labor between prophet and statesperson is a safer second-best proposition because (to paraphrase Madison) we will too rarely have anyone resembling a Lincoln at the helm.[85] My further point is this: to the extent that Niebuhr flirted with the notion of Lincoln as a complete political figure not in need of moral pressure from abolitionists, Niebuhr was quite simply wrong. As the young Richard Hofstadter in *The American Political Tradition* and others after him have demonstrated, Lincoln was hardly a racial egalitarian and abolitionist agitation from the likes of Wendell Phillips, Garrison, and Frederick Douglas was instrumental in creating a northern climate of opinion against slavery that, in President Lincoln's own words, 'no statesman could afford to ignore'.[86]

In effect, Niebuhr granted the limitations of relying on the historical Lincoln alone by moving to identify the prophet King as closest to his model of a democratic hero in current times.[87] At the same time, not even King could fill such a tall order. King's pacifism faded away as a barrier preventing Niebuhr from granting the constructive power of his progressive witness. That separates

---

[84] Niebuhr, 'The Religion of Abraham Lincoln', *Christian Century*, 10 Feb. 10, 1965, 172–5. For a recent biographical treatment of Lincoln in the Niebuhrian mold, see William A. Miller, *President Lincoln: The Duty of a Statesman* (New York: Vintage, 2008).

[85] 'Enlightened statesmen will not always be at the helm.' Madison, 'Federalist 10' in Clinton Rossiter (ed.), *The Federalist Papers* (New York: New American Library, 1961), 80.

[86] Hofstadter, 172–210, at 143. See also Foner, 'Our Lincoln', *The Nation*, 26 Jan. 2009, 16–19 ('The destruction of slavery during the war offers an example, as relevant today as in Lincoln's time, of how the combination of an engaged social movement and an enlightened leader can produce progressive social change') and 'Tichenor, Leaders, Citizenship Movements, and the Politics Rivalries Make', in *Formative Acts*, 241–68, 253, 257. For a sophisticated articulation of the dynamic tension between prophet and statesman in the mode envisioned by Niebuhr, see abolitionist Frederick Douglass' April 1876 speech at the unveiling of the Freedman's Memorial Monument to Lincoln in John W. Blassingame and John R. McKivigan (eds.), *The Frederick Douglass Papers; Series One: Speeches, Debates, and Interviews, Volume 4: 1864–1880* (New Haven: Yale University Press, 1991), 427–40, 436 ('Viewed from the genuine abolition ground, Mr. Lincoln seemed tardy, cold, dull, and indifferent; but measuring him by the sentiment of his country, a sentiment he was bound as a statesman to consult, he was swift, zealous, radical, and determined').

[87] Halliwell, 260. See also Rasmussen, 'Niebuhr's Theory of Power: Social Power and Its Redemption', in Gaudin and Hall (eds.), *Reinhold Niebuhr: A Centenary Appraisal* (Atlanta: Scholars Press, 1994), 158–171, 165.

the later Niebuhr from such avowed followers as Beinart who decry the pacifist tendencies in modern anti-war movements from Vietnam to Iraq.[88] At the same time, however, Niebuhr rightly would have never imagined King or any other pacifist joining Lincoln in the ranks of the Presidency.

Thus any urge in Niebuhr to find the complete democratic hero fails to take precedence over his wise division of labor between statesman and prophet. Resisting the impulse to rely on such a fictional figure is particularly important as Barack Obama moves through his presidency. While invoking Lincoln the statesman and King the prophet as guiding lights, our new President seems to understand in a more or less Niebuhrian way the impossibility of fulfilling the unified statesman-prophet ideal.[89] Yet it is equally important for grassroots progressives and their intellectual supporters to realize that President Obama is a statesman who cannot serve as their prophetic tribune.

None of this means that independent prophetic witness should uncritically submit to the statesmanship of a President Obama. That was Niebuhr's mistake in defending Adlai Stevenson's call to go slow on civil rights during the 1950s. As a political consultant, I can certainly appreciate Niebuhr's plea in *An Interpretation of Christian Ethics* for prophets to comprehend the exigencies of statesmanship and provide what Michael Walzer has subsequently called 'connected criticism'.[90] But Walzer's colleague and fellow Jewish intellectual Irving Howe was certainly correct in the 1950s to ask what could possibly be Christian about Niebuhr's support for Stevenson over King on civil rights.[91]

Niebuhr's lack of prophetic force during the 1950s serves as fodder for critics—ranging from political theorist Wilson Carey McWilliams to theologian Stanley Hauerwas[92]—who conclude that Niebuhr's thought demonstrated

---

[88] Incongruously, however, Beinart embraces the pacifist King without critical comment. See *Good Fight*, 27, 31, 37, 47.

[89] See Barack Obama, *The Audacity of Hope* (New York: Crown Publishers, 2006), 97–98 ('I'm reminded that deliberation and the constitutional order may be the luxury of the powerful, and that it has sometimes been the cranks, the zealots, the prophets, the agitators . . . that have fought for a new order . . . I'm left then with Lincoln who understood both the deliberative function of our democracy and the limits of such deliberation').

[90] Walzer, *Social Criticism* and *Company of Critics*.

[91] Howe, 'Reverberations in the North', *Dissent*, Spring 1956, 121–3, at 123.

[92] McWilliams, 'Reinhold Niebuhr: New Orthodoxy for Old Liberalism', *American Political Science Review* (Dec. 1962), 847–85; Hauerwas, *With the Grain of Universe: The Church's Witness and Natural Theology* (Grand Rapids: Brazos Press, 2001), 87–140; *Wilderness Wanderings: Probing Twentieth-Century Theology and Philosophy* (Boulder: Westview Press, 1997), 32–61; *Dispatches From the Front: Theological Engagements with the Secular* (Durham: Duke University Press, 1994), 91–106. But for a more discriminating judgment, see Hauerwas, 'The Search for the Historical Niebuhr', *Review of Politics*, Jul. 1976, 452–4. And, for a revised view from a McWilliams student, see Patrick Deneen, *Democratic Faith* (Princeton: Princeton University Press, 2005), 239–69. For the challenges that King's example poses to Hauerwas' own political position, see Beach-Verhey, 'Exemplifying Public Discourse: Christian Faith, American

nothing distinctively Christian or otherwise independent from the secular mainstream liberalism of his times. Niebuhr's shortcomings in the 1950s indeed represent a sobering historical lesson for those of us today who profess to be Christians but have concentrated too much on the world of statesmanship. Although statesmanship is an integral part of his legacy, Niebuhr deserves revival—and revision—today because a prophetic side worked in creative tension with statesmanship during his earlier as well as later thought.

Democracy, and Martin Luther King Jr.', *Journal of the Society of Christian Ethics*, 24/2 (2004), 115–36. See also Jeffrey Stout, *Democracy and Tradition* (Princeton: Princeton University Press, 2004).

3

Niebuhr's 'Nature of Man' and Christian Realism

Jean Bethke Elshtain

Reinhold Niebuhr's theological anthropology receives less critical attention than his direct pronouncements on political and social matters, especially those that touch on conflict and war. But Christian realism of the Niebuhrian sort turns on a cluster of interlocked features, including theological realism with its attendant commitment to a particular account of the nature of human beings after the fall. To explore Niebuhr on this issue, I will turn to his major work, *The Nature and Destiny of Man*.[1] In the first volume of this work, Niebuhr's Gifford Lectures, Niebuhr critiques models of man (and I will use 'man' as Niebuhr does as an inclusive term meaning 'all human persons') he finds woefully inadequate even as he unpacks his own views. In our era, when talk of 'human nature' is proscribed in many circles as tales of 'constructionism' dominate—as if human beings are infinitely malleable and entirely 'constructed' out of features of the culture in which they find themselves—Niebuhr's views are a refreshing tonic. What do we make of what we are given? And what is given in the first instance?

To appreciate Niebuhr's efforts is not, of course, to endorse them perforce. One must ask certain questions: Are his views adequate and persuasive? Is there a clear connection between his theological anthropology and his political and social arguments and conclusions? If there are flaws or shortcomings in Niebuhr's understanding of the 'nature of man' does this undercut his Christian realism in any significant way? These and other considerations will be examined in this essay.

---

[1] Reinhold Niebuhr, *The Nature and Destiny of Man*, i: *Human Nature* (New York: Macmillan, 1964; first published in 1941).

WHITHER HUMAN NATURE?

When I studied political theory in the late 1960s and early 1970s, it was still possible to talk about human nature without being accused of 'essentialism', that cardinal sin of the present moment. Alas, the talk was often rote and little in-depth exploration of the matter was undertaken. I recall our class discussions about Machiavelli, Hobbes, Locke, Rousseau, and others and, as I do so, I cannot recapitulate any serious treatment of the ways in which the theorist's anthropology—his understanding of human beings—was taken up in any depth. This is a remarkable thing, for conclusions about human nature are inescapable in the thinkers I note above, and the list is by no means exhaustive. When a theorist, Thomas Hobbes in this case, begins making his case about the need for a social contract culminating in the creation of a 'Leviathan', he does so in book I, chapter 1, with a discussion 'Of Man'.[2] Unless one appreciates Hobbes on this issue, his culminating presentations of the necessity for, and structure of, the 'Leviathan' become opaque, if not unintelligible altogether.

Given our lack of attention to such matters, we rarely asked questions about whether Hobbes' or any other theorist's anthropology was convincing, whether it accounted for the cumulative evidence on how human beings act and behave, whether it appreciated the complex nature of human embodiment, and so forth. As this dynamic played out in the study of historic political thought, in the empirical social sciences human nature took a serious nose-dive. That era was dominated by a very thin account of human beings central to 'behaviorism'. Rarely discussed explicitly, the implicit idea was that human beings behave according to their predictable responses to certain external stimuli. Given its overall radical inadequacy to explain political phenomena, behaviorism was discredited in time but the great gap where a sophisticated account of human beings should have been remained. There were critiques—I think here of sociologist Dennis Wrong's argument against the 'oversocialized' account of man in the social sciences—but very few constructive arguments about what did, indeed, count as a defensible account of human nature.[3]

One text that confronted this question head-on was Kenneth N. Waltz's classic, *Man, the State and War*.[4] Indeed, Waltz made this a linchpin of his critique of simplistic and reductionistic accounts of 'why war': all began with

---

[2] Thomas Hobbes, *The Leviathan* (New York: Collier Books, 1966).
[3] Dennis Wrong, "The Oversocialized Conception of Man in Modern Sociology," *American Sociological Review*, 26 (1961), 183–93.
[4] Kenneth N. Waltz, *Man, the State and War* (New York: Columbia University Press, 1958).

a crude version of human beings, most of them breathtakingly naïve.[5] Waltz insists that one ask certain critical questions of a thinker's understanding of why wars occur. As he does so, he offers insight into the manner in which a critical analysis of theories of human nature can be assessed. For example: is the theorist's image an adequate one? Can it account for the full repertoire of human actions? If a thinker locates some major outcome—war, in his book— to human nature, how does he propose to change human nature?

Often brilliant on deconstruction, Waltz offers no constructive account of his own that might help us to flesh out an adequate view of human nature. Apropos this very point, it is interesting indeed that Niebuhr hovers over Waltz's text but alights, or is permitted to alight, nowhere. It seems clear that Waltz did not want to get on the treacherous ground of theology or anything that smacked of 'metaphysics', a forbidden topic in social science. One imagines a huge sign that proclaims 'Off Limits' at the border of the territory of theological and ethical anthropology. Moreover, a form of moral realism may be assumed tacitly by some thinkers—else how could they critique systems of thought that ushered into pernicious systems of politics—but this, too, went untheorized, unthought, really. Because Waltz represents the best of what serious scholars in political science were writing a few decades ago, one can readily see the problem. Niebuhr could be mentioned but not unpacked thoroughly because, to do so, would require delving into matters that were not within the purview of political science.

Niebuhr, however, moved from theology to politics with ease. He makes explicit much of what was either 'off limits' or implicit in the political philosophy and theory of his time. As one examines Niebuhr's account, one is struck yet again by the damage done to both theology and politics when these subject matters were prised apart—especially from the political end. That is a question I cannot go into in detail here although I have explored it elsewhere.[6] For Niebuhr, nothing of what he offered by way of historical or political analysis could have been advanced in a persuasive manner without the connective tissue afforded by the ways in which he weaves together metaphysical, theological, moral, and political realism, a point made brilliantly by Robin Lovin in his important work, *Reinhold Niebuhr and Christian Realism*.[7] Given this interlocking analysis, it is no surprise that Niebuhr's

---

[5] These naive accounts were most visible in the social sciences, especially psychology, argued Waltz, and he has a great deal of fun exposing the flimsiness of such arguments.

[6] See, for example, the discussion in my Gifford Lectures, *Sovereignty: God, State, and Self* (New York: Basic Books, 2008).

[7] Robin Lovin, *Reinhold Niebuhr and Christian Realism* (Cambridge: Cambridge University Press, 1995). To this one must add his most recent work, *Christian Realism and the New Realities* (Cambridge: Cambridge University Press, 2008).

views on human nature made little headway in the political and social thinking of his time—at least explicitly—even as his political positions were analyzed, applauded, and criticized routinely.

The separation of subject matters—as I have already noted—explains part of this. But another inescapable issue is the fact that when one makes interventions in the political arena, one is not obliged to put on offer *every* assumption with which one works. For example: suppose I state my opposition to a measure that will weaken protection for endangered species. Am I obliged to lay out the doctrine of creation to which I am committed in order to state my political point? The answer is 'no'. I *may* be called upon to do that in some extensive and exploratory context where philosophic matters are in play explicitly but that is simply not the case in the hurly-burly of political argumentation, particularly in this era of sound-bytes and visual bytes.

Similarly, in his hundreds of 'op-eds' and interventions, Niebuhr considered himself under no obligation to preface his position by unpacking his anthropological presuppositions. They *were* there, of course, but, given the nature of political debate, they remained unarticulated. If these sorts of interventions are what one knows of Niebuhr, it is altogether too easy to ignore the heart of the matter for him, namely, 'what is man that thou are mindful of him' and, for our purposes, 'what is man that he has created political worlds that, from the beginning, were marred by conflict, violence, disorder, and duplicity'? That is not all of it, not the full story, of course. But it is a central feature of that story and it is one the optimistic social scientists of Niebuhr's time did not want to hear.

NIEBUHR ON THE 'NATURE OF MAN': THE GOOD, THE BAD, AND THE UGLY

In a compelling work on Niebuhr, Langdon Gilkey insists that 'Niebuhr's theology is as important in understanding him as are his political and ethical insights'; moreover, when this theology takes up human nature, 'the true or essential self', Niebuhr declares that the self 'is utterly dependent on God' yet is also 'free to be fully itself. The true self is the self that finds itself freely in its dependence on God.'[8] The implication here is that, absent its theological underpinnings, Niebuhr's political views amount to the contributions made

---

[8] Langdon Gilkey, *On Niebuhr: A Theological Study* (Chicago: University of Chicago Press, 2001), 188 (quoted material before semicolon), 193 (quoted material after semicolon).

by a serious scholar to serious debates but the deeper truth claims that underlay that scholar's analysis go undiscussed—are never part of the debate. Now, as I noted above, it is the nature of hotly contested political disputes that, most of the time, we are not obliged to articulate the fullness of our positions. But we must be prepared to thus articulate should the occasion arise. This is where so many fall short.

When asked whether their commitment to some public policy turns on an unstated anthropology—a human nature of some sort—most contemporary political advocates will respond with a rather blank stare: What? Really? In this way, all manner of nonsense gets proliferated as political claims are not measured against what we actually know of what makes human beings tick. Moreover, given that every unrealistic account of human nature has fallen apart under historical pressure, the fact that such accounts continue to proliferate is not only frustrating, it undermines attempts to offer a more subtle and comprehensive account.

Of this Niebuhr was well aware. Indeed, some of his own early views are culpable on this score. The Fellowship of Reconciliation to which he belonged before the rise of Hitlerism accepted an account of human beings that construed us as always in touch, or capable of being in touch, with what Abraham Lincoln called 'the better angels of our nature'. This doesn't hold up under scrutiny, no more than does a Marxist anthropology. Given that Niebuhr's early work is laced through and through with Marxist categories and terminology—including repetition of 'proletariat' and 'bourgeoisie'—it is surprising that he did not seem to pause and to ask systematically whether or not the anthropology with which Marxists worked was adequate. One assumes that he did this but that, on the whole, decided that his overall social and political analysis gained sufficient analytic power from key Marxist categories such that its foundational weakness could be bypassed for political ends and purposes. This no doubt made it easier for him to suggest that, although no group of human beings can possibly acquire moral perfection, somehow the 'proletariat' is the more likely repository of an ethic of justice than the 'bourgeoisie', and the like.[9]

Yet, according to Niebuhr himself, every advocacy will be marred by pride or anxiety. It follows necessarily that a flawed anthropology is going to mar the specific political conclusions that are heavily dependent on it and this did indeed happen in Niebuhr's case. The 'proletariat' is no less subject to corruption than the 'bourgeoisie'. Niebuhr knew this but downplayed it, at times, because he had a particular political point to make. Because Marxism

---

[9] The text in which these views are more fully on display is, of course, *Moral Man and Immoral Society* (Louisville: Westminster John Knox Press, 2001; first published in 1932).

turns on an entirely unreal notion of human freedom and human identity, on our ability to transcend all particular attachments (whether to family, faith, or nation), one must be wary of its political advocacy. We know that such transcendence is not only impossible, it is undesirable and invites horrors of specific sorts.[10] Of course, uncritical overattachment to particulars also trails troubles in its wake but the main point, for now, is that there is a worm in the apple from the beginning with Marxism—there has to be—for any Christian thinker. I do not understand how one can endorse Marxist categories and conclusions without buying into its extraordinarily naïve and utopian anthropology. Given that Marxism's equally implausible historic teleology is conceptually linked to the anthropology, that, too, undermines the credibility of its political conclusions, a point Niebuhr makes explicit in the volume under consideration.

Unsurprisingly, then, Niebuhr moved away from both pacifistic and Marxist orientations over time. He was driven in part by events in the 'real world', including the pernicious behavior of Marxists in power and the culpably inadequate nature of accommodationist/quasi-pacifist commitments when dealing with a Hitler or a Stalin. In this way, he moved more explicitly and deeply to a Christian understanding of human beings as torn creatures, always tempted by *superbia* (pride) and the *libido dominandi* (the lust to dominate.) If, as Niebuhr contends, modern culture is a battleground between two opposing views of human nature, it behooves us to appreciate what is at stake in those opposing views. Niebuhr's most complete answer to that question appears in Volume I of his Gifford Lectures, *The Nature and Destiny of Man*. It is only when we appreciate his specific endorsement of a specific understanding of the human person that we can ask the analytic questions concerning the coherence of his perspective overall.

Niebuhr opens his analysis by noting that, as St Augustine insisted, man is a 'problem to himself' as much as he is to others. To unpack this question, we must begin with

two facts about man not usually appreciated with equal sympathy. The obvious fact that man is a child of nature, subject to its vicissitudes, compelled by its necessities, driven by its impulses, and confined within the brevity of the years which nature permits its varied organic form, allowing them some, but not too much, latitude. The

---

[10] Even in *The Nature and Destiny of Man*, Niebuhr is too kind to Marxism, too harsh to Freud, with whom Marx is compared. Freud was no simple hedonist, for one thing. Because he construes Freud as such a hedonist, and declares Marx to have nothing in common with this, Marxism comes off looking more profound than it really is, it seems to me, but this is a point better argued elsewhere.

other less obvious fact is that man is a spirit who stands outside of nature, life, himself, his reason and the world.[11]

Niebuhr adds that it is our capacity for 'self-transcendence' that contemporary rationalists fail to understand and this failure, in turn, mars their attempts to fathom human nature. This leads him to the two broad perspectives he sees in contention in modernity. The first is heavily indebted to the views of classical antiquity, brought into the present time. The second is what he calls, simply, the biblical view. The classical view—and, remember, I am not here so much assessing the adequacy of Niebuhr's treatment as unpacking it—privileges purely intellectual activity. Thus, 'Plato and Aristotle . . . share a common rationalism; and also a common dualism which is explicit in the case of Plato and implicit and covert in the case of Aristotle'.[12] The dualism he associates (problematically, I believe) with both Plato and Aristotle invites 'identifying the body with evil and assuming the essential goodness of mind or spirit', the very position, taking the form of Manicheanism, that St. Augustine so thoroughly and wittily trounces in his masterwork, *The City of God*.[13] Let's call the classical view, brought forward to the present, the 'rationalistic account' (RA): intellection trumps all and essentially defines and distinguishes that which is human. The bodily is inessential in defining us. (How inessential, polluted, etc., the body is varies from thinker to thinker over time, of course.)

An alternative account is the Christian view, biblically derived. Let's call it the Christian Account (CA). This view is incarnational: God created the world and creation is good. As part of God's creation, the human being, body and soul, is also good, although human beings, through their disobedience in the garden, forever after darkened human nature, both body and soul. Nothing escaped. Still it cannot be said that the body is either evil per se or inessential. Our physical being is further enhanced by the fact that God Himself came to earth in human form, was Incarnate as Jesus. This redeems our physical existence even as Christ's suffering on the Cross offers God's judgment on a sinful world.

The high estimate of the human stature implied in the concept of 'image of God' stands in paradoxical juxtaposition to the low estimate of human virtue in Christian thought. . . . The Christian estimate of human evil is so serious precisely because it places evil at the very centre of human personality: in the will.

Still, our 'essence is free self-determination'. It is our tragedy that sin invites the wrongful use of this freedom.[14]

---

[11] *Nature and Destiny of Man*, 3.
[12] Ibid. 7.   [13] Ibid. 7.   [14] Ibid. 16.

It is this apparent paradox—being both 'free' and 'bound'—that serves as a stumbling block to moderns, to the extent that it is considered by the adherents of RA. They would no doubt consider this paradox a logical incoherence and dismiss it thereby. As Niebuhr continues, he insists—against the dominant trends of Western culture—that man is not and can never be wholly self-sufficing. Also, it is *only* within the Christian faith, Niebuhr insists, that man can truly appreciate the reality of evil in himself but, at the same time, escape the error of attributing that evil to anyone but himself. (So we get no 'the devil made me do it' or 'history demands': that sort of thing.) Thus Niebuhr counters the classical understanding that feeds into RA with its view of the body as inessential, even polluted, and its refusal to come to grips with sin and evil.

What did modernity do with these competing views? Niebuhr identifies a variety of trends that run alongside the RA. Romanticism and vitalism present themselves as alternatives but each is deeply flawed. Any rebellion against the notion that man is permanently alienated from the full ground of his being is anathema to both the romantic and the vitalist. Romantics strive to restore our lost wholeness. Niebuhr astutely identifies trends in the 1960s—with Herbert Marcuse and the notion of 'surplus repression' and that sort of thing—with the romantic revolt. These revolts against both RA and CA are extraordinarily naïve about sin. (The RA account is, as well, but, for the moment I am concentrating on the romanticist-vitalist strain that rejects both CA and RA.) One feature of the outburst against sin and evil is its 'optimistic treatment of the problem of evil. Modern man has an essentially easy conscience . . . The idea that man is sinful at the very centre of his personality, that is in his will, is universally rejected.'[15] In my work I·have called this the shift from 'sin' to 'syndromes'.

Romantics and vitalists promote the extraordinary optimism that once flawed social forms are corrected, all will be well. Remove repression and we will live in a polymorphously perverse paradise where there is plenty for everyone. Remove oppression and we will live in a world of universal justice. The RA is usually not so simple-minded, for he or she works with a rather more complex anthropology. But there is a flaw at its core, namely, the view that the 'root of his [man's] evil' lies 'in his involvement in natural impulses and natural necessities from which it hopes to free him by the increase of his rational faculties'.[16] Would it were so simple. This optimistic view is tied to a teleology of progress: we are slowly but surely moving 'toward some kind of perfect society'.[17] All defects will eventually 'be sloughed off by a new education or a new social organization'.[18]

---

[15] Ibid. 23.   [16] Ibid. 23.   [17] Ibid.   [18] Ibid. 25.

Christianity rests uneasily with any and all forms of idealism. At this moment, one might echo what Charles Taylor has called the 'rotten deal' modernity has deeded us in this matter, namely, hyper-rationalism, on the one hand, and hyper-subjectivism, on the other. We are enjoined never to challenge someone else's 'reality'. On the other hand, in public policy and scientific (or pseudo-scientific) matters we are treated to proclamations of absolute certainty as this is what a certain 'model' or rationalist account dictates. We also find new forms of determinism, mostly from the naturalistic side. We are in the throes, for example, of a wave of what might be called 'genetic fundamentalism' as the answer to who we are comes back: we are our DNA. More and more persons are obsessed to find out what 'blood' might course through their veins, in effect, and this will give them the rock-bottom truth about themselves. Niebuhr, were he still with us, would have a field-day with this sort of thing. He rejected all determinisms, of course, but he would be both amused and appalled at the pseudo-sophistication at work in contemporary determinisms.

Niebuhr stresses the capacity of human beings for a form of self-transcendence that never ushers into a totalized vision that we can altogether transcend the terms of our material existence. He links this self-transcendence to that which is 'spirit' in man—thus courting dualism, I fear—and describes this transcendence, in part, as a form of heightened sensibility of individuality. As with most Niebuhrian insights, there is a danger if a moment of truth is taken too far. This individuality may become detethered from concrete realities and turn idolatrous as human beings worship their own pride and power. The self can become absorbed into a variety of categories: we are either all spirit and a shadowy universalism takes over; or all 'natural' and various accounts of us of as biological creatures—the DNA version being prevalent among us, as I have already suggested—take over. Tossed to and fro in this manner, it is small wonder that modern man is confused and abandons complexity for the simplistic; abandons the realistic for an idealism of one sort or another. All RA accounts lend themselves to flights into some form or another of idealism; CA, taken in toto, does not. Thus it is bypassed, remains inarticulate, or is rejected outright.

We have, Niebuhr laments, lost the resources with which to 'modify or to defy' certain tendencies.

Without the presuppositions of the Christian faith the individual is either nothing or becomes everything. In the Christian faith man's insignificance as a creature, involved in the process of nature and time, is lifted into significance by the mercy and power of God in which his life is sustained . . . It is because man is inevitably involved in this primal sin [self-pride] that he is bound to meet God first of all as a judge, who humbles his pride and brings his vain imagination to naught.[19]

Modern man has, altogether, made things much too easy for himself—hence, his uneasy consciousness. The Christian drama of fall, redemption, salvation seems altogether too primitive. We are to urged to reject such accounts and to slough them off as adolescent; hence, 'no cumulation of contradictory evidence seems to disturb modern man's good opinion of himself.'[20] When things go awry, we can just blame corrupting institutions. Somehow, if we can gerrymander this or fix that, we can perfect ourselves. We forget—as did the Marxists, one might add—that our alienation simply is the human condition.

At this point, Niebuhr connects his anthropology to the problems with which he dealt throughout his life, namely, the problems of human living-together, the trials and tribulations of politics and government. What our culture does is to attribute evils 'to specific historic causes without inquiring how such particular causes could have arisen'. In so doing, we assume 'a voluntarism in . . . social theory which [our] deterministic psychology [or biology] denies'.[21] At this point, Niebuhr also indicts Marxism, for its view of human nature derives evil from faults in economic organization, with oppressive governments being the direct consequence of such organization. The home-grown school of American pragmatism that Niebuhr locates in the naturalistic school of explanation also winds up with naïve answers and solutions to complex questions. John Dewey, for example, held to a 'cultural lag' theory of human evil—we just haven't caught up and we remain entangled in the coils of old notions—but sooner or later a persuasive RA will overtake us. At that point we will have a society 'which will ultimately be governed purely by rational suasion rather than force'.[22]

For correctives and a constructive alternative Niebuhr unpacks the CA, including the doctrine of evil. Transcendence is preserved and fallenness is accounted for. Judgment and mercy are kept together rather than driven apart. Given the CA account of sin, biblically derived, that addresses the destructiveness wrought by man's rebellion against God, the CA provides 'an interpretation of history in which judgment upon sin becomes the first category of interpretation'.[23] Let's call this a hermeneutics of sin. This hermeneutics of sin helps us to appreciate that there will never, ever, be a time in history free from violence, horror, and cruelty. We can and must work toward a world less violent, horrific, and cruel. But we cannot definitively cure the

---

[19] *Nature and Destiny of Man*, 92.   [20] Ibid. 94.   [21] Ibid. 99.
[22] Ibid. 113.   [23] Ibid. 140.

universe. Those who attempt such cures wind up with wild moralistic crusades that trail even further horror in their wake.[24]

Among liberals—and Niebuhr thus identified himself—there is a tendency to overstate the benefits of social change, to embrace a vision of progress that is, in the final analysis, unsustainable. Liberal Protestantism is culpable as well for having bleached out so much complexity and for having abandoned the CA for a far more optimistic account of man and culture (a kind of secular post-millennialism). But sin is not just a mistake, an error.[25] Our anxieties, pridefulness, greed are never suspended. Thus we are susceptible to ideologies and manifestations of all kind, utopias of various stripes, whether of the totalitarian variety or the pseudo-scientist variety. Current RA cannot begin to come to grips, then, with our self-transcendence, our finiteness, and our evil—all at once. The CA can and that is why it should be embraced.[26]

The contemporary non-Christian Realist appreciates at least part of the story. He or she appreciates the tendency toward pridefulness; our susceptibility faced with triumphalist prospects. Realists take note of this, whether they hold to the full CA or not. What the CA adds is depth and breadth, including our capacity for forgiveness, charity, and reconciliation. Many hard-core Realists, in denying or ignoring any possibility that moral motives may be at work in politics, including international politics, sell us short.

Nevertheless, Niebuhr suggests that their wariness is far more welcome, and to be endorsed, than simplistic RA accounts. The Christian doctrine of sin offends adherents of the RA. So be it. There is no way to evade real moral dilemmas or human weakness. At the same time, however, we must give due credit to our responsibility, our freedom, our capacity for self-criticism and subsequent remorse and repentance. After all, Niebuhr reminds us, the great theological virtue is hope—realistic hope not silly, overly optimistic hope that is not hope at all but, rather, optimism—not the same thing. Evil and sin 'cannot completely destroy the goodness of what God has created in man',

---

[24] See, for example, the discussion of the French Revolution in my *Sovereignty: God, State, and Self* (New York: Basic Books, 2008). I draw upon both Albert Camus and Dietrich Bonhoeffer in advancing my account.

[25] Recently I witnessed this scene: a troubled young woman confessed her sins to a local pastor. The pastor was very kind, very motherly as she listened. As the young woman said, again, 'I've sinned', the pastor leapt in: 'You made a mistake'. I nearly fell off my chair but it was my job to listen and not to intervene—not an easy task, as it turned out, given what transpired. The word 'mistake' came nowhere near dealing with the anguish the young woman felt. In this way, in the name of being charitable, we diminish people's sorrow and troubles and deprive them of the depth of that which they are themselves feeling.

[26] See, for example, ibid. 150.

hence, our capacity to hope.[27] The CA helps us to recognize evil because it emerges against a backdrop of that which is good—something too many contemporary Realists ignore. Niebuhr does not accept every version of the CA. He charges the Catholics, for example, with falling on the optimistic side of the ledger. He also gives us the 'stuff' out of which a critique of the so-called Christian Left could be mounted. (Given that Niebuhr is so clearly associated with opposition to the 'Christian Right', to those who are excessively fundamentalist and literalist, it is more interesting to consider what he has to say on the other side of the CA-divide.)

Among other things, his words suggest that, e.g., the Catholic 'preferential option for the poor' may involve a misinterpretation of the Scriptural message insofar as no one is any less a sinner for being a victim. The poor may be less responsible for a given state of affairs but that, by no means, means that they should be treated sentimentally or as a pure repository of goodness and unselfishness. He writes:

The anti-aristocratic emphasis of the Bible has been interpreted by certain types of sectarian Christianity and by modern secular radicalism in too simple politico-moral terms. Jesus is reduced in this type of thought to the stature of a leader of a proletarian revolt against the rich ... Capitalists are not greater sinners than poor labourers by any natural depravity...A too simple social radicalism does not recognize how quickly the poor, the weak, and the despised of yesterday, may, on gaining a social victory over their detractors, exhibit the same arrogance and the same will-to-power which they abhorred in their opponents and which they were inclined to regard as a congenital sin of their enemies.[28]

To sum up, it is very easy for illusory visions of politics and history to overtake us should we rely on overly optimistic views of human beings. The CA, by contrast, affords us a position of depth and breadth. We come to understand human tragedy and irony, the paradox of man as both wise and wicked, horrific and loving. The world is an arena of moral striving—something Realists—not Christian Realists but Secular Realists—frequently forget. No overarching ideology can or should be endorsed wholesale. No collectivity of human beings is free from dangerous triumphalism, even to a 'good' end.

---

[27] Ibid. 267.
[28] Ibid. 225–6. On this score, it should be noted that Niebuhr is too often associated with a simple kind of Christian Left position: the Christian Right is demonized; the US government, at least under former President Bush, is demonized even as under President Obama it is lionized as an unalloyed source of good, and so on. Niebuhr would have none of this, of course, as he detested ideologies and the trapping of interpretations inside ideologies that distort such interpretations, whether of the CA or some other.

WHITHER NIEBUHR AND REALISM?

Can the post-modern mind of the present moment comprehend Niebuhr's CA? I doubt it. In Western Europe, Christianity has pretty much evaporated and been reduced to thin rituals at certain key moments: baptism, marriage, funerals— although even that is disappearing. (I should note the growth of Islam, including in its dangerous radical variety, but that is the subject of another essay.) Key aspects of CA are waning or on their way out, including Incarnation and Resurrection, simple untelligible to a certain version of the 'modern mind'. (Crucifixion is a historically established fact so it can remain.) Do we truly believe that God is sovereign over history? Do we truly believe that God became incarnate, died for our sins, and was raised again? Not really, taken in the main.

What does this do to the remainder of the CA? It weakens it at best. Moreover, Niebuhr could assume a majoritarian Protestant Christian culture when he was writing in the 1930s and through the 1950s, a kind of civic consensus in the United States. That, too, is gone. The mainline tradition he represented is by now thinned out and on the wane. The evangelical tradition is alive and well—and evangelical Christianity should by no means be equated with fundamentalism as these are different phenomena—but most Niebuhrians repudiate it as promoting an overly simplistic CA. At least the evangelicals keep alive sin and redemption although, at the same time, too many look to government, or to policies they endorse, in an overly optimistic way that may lend itself to a crusading mentality. The Catholic Church comes closest to maintaining the full panoply of the CA. Of course, Niebuhr taxed Catholics with having concentrated on sin, which is good, but with overemphasizing certain social virtues, or their possibility as well. Were he alive, Niebuhr would surely find much to endorse in the social teachings of Pope John Paul II and in Pope Benedict's sophisticated reprise of the CA that keeps alive what Benedict calls a necessary connection to classical antiquity.

When Niebuhrians—and not they alone—ask where our contemporary Niebuhr is or might come from, they are asking a question that is moot from the start. There cannot be a contemporary Niebuhr as the culture that gave rise to Niebuhr and which he could assume, no longer exists. If the heart of the CA is that sin and freedom go together, we are enthralled by a sinless freedom and that is a very dangerous thing indeed. Gilkey alerts us to the fact that Niebuhr always recognized 'the problem of a translation, so to speak, of an existential and inward resolution into the public, historical sphere and he seeks to deal with it'.[29]

---

[29] Much easier to effect that translation in the face of a consensus than in a situation of fragmentation, with atheists and agnostics the fastest growing 'group'. See Gilkey, *On Niebuhr*, 194.

That translation becomes ever more difficult as the faith that sustained it recedes. Niebuhr was always clear in his version of Christian Realism that the adherent of the CA need not bring the full panoply of his or her beliefs to bear when endorsing any specific policy question or programmatic possibility. At the same time, one can posit two people who share an identical CA but who differ on the policy implications. Christian Realism does not guarantee any sort of consensus on policy questions, although highly politicized Niebuhrians seem to think so. This came our clearly during the Iraq War. I recall listening to Niebuhr papers that offered the most extraordinary demonization of the Bush Administration, the effect of which was an excessive moralism and idealism attached to their own anti-Iraq War accounts. Points of view that differed from their own were trivialized and even demonized. That is surely not the Niebuhrian way.

Politicized Niebuhrianism aside—and another interesting question would be whether Niebuhr himself encouraged the tendency toward excessive politicization given the focus of his public ministry—Niebuhr would have much to offer where our own company of RA aficionados is concerned. Take, for example, the idealism of contemporary Kantianism. 'Peace', Kant opined, 'is the end of all hostilities so that even to modify it by 'perpetual' smacks of pleonasm', or superfluous use, meaning more than necessary.[30] All dealings between states must be submitted to full transparency, with nothing held in reserve. All treaties that end particular wars but do not end the state of war must be rejected, and so on. In contemporary neo-Kantian versions of peace, international law and its tribunals play something of the part Kant assigned to moral philosophers—they are allegedly above the fray; no one would suspect them of being self-interested; they are incapable of forming cliques, and so on. If this be not true, then morality is just prudence and this is no morality at all.

Neo-Kantianism cannot appreciate the tragedy that on this earth even good and decent principles cannot be wholly realized. Hence, calls for a lesser evil or for what I call 'minimally decent states' are taxed with being disguised forms of ethnocentrism or some such. The contemporary neo-Kantian proffers a kind of fantasy United Nations—quite unlike the one we actually have—tethered to a universally accepted, endorsed, and self-enforced international law—although just how all this is to be accomplished is rather thin. A Christian Realist of the Niebuhrian sort would ask how a United Nations composed overwhelmingly of delegates from undemocratic and corrupt regimes can legislate in a wholly impartial and moral way, or why an International Court of Justice dominated by Western Europeans is somehow

---

[30] Immanuel Kant, *Perpetual Peace and Other Essays on Politics, History and Morals*, trans. Ted Humphrey (Indianapolis: Hackett Publishing, 1983), 107.

universally valid. The Kantian vision relies on a dualistic contrast between 'perpetual peace' and 'perpetual war', ignoring or downplaying moral and political ambiguity and nuance, the smudginess of real human lives and history.

The new neo-Kantianism, this variant on the RA, is an untethered idealism that hopes for the triumph of good will and a world in which international bodies supplant states and international law supersedes any and all civic law. This, allegedly, will lead to or is itself part and parcel of the definitive abandonment of the use of force in international affairs.

One readily sees that Niebuhr's Christian Realism remains powerful as a solvent of such simplistic idealisms. As critique, it is alive and well, at least in some circles. As a constructive account, however, it has faltered as the CA has thinned out and been abandoned. Niebuhr would surely agree with the powerful insights proffered by T. S. Eliot in his poem, Choruses from 'The Rock':

> 'It is hard for those who live near a Bank
> To doubt the security of their money.
> It is hard for those who live near a Police Station
> To believe in the triumph of violence.
> Do you think that Faith has conquered the World
> And that Lions no longer need keepers?'

Puncturing illusions, including the illusion that moral suasion alone suffices in a dangerous world, is a great strength of Christian Realism. At the same time, the constructive CA, although not lost to us completely, is more difficult to hold together. This essay has already grown beyond a reasonable length, so let me conclude by posing some questions that suggest the need for further examinations, interpretations, and analyses:

Is it reasonable and legitimate to claim that one's position is a Niebuhrian one unless one adheres to the CA as did Niebuhr?
Is it possible to disentangle Niebuhr's anthropology from his other commitments without a loss in coherence?
Can Christian Realism as a thought-through position remain a vibrant option in a Western world within which faith is under constant pressure and the story that made so much sense for so many centuries, as Charles Taylor has pointed out, now makes so little sense to so many?[31]

I am loath to end with a series of questions but they do reflect what I take to be our current situation. Let me add, then, by way of affirmation, that what we might call a 'Niebuhrian sensibility' or 'Niebuhrian disposition' can and does

---

[31] See his masterwork, *A Secular Age* (Cambridge, MA: Harvard University Press, 2007).

exist absent the full embrace of the CA. One finds it in the skepticism of non-Christian Realism concerning the use and abuse of power. One finds it in all those aware of the ironies of history and of how our best-laid plans go astray. The temptation, however, is for the Realist absent the CA to focus only on power and violence and to repudiate the force of moral purposes and motivations in collective action. The temptation for the skeptic and ironist is that he or she may be paralyzed from endorsing much of anything. It seems, then, that we need Niebuhr and yet we cannot quite fully embrace him—the 'we' in this instance being the prototypical modern man or woman. *That* is our dilemma. How would Niebuhr help us to think our way through it? Another essay for another time.

4

Radical Orthodoxy's
Critique of Niebuhr

Ben Quash

INTRODUCTION

Reinhold Niebuhr's 'Christian realism' was in significant part a rejection of the pacifism and optimism of the Social Gospel movement in the United States. Even though Niebuhr had initially been sympathetic to the movement, he came to dismiss its belief that the realization of the kingdom of God, proclaimed by Jesus, could be expected in the foreseeable future. He thought the movement's great confidence in human progress was naïve, and that its belief in education's power to foster a law of love (and thus to eradicate the sin of selfishness from individuals and institutions) lacked a proper understanding of original sin.

Recognizing the force of Niebuhr's criticisms of the Social Gospel movement, this chapter sets out to ask whether Niebuhr's thought is as effective a riposte to another and much more recent strand of thought in Christian ethics: the ecclesially centered ethics of Radical Orthodoxy. Measuring Radical Orthodoxy's thought against Niebuhr's is given added interest by the fact that Radical Orthodox thinkers themselves—and especially John Milbank—have explicitly and critically engaged Niebuhr, and have described what they see as the 'poverty' of his idea of Christian realism for contemporary ethics.[1]

Though quite distinct from the Social Gospel movement, Radical Orthodoxy has what superficially might seem to be correlates for the social gospellers' optimism and pacifism. It is robustly confident that that Church exists as the embodiment of a uniquely counter-cultural and divinely informed

---

[1] See John Milbank, 'The Poverty of Niebuhrianism', in *The Word Made Strange: Theology, Language, Culture* (Oxford: Blackwell, 1997), 249. I shall be referring principally to this essay in what I write here, taking Milbank to be the best (as he is also the originating) expositor of Radical Orthodoxy's theological approach, and acknowledging this essay to be his most sustained and direct response to Niebuhr's thought.

sociality in the face of the modern West's catastrophic embrace of various secular ideologies. This is a *real* embodiment, *now,* and Radical Orthodoxy has little truck with attempts to assimilate the Church's everyday structures and patterns of life to those of other human institutions or cultures.[2] (Its 'optimism' therefore takes on the appearance for some of a sort of ecclesial triumphalism.) At the same time, it asserts in an Augustinian vein (against the hidden Nietzschianism it discerns in liberal secular thought[3]) the ontological priority of peace. That is to say, it holds up the Christian metanarrative (displayed in scripture's accounts of creation's good beginnings, and enacted by Christ in his trustful refusal of violence) as a unique source of confidence that there is something more ultimate in the world, more fundamental, than conflict between the hungry interests of competing individual creatures. The 'pacific' vision of Radical Orthodoxy is a belief in the possibility of 'threading . . . event to event [in world history] in peace, and the trust that the *entire* labyrinth can eventually be so interwoven in harmony'.[4] To participate in being in the fullest possible way involves living out of this deep confidence in peace as the origin and end of the world's story.

CONTESTING THE 'REAL' ON THE GROUND OF HISTORY

At the heart of the confrontation between Niebuhr's 'realist' and Milbank's radically orthodox theology is precisely the interpretation of the 'real', and their respective claims to have a suitably developed historical sense of it. On the face of it, neither would be likely to deny the truth of the liberation theologian José Miguez Bonino's statement that '[t]ruth is at the level of history, not in the realm of ideas'.[5] Both are concerned with the irreducible embodiment in history of Christian claims to insight. For Niebuhr, historical experience educates us in the limits of what we may expect from our own moral efforts. It thus has a chastening effect on a common Christian temptation, namely, that of being irresponsibly *gung ho* about our human capacity to overcome the constraints of life in the world. But to make this claim about limits Niebuhr seems to have too secure a grasp on what is always and

---

[2] '[O]ne must . . . sketch out a "counter-history" of ecclesial origination [and] the "counter-ethics", or the different practice, which emerges . . . [whereupon] Christianity starts to appear— even "objectively"—as not just different, but as *the* difference from all other cultural systems' (John Milbank, *Theology and Social Theory* (Oxford: Blackwell, 1990), 381).

[3] See ibid. 262.

[4] Milbank, 'The Poverty of Niebuhrianism', 249.

[5] José Miguez Bonino, *Revolutionary Theology Comes of Age* (London: SPCK, 1975), 72.

everywhere true in history; in other words, he claims a *necessity* for what may only be *contingencies* in historical experience (even if exceptionless or nearly exceptionless contingencies), and to do this, he makes a claim that is itself a- or supra-historical. He makes a claim about 'nature' rather than about history: about *human* 'nature', and the 'nature' of original sin.[6] Milbank's version of Radical Orthodoxy is, by contrast, both more modest and more bold in its alleged historicity. It claims to operate without a viewing platform above history, but strictly from 'in the midst' of historical process.

All historical understanding, it claims, is mediated by language and culture, and the Christian's is no exception. 'Christians, like everyone else, are scions of language, bound to structures in which reality is already "worked over"';[7] '[o]ur historical and moral existence [belongs] entirely inside a world of signs which at all points depends upon convention'.[8] In the light of this modesty, Radical Orthodoxy refuses to absolutize specific examples of tragic failure (even when aggregated) in the service of a theory of sinful finitude. To be in the middle of history also means to be in a position to be surprised by it: '[j]ust because the entire world only arrives to us as language, so also language only arrives to us as the world, whose specificities surprise us and remain beyond our grasp and control'.[9] It thus argues for a caution about turning the statement 'it was ever thus' into the claim 'it must ever be thus'. But then comes its bold move. For Milbank's Radical Orthodoxy, history is the site of a unique disclosure: the resurrection of Christ. The Christian imagination's exploration of the implications of this event (an event *within* history) can deliver a persuasively beautiful and unusually comprehensive account of *how* and *for what* all things hold together. Of course, there is no way independently to verify the superiority of truth claims about the resurrection in relation to other (non-Christian) truth claims—for example, by reference to some neutrally and generally available concept of the 'real'. They are claims, as we have noted, that are sustained within Christian 'conventions' of language and culture, and there is no way to step outside such conventions. Such conventions are the only way in which humans can relate to the real; mediation in languages and in specific cultures is the way in which the real is real for people at all. But Christian truth claims of this kind, Radical Orthodoxy supposes, retain a power to out-narrate those around them, and are attractive for having this power. Moreover, in ethical terms, they equip the Church with a capacity

---

[6] This despite his explicit statement that '[a]lmost all the misinterpretations of human selfhood and the drama of history in the modern day are derived from the effort to reduce human existence to the coherence of nature' (Reinhold Niebuhr, *Christian Realism and Political Problems* (London: Faber and Faber, 1954), 187).

[7] Milbank, 'The Poverty of Niebuhrianism', 250.

[8] Ibid. 249.   [9] Ibid.

to question the 'givens' of situations or world-descriptions with which it is presented. The Church can hold onto 'the possibility of atonement, and an atoning process' even when faced with an ' "academically precise" tracing of catastrophe' in world history'.[10]

Now Niebuhr's project is not well described as only an exercise in the tracing of catastrophe in world history. It had a far more positively constructive intention to it than that would allow. But it does generate, at various stages of its development, certain alleged 'givens' whose givenness Radical Orthodoxy would want at least to query. For example, in *Moral Man and Immoral Society* (1932) Niebuhr makes a distinction between individual face-to-face relations, which have the capacity to be unselfish, and interactions between one group and another, where such unselfishness is virtually impossible.[11] Furthermore, in *An Interpretation of Christian Ethics* (1936)[12] Niebuhr describes love as an 'impossible possibility', and suggests justice as a more suitable term for economic and political discourse (this is echoed again, classically, in 1944: 'Man's capacity for justice makes democracy possible; but man's inclination to injustice makes democracy necessary'[13]). Then, in *The Nature and Destiny of Man* (1941, 1943), Niebuhr focuses more explicitly on the question of sin, arguing that the doctrine of original sin is the only empirically verifiable doctrine of the Christian faith. It is the limitation imposed by sin that keeps humanity in the finite and prevents its realizing its destiny in the infinite (Niebuhr regards the agape love of Jesus as a religious ideal that could not be treated as normative ethic).[14] Justice therefore requires coercion to balance out social disparities and resist tyranny. And all of these 'givens' contribute to his notion of realism, which can be summed up as follows:

[Man's] concern for some centuries to come is not the creation of an ideal society in which there will be uncoerced and perfect peace and justice, but a society in which there will be enough justice, and in which coercion will be sufficiently non-violent to prevent his common enterprise from issuing into complete disaster.[15]

[10] Ibid. 248.
[11] Reinhold Niebuhr, *Moral Man and Immoral Society: A Study in Ethics and Politics* (London: C. Scribner's Sons, 1933).
[12] Reinhold Niebuhr, *An Interpretation of Christian Ethics* (London: SCM, 1936).
[13] Reinhold Niebuhr, *The Children of Light and the Children of Darkness* (London: Nisbet and Co., 1945), xii–xiv.
[14] Reinhold Niebuhr, *The Nature and Destiny of Man: A Christian Interpretation* (London: Nisbet and Co., 1941–3).
[15] Niebuhr, *Moral Man and Immoral Society*, 22.

Radical Orthodoxy, by contrast, resists this set of claims—which together seem to rule out the possibility of a genuine Christian politics. (1) It objects to what it sees as Niebuhr's negative appraisal of human finitude whereby the limits of human achievement are viewed as intrinsically tragic because they are always bound to fall short of some higher ideal, an ideal which exists *outside or above* human history. Instead, it wants to see finitude as quite compatible with conformity to and expression of God's goodness in human life—indeed, as the precondition of participation in the goodness of being. (2) It objects to what it sees—latent in the logic of Niebuhr's position and explicit in the work of later Niebuhrians—as an inadequate doctrine of sin: sin conceived as the property of individuals (every and each individual) by virtue of their ahistorical relation to some foundational defect in the fallen constitution of humanity, rather than being mediated historically and as always also a condition of the larger cultures and societies in which individuals live. It would of course be unfair to Niebuhr to suggest that he was anything less than highly sensitive to the deficiencies of political and social institutions, and Milbank may skip a little too quickly over this point. But the core point of the radically orthodox critique here is that, just like the ideals of Christian love to which Christians aspire in their finitude, so also sin ought not to be located ahistorically outside material creation. To do so is to mistake its seriousness. Milbank wants to say that sin is both less than Niebuhr says it is, by claiming its contingency (rather than its ideality), and also to assert even more strongly than Niebuhr does its total historical force (its universality)—at all levels of human and natural life. (3) Finally, Radical Orthodoxy objects to the Niebuhrian claim to know the constraints of the 'practicable', or the morally realizable, too much in advance, as well as its tendency to tie practicability too much to what the individual can will and achieve. Here, again, we encounter Radical Orthodoxy's suspicion of a Niebuhrian individualism. Milbank writes:

Because Niebuhr thinks of ethics in terms of private assent to the intrinsic goodness of certain ideals of action—the realm of the spirit—he thinks of the external, historical world as the merely physical sphere of cause and effect . . . The private realm of ideal obligation and the public realm of cause and effect only interact at certain points—namely the moments of ethical decision.[16]

If for Niebuhr the most one can hope for in a Christian attitude to politics is the strategic modification and application of specific aspects of an agapaic ideal, then Radical Orthodoxy rejects this as a failure of imagination. It rejects what it sees as the Niebuhrian view that 'politics is basically technology, a

---

[16] Milbank, 'The Poverty of Niebuhrianism', 245.

matter of the manipulation of physical forces';[17] and that love is only ever 'a *secondary* intrusion upon a pattern fundamentally governed by power relations'.[18] Christianity, says Radical Orthodoxy, can give an account of human communal existence which does not just explain it in terms of what is 'given and instinctive' while having little positive value as regards morality (which is in quasi-Stoic fashion exercised by the *individual will* acting responsibly). Christianity will do better if it can see the created solidarities of human community as a medium for vocational response to God, and as capable of gracious and dramatic transformation in themselves. The Church is where this transformation may already be discerned, Radical Orthodoxy argues. The Church and its sacraments are Christianity's politics:

the 'apolitical' character of the New Testament signals the ultimate replacement of the coercive *polis* and *imperium*, the structures of ancient society, by the persuasive Church, rather than any withdrawing from a realm of self-sufficient political life.[19]

In other words, Radical Orthodoxy is prepared to look hopefully for the emergence of radical newness in history, in the face of its apparent givens, and to believe that the Church—originating (as it were *ex nihilo*) from the generative form of life communicated to the world by Son and Spirit—is just such a new reality, which at the same time recalls the world to its deepest truth.

This is perhaps a good moment to step back from the particular lines of controversy between the Niebuhrian and radically orthodox outlooks, and to ask what might be some of the broader issues at stake in their disagreements, and how these might relate to other kinds of Christian radicalism and compromise. We will be helped in this by Dietrich Bonhoeffer's well-tried categories of the 'ultimate' and the 'penultimate', as outlined in his *Ethics*.[20]

THE RELATION OF ULTIMATE TO PENULTIMATE

'Faith promises and demonstrates as realized in Christ a utopia that consists in a world totally reconciled, a world that is the fulfilment of what we are creating here on earth with feeling and love.' So writes Leonardo Boff.[21] And even if we may have qualms about the use of a word like utopia here, the point of Boff's use of it is surely partly to subvert it, for this utopia is not a Butlerian

---

[17] Ibid. 241.   [18] Ibid. 240.   [19] Ibid. 251.
[20] Dietrich Bonhoeffer, *Ethics*, ed. Eberhard Bethge (London: SCM, 1955), 79–100.
[21] Leonardo Boff, *Jesus Christ Liberator: A Critical Christology for Our Time* (London: SPCK, 1980), 45.

'Erewhon'[22] but is *realized* in Christ. If such a conviction is recognized as a proper starting place for Christian belief, then whenever the 'ideal' and the 'actual' are separated in Christian thought it will have to be said that they are *falsely* separated. This world is decisively vindicated and reconciled by the death and resurrection of Christ, and in the movement of affirming this fact Christians are called to *respond* to the recognition of it, and to *participate* in its realization. There is to be no dichotomy between some transcendent fact and the response of creation to that fact. It is not appropriate to counsel despair about the inevitability of a divide between the two, and to advocate acquiescence in the inadequacies and compromises of the 'actual'. Humanity's task is to seek to conform itself to that destiny which has been revealed as its proper destiny. As Oliver O'Donovan argues in a discussion of the Epistle to Hebrews, God's work is complete (or, as Boff would put it, 'realized in Christ'), and what remains is for us to *enter* that sabbath rest which is waiting for us: 'Historical fulfilment means our entry into a completeness which is already present in the universe. Our sabbath rest is, as it were, a catching up with God's.'[23] O'Donovan and Boff may be very different thinkers indeed, but both take the idea of grace in Christ with the greatest seriousness, and both look for the presence and force of that idea in the practical realm. For both it is, in the end, from the idea of grace that Christianity lives and speaks in the world. Where an account of grace is lacking, Christian analyses of the world lose their integrity and authenticity.

However, as Bonhoeffer reminds us, this does not mean there is no longer any distinction to be drawn between the 'ultimate' and the 'penultimate'. Getting both right, and getting the *relation between them* right, is the challenge facing the theological ethicist. Radical versions of Christianity—whether liberationist, Barthian, or something else again (radically orthodox, perhaps)—might well always be drawn to concentrate on something like Bonhoeffer's 'ultimate', but if they neglect the penultimate they may do so to their detriment. Any emphasis on the ultimate which asserts that grace has worked and works through Jesus Christ even in the present moment, must be led—even though always in the *priority* of this assumption—to encounter the penultimate. It will do so, usually, in a critical frame of mind, but also, properly, in one that accords the penultimate its own relative sphere (provided that, as penultimate, it does not claim its own absolute self-sufficiency), and is patient with it. Meanwhile, an emphasis on the penultimate—when not approached *through* the ultimate (i.e. when the priority of the ultimate is not clearly acknowledged)—risks forgetting grace and

[22] Samuel Butler's (1835–1902) satirically drawn, fantasy utopia (the 'nowhere', of which 'Erewhon' is an anagram).
[23] Oliver O'Donovan, *Resurrection and Moral Order* (Leicester: IVP, 1986), 62.

its immanence. This will be the perennial risk to less obviously 'radical' forms of Christianity.

Niebuhr argues against his 'morally perfectionist' brother (H. Richard Niebuhr) in the following terms: 'as long as the world of man remains a place where nature and God, the real and the ideal, meet, human progress will depend upon the judicious use of the forces of nature in the service of the ideal'.[24] It is on grounds such as these, as Stanley Hauerwas notes, that Niebuhr supposes the 'inevitable and ambiguous means of coercion'[25] to have a necessary part to play in the struggle for justice. Niebuhr fully accepts that our perseverance in this struggle is to be fuelled by hope in the ultimate—a hope that realizes that its fulfilment rests beyond history. But he sees no alternative to the need for discerning and pragmatic action in the present which will make historical existence more *nearly* just and less violent.

Radical Orthodoxy, as we have begun to see in this chapter, proffers its own suggestions for how Christian radicalism can be more thoroughly *Christian*. It does not claim to 'represent' an objective social reality in allegedly scientific terms; instead, the social knowledge it advocates is 'the continuation of ecclesial practice, the imagination in action of a peaceful, reconciled social order, beyond even the violence of legality'.[26] The logic of Christianity involves the claim that the interruption of history by Christ and his bride, the Church, is the most fundamental of events. In the Church, as it is shaped by the narratives of Jesus Christ, we see the concrete (and not ideal) possibility of a non-violent practice in a life lived by faith. 'Knowing the shape of sin', writes Milbank, 'and the shape of its refusal, we can at last be radically changed'.[27] We are to imitate Jesus' life, and also his end. The kingdom means bearing the burdens of others, even of our accusers, and this is what Paul seems to mean when he talks about 'filling up what is lacking in the sufferings of Christ' (Col. 1:24). Radical Orthodoxy urges the Church to go beyond considerations of desert and non-desert (this is a crucial way in which it seeks to go beyond the present 'horizon'): 'there is a way to act in a violent world which assumes the ontological priority of non-violence, and this way is called "forgiveness of

---

[24] Reinhold Niebuhr, 'Must We Do Nothing?', in Harold E. Fey and Margaret Frakes (eds.), *The Christian Century Reader: Representative Articles, Editorials, and Poems Selected from More than Fifty Years of the Christian Century* (New York: Association Press, 1962), 226–7.

[25] Stanley Hauerwas, *The Peaceable Kingdom: A Primer in Christian Ethics* (London: SCM, 1984), 140–1.

[26] Richard H. Roberts, 'Theology and the Social Sciences', in David F. Ford with Rachel Muers (eds.), *The Modern Theologians: An Introduction to Christian Theology Since 1918*, 3rd edn. (Oxford: Blackwell, 2005), 380.

[27] Milbank, *Theology and Social Theory*, 397.

sins"'.[28] The one way to respond to sinfulness that is not itself sinful is 'to anticipate heaven, and act as if [another's] sin was not there, by offering reconciliation...beyond the bounds of any given "responsibility"'.[29] Otherwise, Christianity, like everything else, is confined within the cycle of the ceaseless exhaustion and return of violence. It may be that such a Christian 'politics', viewed in a Niebuhrian light, will be dismissed as not taking the *penultimate* seriously enough, however clear-sighted its assessment and embrace of the cost of pursuing its beliefs. We will look more closely at this potential criticism in the closing section of this chapter. What cannot be said, though, is that it fails to take grace sufficiently seriously. It appreciates that the cross of Christ may demand a self-denial which no social norms can require.

The radically orthodox emphasis on openness to grace, which is akin to a disposition of wonder, needs to be related to the debate sketched earlier between Niebuhr and Milbank about what is *contingent* and what is *necessary* in historical life. In particular, the argument over the contingency or necessity of sin is at the heart of what divides them, for this issue contains within it the various other issues we have touched on: of whether finitude is always an obstacle to moral goodness, whether the Church can truly be conformed to Christ on this side of the parousia, and whether as a consequence there can be a true Christian politics. In fact, the difference between their positions is very subtle, though very important. Radical Orthodoxy takes Niebuhr to be saying that sin is a 'given' in the sense of being a *universal and also necessary* condition, a condition that is well described as tragic. Even though Niebuhr wants to hold on to the fact that Christianity is 'beyond tragedy' insofar as it regards evil as 'finally under the dominion of a good God', he still claims that evil is 'an inevitable concomitant of even the highest spiritual enterprises'.[30] Those who make the attempt to bring society under the dominion of love will die on the cross. Niebuhrianism, in other words (and despite its caveats), implies a world tragic *by nature*. Radical Orthodoxy itself wants to assert that sin is a *universal and yet contingent* condition. There may well be a ubiquity *in fact* to tragic experience, but to claim that tragedy is a necessary and original feature of the world *in principle* would be to give it a primordial status wholly at odds with Christianity's claims about the origination of all things only in God's goodness and grace. By insisting that we ought not to live in the assumption that tragedy is definitive of our world, and by living in the continual (even if apparently counter-intuitive) expectation that things could be otherwise, Christians bear witness to the possibility that sin's

---

[28] Milbank, *Theology and Social Theory*, 411.   [29] Ibid.
[30] Reinhold Niebuhr, *Beyond Tragedy: Essays on the Christian Interpretation of History* (London: Nisbet and Co., 1938), pp. x–xi.

power is breakable. Indeed, in Christ it *has been* broken, and on this basis Christians are called—collectively, in the Church—to live in a way that denies sin (or tragedy) this original or necessary status. This is why Milbank writes:

I fully accept [Niebuhr's] view that the nature of our present historical condition is such that we are faced with tragic dilemmas in which it is impossible to avoid some complicity in evil . . . What I do quarrel with is the attempt to ground these claims . . . in certain notions about 'human nature' . . . [31]

Milbank himself has attractively explored the ability of Shakespeare's play *The Winter's Tale* to illustrate just this *relativization* of tragedy without an *evasion* of tragedy.[32] His point is not that Christianity should skip lightly or comedically over sin (and on this point he and Niebuhr would surely agree). His point is that—even before the full realization of the eschaton—Christianity should not let it have the last word. There is in history something to contrast with tragedy, something which is not so much comedy as, well, *grace*. (And Shakespeare's 'Romance' form might be the literary genre that least inadequately shows grace's appearance.) *The Winter's Tale* is readable as an affirmation of Radical Orthodoxy—affirmation specifically of its distrust of a Niebuhrian deference to tragedy, especially where this deference threatens to become an *absolutizing* of tragedy.

It is important to acknowledge, of course, that the pain and suffering—the sheer destructiveness of the human behaviour in the play—is every bit as serious as in Shakespeare's tragedies. The scale of this destruction—and its sixteen long years of alienation—completely removes *The Winter's Tale* from the world of the comedies. And we know we are closer here than in the comedies to the Genesis account of the world of death and suffering to which our sin contributes. But this is not the end of the story either for Christian theology or for *The Winter's Tale*. Leontes inaugurates a world we recognize: a world of the tragic. As Milbank points out, he cannot be reconciled to what he has done, because those he has done it to are irretrievably lost. He can be punished but never, never forgiven. This is the tragic, inconsolable world of Lear's 'Never' uttered at the death of Cordelia over and over again. Nothing can compensate for what has happened, since it is unique, irreplaceable ones who have been betrayed. Only reconciliation with them could cancel out the deed, and that is impossible, since they are dead (and lost). Christianity, in its account of the fall and of human sin, does not attempt to escape from or deny this world. It recognizes the truth of the description (so far so Niebuhrian).

---

[31] Milbank, 'The Poverty of Niebuhrianism', 234–5.
[32] John Milbank, 'The Midwinter Sacrifice: A Sequel to "Can Morality Be Christian?"' in *Studies in Christian Ethics*, 10/2 (1997), 13–38.

But, in line with Radical Orthodoxy's emphasis, it knows it may not be immobilized by what might seem the tragic implications of this vision; the possibility of punishment but the impossibility of real reconciliation; the force of Lear's 'Never'. Why not? The answer lies in the possibility of an unexpected arrival (just as Sicily's redemption lay hidden in the arrival of Perdita from her place of hiding in Bohemia). This possibility *relativizes* our grasp on the world we think we know; the tragic world, in which loss is loss and *no* gift could ever redeem this cycle. The tragic condition may be *universally* true of our world, but the assertion of the possibility of an arrival—another way forward— makes the tragic condition less than absolute; less than final. God's grace is something more final than the apparently universal story of sin and its consequences. This is the crux of Radical Orthodoxy's resistance to a false despair at what may be expected in the world's life.

Radical Orthodoxy's theological vision is one whose confidence in the dismissal of tragic 'givens' offers much to energize the Church. In its continued acknowledgement of the power and purchase of sin, its optimism and its call to live out a narrative of the ultimacy of peace do not deserve to be dismissed along with the social gospellers whom Niebuhr had in his sights. It is not (in *that* respect) *naïve*, as Niebuhr thought the Social Gospel movement was. Radical Orthodoxy celebrates grace as the excessive possibilities that are in the world at points where we too frequently think there are no such possibilities, and it celebrates faith as life lived in openness to these excessive possibilities. It celebrates forgiveness as possible because evil is not ultimate (forgiveness wouldn't be possible otherwise), and it celebrates resurrection as possible because death is not ultimate (resurrection wouldn't be possible otherwise). In such ways, it claims it is being 'realistic', and more realistic than those who would artificially foreclose all these possibilities.

CONCLUDING REMARKS: THE CONTINUING IMPORTANCE OF NIEBUHR'S EXAMPLE

In these closing remarks, I want to show how Radical Orthodoxy might still need to listen to ongoing calls (from various quarters) that Christian theology be open to learning about what the 'real' is from outside its own disciplinary enclave. Niebuhr might not be theology's only teacher in a contemporary context, but such 'listening' by theology will be true to a good Niebuhrian tradition, and will have vital benefits for theology still.

Despite its vigorous and valuable attempt to reverse a contemporary contraction in the Christian imagination that is *disguised* as realism, Radical Orthodoxy can afford to extend its existing openness (to grace in history and the material creation) into an openness to certain other disciplines and their ways of reading the signs which creation proffers. Admittedly, and as Milbank so devastatingly argues in *Theology and Social Theory*, certain kinds of social science are prisoners of an ideology that is congenitally opposed to Christian truth claims. Their pretensions to 'scientific' analysis need to be treated with the same caution as (so Niebuhr recognized) certain Marxian ones. But as Richard Roberts has insisted, 'sociology and theology . . . cannot afford to neglect or express contempt for *ethnography* [my emphasis], that is, the effective representation and interpretation of what is actually happening in human lives'.[33]

There are irresponsibly shallow ways of studying social reality, its obligations, bonds and values. Timothy Jenkins has highlighted the destructive effects of 'premature generalisations and imponderable universals' on critical thinking in relation to the social. Any critical understanding, he argues, must include 'some estimate of the limits of its own applicability'.[34] Rejecting grand theories and artificial ordering principles alien to the subject matter in hand, he gives us an acute and proper sense of the 'difficult-to-handle'—of the intractabilities and imponderables that encounter those who try to make sense in a sustained way. It is worth considering in this connection how over-reaching and immodest the scales and perspectives adopted by theologians have been prone to be, and how little attention is paid in the ethical dimensions of such theologies to the 'middle-distance' loyalties, solidarities, compulsions, desires, and habits that are the actual medium in which human lives come to a perception of what their salvation might consist in. It is potentially a chastening experience. For theologians are rather too ready to invoke what we might call 'ultimate horizons', especially in the newly eschatological and global purviews of many twentieth- and twenty-first-century theological projects.

Niebuhr, we may conjecture, would have recognized much of the force of Jenkins's concerns. Radical Orthodoxy's weakness, by contrast, is perhaps that there is so little ethnography in its thought. For a movement so concerned to emphasize the contingency of ideas, there is very little attention given to particular, concrete, human realities. I suggest that this represents a serious falling short *in Radical Orthodoxy's own terms*. It has been said that to read

---

[33] Roberts, 'Theology and the Social Sciences', 381.
[34] Timothy Jenkins, *Religion in English Everyday Life: An Ethnographic Approach* (Oxford: Berghahn, 1999), 230.

Milbank is to read what all too often seems to be a story about 'magic texts', which have their own life, and are highly contagious. The story of modern thought is told through the mysterious influence with which certain key texts influence and corrupt successive texts, in long genealogical processions. The names of thinkers are used to represent 'positions', and these positions are then displayed in complex synthetic relationships or else in their oppositions. This, as is remarked from time to time in critical responses to Radical Orthodoxy, is the rather procrustean hermeneutic of the 'history of ideas'. It should be recognized that there are *positive* chains of 'magic texts' for Milbank, too, parallel to the dominant and malign strains of modernity. '[O]ther early modern thinkers', he writes (drawing a contrast with a Hobbesian tradition), '[inaugurate] a kind of "counter-modernity" which later, through the writings of Vico, Hamann, Herder, Coleridge, Kierkegaard and Blondel, continues to shadow actual, secular modernity.'[35] We may remind ourselves again here of Jenkins's warnings, who (when defending the value of the modest, attentive, social anthropological approach) states that: '[A] "high structuralist" view is characterised by what we might call a flatness of vision, whereby all history is reduced to narrative elements and organized into texts.'[36]

'Bold theological constructions involve corrigible claims', says another distinctively Anglican voice in this debate. Such claims 'can and should be brought into close contact with the realities that they purport to represent, and tested by those realities':

As a first example, one might consider the potential *repair* of Radical Orthodoxy: the wager that the theological boldness of Radical Orthodoxy can be deepened, made more powerful, and made more effective if it is interrupted both by greater historical attentiveness (including social-historical attentiveness) to the intellectual traditions that it mines so confidently, and by greater ethnographic attentiveness to the political worlds about which it speaks so stridently. This interruption is not, however, intended as a dismissal or disproof of Radical Orthodoxy, but as its over-acceptance and repair.[37]

This is perhaps the kind of debate where a revived attention to Niebuhr's sense of critical obligation to his context has its place, and (without sapping any of their energy) has not only a corrective but potentially an enhancing contribution to make to some of the most dynamic initiatives in recent theological thought.

[35] Milbank, *Theology and Social Theory*, 4.
[36] Jenkins, *Religion in English Everyday Life*, 144.
[37] Mike Higton, unpublished paper on 'Description', 2004.

5

The Nature and Destiny of Serious Theology

Samuel Wells

One habit that seems to have taken hold among the professional classes in contemporary America is as follows. A person making a presentation hesitates for a moment, as if fighting an inner battle between duty and indiscretion, and then, summoning courage, says, 'Okay, in the interests of full disclosure . . .' before telling the members of the audience or group something quite personal they really didn't have any need or reason to know.

Thus, in the interests of full disclosure, I might mention that my grandfather presided at Ursula and Reinhold Niebuhr's wedding. Indeed, because Ursula Keppel-Compton was a longstanding family friend, her signed copies of her husband's great works held honoured places in my father's library. They still do in mine. My father, a man who to the end of his days shivered to recall the deeds he was required to do as a soldier in the Second World War, was among a generation of clergy who took Niebuhr's template for the Christian's place in society as a default setting for all subsequent discussion of social ethics.

So to write a book, as I wrote *God's Companions*, in part as a sustained attempt to portray an ethic in almost wholesale contrast to Niebuhr, and to dedicate that book to my late father, may have seemed a curious thing to do. The invitation to write this present essay is an opportunity to explore some of the journey that has led me to think outside some of the categories that Niebuhr displays so compellingly.

The essay is in five parts. First, I take Niebuhr's essay 'Why the Christian Church is not Pacifist', and set out its arguments as a characteristic Niebuhr manifesto.[1] Next, I explore two weaknesses of the essay—its inadequate

---

[1] Reinhold Niebuhr, 'Why the Christian Church is not Pacifist', in *Christianity and Power Politics* (New York: Scribner's, 1940), cited in the text as *CPP* page citations in the text. I am choosing this essay as an articulation of Niebuhr's mature position on the issue. Niebuhr's thought evolved and changed in the course of his life, and has been variously claimed, as the first two essays in this book by Lovin and McCorkle bring out very strongly. For example, Niebuhr did think there was an important place for non-violent resistance in certain circumstances, as he

account of pacifism and its impoverished account of realism. Third, I argue
that at the heart of Niebuhr's theology, and significant in both the weaknesses
already named, is his particular reading of the parable of the wheat and the
tares (Matthew 13). This parable concerns the nature and destiny of humanity
in the face of evil. I find Niebuhr's treatment of the parable seriously flawed.
Fourth, I suggest what a Christian pacifism free of Niebuhr's assumptions
might look like. Finally, I explore what might make for a more appropriate
sense of Christian realism than that offered by Niebuhr.

'WHY THE CHRISTIAN CHURCH IS NOT PACIFIST'

On the eve of America's entry into the Second World War, Niebuhr sets out
the case for Christian realism by dismantling the case for Christian pacifism.
He perceives two kinds of pacifism. The first might be called sectarian
pacifism—as propounded by the medieval ascetics and by the sixteenth-
century radical reformers. This represents Christian perfectionism—'a genuine impulse in the heart of Christianity, the impulse to take the law of Christ
seriously and not allow the political strategies, which the sinful character of
[humanity] makes necessary, to become final norms' (*CPP* 4). This was never
a fully-fledged political alternative. It

> did not give itself to the illusion that it had discovered a method for eliminating the
> element of conflict from political strategies. On the contrary, it regarded the mystery
> of evil as beyond its power of solution. It was content to set up the most perfect and
> unselfish individual life as a symbol of the Kingdom of God. It knew this could only be
> done by disavowing the political task and by freeing the individual of all responsibility
> for social justice. (*CPP* 5)

This *historical* strand of pacifism is a valuable reminder of the difference
between relative norms and final norms. But those who advocate for the
alternative *contemporary* strand of humanistic pacifism are propounding
nothing less than a heresy.

> Presumably inspired by the Christian gospel, they have really absorbed the Renais-
> sance faith in the goodness of [humanity], have rejected the Christian doctrine of
> original sin as an outmoded bit of pessimism, have reinterpreted the Cross so that it is
> made to stand for the absurd idea that perfect love is guaranteed a simple victory over

---

argued in *Moral Man and Immoral Society.* Likewise the normative aspect of the ethical ideal is
strong in *An Interpretation of Christian Ethics*, but had been set aside by the time he wrote 'Why
the Christian Church is not Pacifist'.

the world, and have rejected all other profound elements of the Christian gospel as 'Pauline' accretions which must be stripped from the 'simple gospel of Jesus'. (*CPP* 5–6)

This, says Niebuhr, has no justification in relation to 'the total gospel' nor any resemblance to any historical reality. It is a 'pathetic alternative' to the Christian faith, because its proponents fail to see the tragedy of the human situation, and 'make Christ into the symbol of their faith in [humanity]' (*CPP* 7). Contemporary pacifism is based on a misreading of human nature, asserting that 'if only [people] loved one another, all the complex, and sometimes horrible, realities of the political order could be dispensed with' (*CPP* 14). But because human beings are sinners, justice requires both coercion (to prevent anarchy) and resistance to coercion (to prevent tyranny). Contemporary pacifism, by withholding all resistance to coercion, expresses a morally perverse preference for tyranny over anarchy, forgetting that the 'momentary' anarchy of war is necessary to overcome tyranny. But Niebuhr maintains that tyranny simply grows if not resisted. Humanity's rebellion against God is 'too serious' (note the word) to be addressed by just 'one more sermon on love' (*CPP* 32).

Niebuhr has no time for the distinction between non-resistance and non-violent resistance—in which the latter 'allows one to resist evil provided the resistance does not involve the destruction of life or property.' He regards this as scripturally unfounded and in any case a less than adequate distinction, probably based on a Platonic preference for the spiritual over the physical. 'Nothing could be plainer than that the ethic [of Scripture] uncompromisingly enjoins non-resistance and not non-violent resistance' (*CPP* 10). Niebuhr does not see himself as bound by this ethic, but feels those who claim to be should at least identify it correctly.

Meanwhile Niebuhr sets out the case for Christian realism. The good news of the gospel, for Niebuhr, 'is that there is a resource of divine mercy which is able to overcome a contradiction within our own souls' (*CPP* 2). That contradiction Niebuhr expresses in characteristic terms from Romans 7: 'though we know we ought to love our neighbor as ourself, there is a "law in our members which wars against the law that is in our mind", so that, in fact, we love ourselves more than our neighbor' (*CPP* 2). Christianity measures 'the full seriousness' (note the word again) 'of sin as a permanent factor in human history.' This is Niebuhr's notion of justification by grace through faith: Christ is the 'impossible possibility'—the gracious pardon of God which is vouchsafed to human beings, in spite of the fact that they never at any stage attain the 'full measure of Christ' and cease to be sinners (*CPP* 3).[2]

---

[2] While Niebuhr believes this notion of justification renders pacifism a heresy, it is interesting to note that it is not an understanding that is Christologically determined.

Christianity is not, for Niebuhr, a challenge to live up to a nigh impossible ideal but a realistic method for dealing with the problem of abiding human sin and thereby achieving justice. The key quality Christianity brings is balance.

> The closest approximation to a love in which life supports life in voluntary community is a justice in which life is prevented from destroying life and the interests of the one are guarded against unjust claims by the other.... Justice is basically dependent upon a balance of power.... [W]ithout the balance of power even the most loving relations may degenerate into unjust relations, and love may become the screen which hides the injustice. (*CPP* 26–7)

Perhaps the following two sentences epitomize Niebuhr's realism.

> There are too many contingent factors in various national and international schemes of justice to justify any qualified endorsement of even the most democratic structure of justice as 'Christian.' Yet it must be obvious that any social structure in which power has been made responsible, and in which anarchy has been overcome by methods of mutual accommodation, is preferable to either anarchy or tyranny. (*CPP* 28)

Notable in these two sentences is Niebuhr's scepticism about realizing any kind of Christian ideal, but his equal confidence that finding a balance between competing forces self-evidently expresses a Christian ethic and is achievable through responsible and serious engagement. This mixture of scepticism toward explicitly theological ethics (portrayed as idealistic) and confidence in his own urbane reasoning (portrayed as realistic) constitutes the characteristic Niebuhrian brand of social ethics.

WHY THE CHRISTIAN CHURCH IS NOT NIEBUHRIAN

In this section I propose that Niebuhr's account of pacifism is inadequate and his account of realism is impoverished.

First, pacifism. Niebuhr's understanding of Jesus' ethic in relation to violence and war can be presented as a syllogism.

> Jesus' ethic—represented in statements such as 'Love your enemies' and 'If anyone strikes you on the cheek, offer the other also'—is an unequivocal deontological opposition to violent conduct. It is an ideal centred on purity and self-denial and not designed to be translated into any realizable social programme.
> Political ethics by contrast must be consequential in reasoning, because they are concerned with achieving a balance between the ideal and the facts, between human community as it might be and sinful existence as it actually is, between history and

the transcendent, in the service of achieving the most extensive possible degree of justice.

Therefore Jesus' ethic should be attended to as a transcendent critique of human justice (an 'impossible possibility'), but it would be wrong to pretend proximate justice were identical to Jesus' ethic, and foolish to try to translate Jesus' ethic into some kind of non-violent political programme.

The problem with Niebuhr's reasoning is his unwillingness to take seriously (note the word again) the full humanity and the full divinity of Christ. The first item of the syllogism above fails to take seriously the humanity of Christ.[3] Jesus is too heavenly minded to be any earthly use. We understand human nature so much better than he did. Meanwhile the second item of the syllogism fails to take seriously the divinity of Christ. There are things we know—the character of justice and the realities of politics—that have more authority than Jesus does; it seems that there is nothing we could discover about Jesus that would shake our certainty about what we know about politics and justice. Thus Jesus emerges as neither fully human nor fully divine: a truly impossible possibility, indeed.

Niebuhr's existing commitments concerning politics and justice circumscribe what he is capable of seeing in Jesus.[4] What he does see is an ethic largely divorced from the doctrinal (or narrative) context that gives it its meaning and power. That doctrinal, narrative context is Jesus' death and resurrection. What Niebuhr does not seem to see is this. Those whom Jesus describes in Luke 6.27–30—those who are your enemies, those who hate you, those who curse you, those who abuse you, those who strike you on the cheek, those who take away your coat, those who beg from you, and those who take away your goods—are those he encounters on his way to Calvary. Jesus went to the cross because he loved his enemies. As he went to the cross he was

[3] This is the view of Richard Hays. 'It is difficult to see how Niebuhr's account of the ethic of Jesus avoids the pitfall of docetism. . . . If Jesus of Nazareth was a historical figure who lived—as all persons in history do—amidst 'contending factions and forces' how could his ethic fail to address the moral problem of human life?' (Richard B. Hays, *The Moral Vision of the New Testament: A Contemporary Introduction to New Testament Ethics* (New York: HarperCollins, 1996), 218).

[4] Larry Rasmussen suggests the problem lies with Niebuhr's individualized anthropology, which inclined him to overlook Jesus' social programme. 'Jesus' piety was social; all aspects of life, including political and economic ones, were related to God in a community that sought to give faith concrete social form. . . . Despite his keen sense of our social nature, Niebuhr's theology implicitly exalts individual and heroic self-sacrifice, to the neglect of mutuality and community, as the most manifest expressions of the Kingdom of God' (Larry Rasmussen, *Reinhold Niebuhr: Theologian of Public Life* (London: Collins, 1988), 40).

hated, he was cursed, he was abused, he was struck, he was stripped of his
clothes and humiliated. This is not an abstract disembodied ideal, but a list of
lived interactions, recorded as injunctions made before the event. Jesus' ethic
is not a series of pious proposals; it is the implication of his incarnation,
crucifixion, resurrection, and ascension. If he was fully human his ethic is
fully realizable by human beings; if he was fully divine his ethic is fully binding
on human beings. Niebuhr's rejection of pacifism proceeds by dismissing
theological pacifism as politically irrelevant and tactical pacifism as political
naivety. But what if theological pacifism is exegetically and theologically
unavoidable, because it is integral to the core tenets of the faith—incarnation,
crucifixion, resurrection, and ascension? What if Jesus brought not a new
ethic or a new law but a new reality, and non-violence was not living up to a
challenge (to use Niebuhr's term, *CPP* 3) but simply recognizing and inhabit-
ing that new reality?

   This brings us, second, to realism. George Hunsinger points out that
Niebuhr contrasts realism with idealism.[5] But there are other alternatives to
realism. Karl Barth, for example, contrasts the real to the unreal. Here is how
Hunsinger contrasts Niebuhr with Barth.

Niebuhr exemplifies the kind of theology which thinks in terms of the real and the
ideal. Niebuhr thought of love, for example, as representing an unattainable ideal.
Although impossible to attain, the love ideal had at least two important functions.
It served constantly to remind us of human sinfulness, and it stood as a warning

---

[5] Niebuhr quotes with approval Machiavelli's definition of the purpose of a realist: 'to follow
the truth of a matter rather than the imagination of it'. Niebuhr concurs with Machiavelli that
idealists are subject to illusions about social realities. The idealist, Niebuhr suggests, is 'the
person who seeks to bring self-interest under the discipline of a more universal law and in
harmony with a more universal good'. But this involves ignoring the forces in human life that
resist universally valid ideals and norms, a disposition that surfaces 'whenever men are inclined
to take the moral pretensions of themselves or their fellow men at face value; for the disposition
to hide self-interest behind the façade of pretended devotion to values transcending self-interest
is well-nigh universal.' On the political plane, 'For the realist, all plans for the future are
dominated by the question: Where do we go from *here?* . . . For the idealist, the primary concern
is not with perennial conditions but with new possibilities, and not with the starting point but
with the goal.' In general, realists seek a balance of power in the interests of justice. Idealists state
the ideal requirements of the situation in as rigorous terms as possible. These summaries are
derived from Harry R. Davis and Robert C. Good (eds.), *Reinhold Niebuhr on Politics: His
Political Philosophy and its Application to Our Age as Expressed in his Writings* (New York:
Scribner's, 1960), 64–5. The distinction between idealism and realism reflects Niebuhr's overarching distinction between love and justice, wherein love is always disinterested, whereas justice
is inherently partial.

against identifying any human achievements or institutions with the absolute. It was a critical standard which (without ever losing its status as an imperative) disclosed that human beings, no matter how hard they might try, would always fall short. Love, for Niebuhr, thus had to be described as an 'impossible possibility', for human nature as such determined what could be called 'real'. Niebuhr's concept of the real was grounded in his anthropology of sin so that love, being unattainable in its essential fullness, could only be conceived as a critical but elusive ideality.

Barth, by contrast, thought in terms of the real and the unreal. Whereas Niebuhr's thinking about 'reality' was anthropocentric, Barth's was theocentric. It was God who set the terms for what was real. Anything opposed, hostile, or contrary to the reality of God was 'unreal' by definition. Therefore for Barth the 'impossible possibility' was not love but sin. Sin (and sinful human beings) existed in a netherworld of unreality. Sin's origin was inexplicable, its status was deeply conflicted, and its destiny was to vanish. Meanwhile, it was actually there and had somehow to be taken into account, but (being essentially absurd) it could only be described in paradoxical terms. It was an impossible possibility and an unreal reality. Since God's love in Jesus Christ established Barth's concept of the real, his anthropology of sin had to be articulated in terms of the shadowy, the conflicted, the unreal (*Church Dogmatics* IV/1, 408–10). Thus Barth and Niebuhr both used the term 'impossible possibility', but in diametrically opposite ways. What for Barth was the touchstone of reality (love) was for Niebuhr the 'impossible possibility', whereas what for Barth was the 'impossible possibility' (sin) was for Niebuhr the touchstone of reality.[6]

Hunsinger exposes how, powerful as Niebuhr's use of the term 'real' may at first appear, that power is based on a very limited exploration of the term's semantic range. It is not just Jesus' love ethic, it is the whole of Jesus' place amid the known territory of the real that is an anomaly. The claim of the New Testament is that Jesus' incarnation, crucifixion, resurrection, and ascension have changed the dimensions and boundaries of the real—not by offering an ideal, but by manifesting and creating a new reality.[7] This is a perspective Niebuhr's twofold universe of the real and the ideal renders him unable to comprehend.

---

[6] George Hunsinger, *How to Read Karl Barth: The Shape of His Theology* (Oxford: Oxford University Press, 1991), 38–9.

[7] For a remarkable proposal describing how Barth's view of the real transforms the foundations of natural theology, see Stanley Hauerwas, *With the Grain of the Universe: The Church's Witness and Natural Theology* (Grand Rapids: Brazos, 2001).

THE NATURE AND DESTINY OF HUMANKIND

Reinhold Niebuhr is not noted for his close exegesis of scripture (except Romans 7, to which he returns as to a transitional object) but on more than one occasion he grounds his version of Christian realism on the parable of the wheat and the tares.[8] Perhaps largely because of his treatment of this parable, it has become one of the most significant passages in the Bible for the way individual Christians and whole denominations have understood their relationship to public life in America in the last century.[9] However, Niebuhr's reading of the parable rests on a mistake. I want to identify that mistake and describe the beginnings of what a Christian response to evil might look like if the parable were read in a more appropriate way.

Here is the parable.

The kingdom of heaven may be compared to someone who sowed good seed in his field; but while everybody was asleep, an enemy came and sowed weeds among the wheat, and then went away. So when the plants came up and bore grain, then the weeds appeared as well. And the slaves of the householder came and said to him, 'Master, did you not sow good seed in your field? Where, then, did these weeds come from?' He answered, 'An enemy has done this.' The slaves said to him, 'Then do you want us to go and gather them?' But he replied, 'No; for in gathering the weeds you would uproot the wheat along with them. Let both of them grow together until the harvest; and at harvest time I will tell the reapers, Collect the weeds first and bind them in bundles to be burned, but gather the wheat into my barn.' (Matthew 13.24–30)

The parable of the wheat and the tares tells us that there is real good in the world, and it is there because God put it there. Then it tells us that there is real evil in the world. (The agricultural historians inform us that this darnel, often translated weeds, looks just like wheat, especially in its early growth, but kills wheat through overwhelming its roots.) Then we are presented with the two great questions, the theological one and the ethical one. The theological question is: Where did the evil come from? The story says, 'An enemy did

---

[8] I owe this insight to Michael Cartwright. See his *Practices, Politics, and Performance: Toward a Communal Hermeneutic for Christian Ethics* (Eugene, OR: Wipf and Stock, 2006), 25–34.

[9] Niebuhr preached on this parable more than once. See Reinhold Niebuhr, *Justice and Mercy: Selections from the Shorter Writings of Reinhold Niebuhr* (New York: Harper and Row, 1974), 51–9; and Robert McAfee Brown (ed.), *The Essential Reinhold Niebuhr: Selected Essays and Addresses* (New Haven: Yale University Press, 1986), 41–8; and, for a different version, Reinhold Niebuhr, 'The Wheat and the Tares', audio tape #N-665 Union Theological Seminary Collection, Richmond, VA.

this.' So the evil in the world does not come from God. We do not discover in this story or elsewhere the character or purposes of God's enemy, but we learn that God for some reason permits evil in the world. But the ethical question is more developed. The ethical question is: Should we pull the weeds out? The clear and perhaps surprising answer is no—for two reasons. First, there is no way to pull the weeds out without pulling the wheat out too. Second, there is going to be a harvest, and that will be the moment when God will sort everything out.

It is hard to exaggerate the importance of this parable in the twentieth-century history of the churches in America. The Niebuhrian reading of the parable of the wheat and the tares is as a lesson in humility. It takes humility for a church or for an individual to realize that it is itself a cocktail of good and evil. Evil is never more likely to be present than in people who think of themselves as unambiguously good. It is no use trying to set up some utopian Christian society, because either at worst you will be humiliated in no time by the reality of the evil you had tried so hard to ignore, or at best you will set yourselves apart in a field of wheat and leave the great field of the world to its own destiny. The best you can hope for as a Christian in the world is not to heal evil or to avoid it, but to live amid the reality of good and evil and try to discern amid many flawed and unsatisfactory possibilities the one that expresses and achieves the greatest good and the least evil. Humility is thus a huge improvement on the naivety that supposes evil can be killed with kindness or the arrogance that suggests it is possible to be a person or a community without evil.[10]

It is important to appreciate how attractive it is to read this as a parable about humility. Church leaders know their own members are far from shining examples of the values they are calling the whole nation to uphold. And so to avoid being laughed out of the public policy debate as fools or hypocrites the churches have in many instances tried to show just how realistic they could be, just how aware they were that the world, like the field, is a mixture of wheat and weeds. The worst thing would be to pretend that we could all be good. Much better to arrange society so that the unavoidable evil that is always there cannot do too much harm.[11]

---

[10] Cartwright points out that, for Niebuhr, the real issue was to oppose a nineteenth-century liberal view of history as progress. Thus the parable demonstrates that history culminates not in the triumph of good over evil but in the growth of good and evil. Here as elsewhere it seems Niebuhr's desire to counter Christian idealism becomes such an overarching need that it distracts his attention from what the parable is really saying.

[11] Robert McAfee Brown works so hard to contradict those who have used Niebuhr's view of sin to underwrite right-wing political platforms that he almost makes Niebuhr's opposition to the philosophy of human progress incomprehensible. Brown quotes as decisive these words in

The trouble with this approach is that it only reads the opening scenes of the parable.[12] It sees the description of the world as a place where evil is intertwined with good and then goes straightaway to the point where it acknowledges that it is pointless and foolish to try to form public policy untainted by evil. In no time it ends up largely giving Christian justifications for actions the public policymakers would have embarked on anyway. The one thing everyone seems to agree on in American foreign policy at the moment is that evil must be sought, found, and rooted out. Yet this is the one thing the parable explicitly states is *not* the way of the gospel. It may not be an exaggeration to say that America is a country whose foreign policy in the early years of the twenty-first century has been based on a misreading of this parable.

The parable of the wheat and the tares turns out not to be about humility but about patience. The sting in the story is not at the beginning where we find that the world is a mixture of good and evil. It is not in the question of where the evil came from and why it is there. The sting in the story is when the farmer says 'Don't gather up the weeds now. Wait till harvest and they will be gathered up in other ways.' The Niebuhrian reading of the parable, the reading that has predominated for most of the last century, ignores the ending. But the ending is the whole point of the parable. The parable is about how we live in the face of undoubted evil. And all our righteous instincts say we must confront evil, fight with it, root it out and burn it up.

But the parable says there are two things wrong with this approach. First, it does not work. You cannot clean up the world.[13] If you set about rooting up evil, you root up the good too. There is no such thing as a clinical bombing campaign. There is no way surgically to extract terrorists from a country

---

Niebuhr's late (1965) book *Man's Nature and his Communities*: '[It is] my strong conviction that a realist conception of human nature should be made the servant of an ethic of progressive justice and should not be made into a bastion of conservatism, particularly a conservatism which defends unjust privileges. I might define this conviction as the guiding principle throughout my mature life of the relation of religious responsibility to political affairs' (Brown, *The Essential Reinhold Niebuhr*, p. xxii).

[12] Richard Hays notes Niebuhr's reluctance to engage scripture systematically. 'Niebuhr employs a relatively narrow range of New Testament texts in the construction of his ethical position. In the gospels...he concentrates on Jesus' sayings to the virtual exclusion of the narrative framework. His reading of Paul is highly selective, focusing on Romans 7...but giving scant weight to Romans 8....Niebuhr makes almost no use of the rest of the New Testament' (*Moral Vision*, 221).

[13] It goes without saying that Niebuhr assumes Christian ethics is written for the benefit of and from the perspective of those who assume they have the power to clean up the world. 'We' for Niebuhr tends to mean 'The Secretary of State and me, his closest adviser'. For a critique of these assumptions, see Samuel Wells, *Improvisation: The Drama of Christian Ethics* (Grand Rapids: Brazos, 2004), ch. 6.

you've invaded. And second, taking it upon yourself to rid the world of evil shows a lack of faith that that is exactly what God will do at the end of history. We either say to ourselves we don't trust God will do it or we say to ourselves we can't wait that long. Those are exactly the two responses this parable is about. The parable is saying God *will* do it and we should wait because only God *can* do it without doing as much harm as good.[14]

The parable is calling Christians to revolutionary patience. The world is full of people who want to take justice into their own hands and see a field with evil in it and are happy just to slash and burn the whole lot. What the world needs is patient people who believe God's judgement will finally do all the sifting that is necessary and in the meantime are content faithfully to tend the farm knowing that that not everything in the field is wheat. The parable suggests the greatest way Christians show their faith in the God revealed in Christ may not be their transformatory intervention, but their revolutionary patience.

WHY THE CHRISTIAN CHURCH MIGHT BE PACIFIST AFTER ALL

What does it mean to say pacifism is primarily a doctrinal, rather than an ethical, issue? What does it mean to say Jesus' incarnation, crucifixion, resurrection, and ascension have transformed the dimensions and boundaries of reality? These are the questions I seek to address in this section.[15]

The first step is to perceive the power of the term sacrifice. Sacrifice gets a bad name when it is used as a transitive verb—something one imposes on or expects of others. Its true meaning in the theological lexicon is as an intransitive verb—something one voluntarily takes upon oneself. The one is a preparedness to lay down one's life that others may die—or even to lay down

---

[14] Cartwright argues that Niebuhr's interpretation of the parable, anxious as it is to avoid the kind of church discipline which seeks to make the political reality of the church visible, follows that of the magisterial reformers. The Anabaptists responded, Cartwright notes, in two ways. 'First, they noted that the magisterial reformers superimposed an identification of the church as 'the field' when, in fact, Jesus' own allegorical explanation is that the field stands for 'the world' not the church. Second, they pointed out to the Swiss Reformers that they themselves killed dissenters, whereas Anabaptists did not kill dissenters' (*Practices*, 33–4).
[15] Much of this section is addressed at greater length in Samuel Wells, 'Sacrificing War', *Journal for Preachers*, 32/1 (Advent 2008), 40–4.

the life of another so that one may oneself live. The other is a preparedness to lay down one's life that others may live—and thus, literally, to make holy.

The second step is to recognize that war and sacrifice lie close to one another in the popular imagination. Once a war begins the lives of the fallen become their own irrefutable logic. That logic is simple: this war must be about something more important than life, otherwise these beloved men and women would not be dead. War becomes the way we know something is true. What is true comes to be defined by the things for which we go to war.

The third step is to name what war is theologically. We believe in war. How we believe in war. Sometimes it seems we believe in war more than we believe in God. It is exhilarating feeling something so deeply that it goes beyond our ability to express it in words. But the truth that war is, is not the truth of Christ. War is indeed a sacrifice. But war is not an atoning sacrifice. It is not a sacrifice that takes away sin. Thus theologically war is a form of worship that claims to make us holy but does not in fact do so. This is a definition of idolatry.

The fourth step is to set the sacrifice that is war alongside the sacrifice of Christ. Consider the story of Abraham's binding of Isaac, in Genesis 22. The poignancy of the story is that Isaac utterly trusts Abraham, and Abraham utterly trusts God. Christians read the story in the light of the death and resurrection of Jesus. They see Jesus reflected in Isaac, because they see Jesus' utter trust for his Father and they see the sacrifice to which Jesus is subject. They see Jesus also reflected in the ram, because, unlike Isaac, Jesus really is sacrificed to the point of death. Jesus is the Lamb of God whose sacrifice delivers us from death. Because of Jesus we can see ourselves as Isaac, bound to death but delivered by grace.

And this is the Christian gospel. All the pointlessness and horror of human existence is drawn into the vortex of the cross. The cross is what happens when unending love becomes bonded to a human nature and imagination that cannot tolerate it. The cross is humanity's allergic reaction to the love of God. But the reason why the cross is good news is that the early church recognized it as the *last* sacrifice, the one that finally took away sin and became the death of war. The sacrifice of the Son of God is the sacrifice to end all sacrifice—the true atoning sacrifice. So the war to end all wars was not the American Civil War or the First or the Second World War: it was the cross. The dividing wall of hostility between us and God has tumbled down. The good news of the cross is fundamentally that the war is over. God gives us the sacrifice that ends all war. Thus war becomes the most profound way in which we show our rejection of God.

And the fifth and final step is to revisit Niebuhrian realism in relation to the power of the final sacrifice. For Christians, the problem with the weapons of war is fundamentally not that they are too strong but that they are too weak.[16] God has shown us how he goes about setting things straight. The way God redeems evil is not by responding in kind but through self-giving, patient, open-hearted non-resistant love. So it is not that war is so powerful that it is more powerful than God. It is that war is a failed attempt to establish our own meaning, when God has already given us the world's meaning in Christ's death and resurrection. Anyone who has really attempted it knows that reconciliation is harder than war. To destroy a bridge takes a second. To build one takes far longer. To kill can take a moment. To forgive can take a lifetime. The qualities that ennoble war are friendship, loyalty, courage, and unselfishness. These qualities are all required to make peace. The trouble is, while we keep war on the table as an option, we never fully use those qualities to make peace. We prop up the weakness of war, and never develop the imagination and creativity that constitute the power of peace.

WHY CHRISTIAN REALISM MAY NOT BE QUITE AS THEOLOGICALLY SERIOUS AS IT MAY APPEAR

My argument has been that Niebuhr's account of realism rests on the rejection of what turns out to be an inadequate account of pacifism—inadequate, because it identifies Jesus with perfectionist ethics rather than Chalcedonian doctrine. This account rests on a misreading of the parable of the wheat and the tares. I have proposed what I regard as a more adequate theological understanding of pacifism. I now conclude with what I suggest might be a more adequate theological account of realism.

My reading of Niebuhr has disclosed two terms that I now take as indicative of Niebuhr's ethic as a whole. In regard to anthropology his key term is sin. (Other anthropologies, notably the humanist/pacifist one, are rejected because they have an unrealistic account of sin.) In regard to social ethics, his key term is balance. (Appropriate political engagement is achievable provided competing interests are held in check.) My response to Niebuhr's realism must therefore be a response to his two key terms. There are two theological points to make.

First, anthropology. It seems for Niebuhr that anthropology governs all else in theology, and that this anthropology is derived from reason and

---

[16] I owe this way of putting the matter to John Howard Yoder. See his 'Living the Disarmed Life', in *A Matter of Life and Death: A Study Guide for Churches on the Nuclear Arms Race* (Washington, DC: Sojourners, 1981), 40–3.

observation rather than from revelation.[17] (In fact, reason and observation seem to be a large constituent element of the term 'serious'.) There is no sign that Christology has any particular role to play in determining, qualifying, or altering this anthropology. By contrast I would argue that for theology to be serious, Christology must govern anthropology. If Christ is fully human and fully divine, he shows us what humanity and God, respectively, truly look like. Leaving aside grand soteriological theories, it is hard to make any sense of the coming of Christ except as an expression, transformation, vindication, or restoration of the everlasting purpose of God to be with humanity. If this relationship is the heart of all things—creation, salvation, and eternal life— then it must be the Real Thing against which all other claims to reality are judged. If this is not regarded as real—if Jesus is not a definitive expression of God or even an unqualified expression of God at all—then there is no clear reason to take Jesus seriously as an ethical guide or example, let alone a philosophical foundation. Niebuhr's work is undoubtedly serious political engagement, but since it seems to set aside the foundation of Christian theology, it is less clear that his work is serious theology. Or is that what serious theology is—placing 'the human predicament' as philosophically prior to the action of God?

Second, ethics. Here, in relation to Christian engagement in politics, the key term is balance. ('Balance' arguably makes up the rest of the content of the term 'serious'.) But here two terms seem to be missing, each of which, I would argue, should govern ethics. One is eschatology. Niebuhr is committed to consequentialist ethics, since he is flexible about means so long as the result is justice. One of the most significant flaws in consequentialist ethics tends to be its perception of time.[18] The timeframe involved in consequentialist

---

[17] Richard Hays expresses this nicely. 'Reason and experience do not contradict Scripture; rather, they show how Scripture should be read. The Bible's anthropology tallies with the evidence rationally discerned. Nonetheless, it is the empirical evidence that is decisive for Niebuhr' (*Moral Vision*, 223).

[18] This point is made most tellingly by John Howard Yoder, who highlights the way the contrast between pacifism and 'responsibility' is in fact a contrast between two different eschatologies. 'The person who says, "You must give up some of your scruples in order to be effective", is still saying that because the goal for the sake of which to be effective is *in principle* a good goal. So the argument which takes the clothing of "principles versus effectiveness" really means this principle versus that principle. It really means that goal, for the sake of which I want you to give up other scruples, is so overridingly important that those other things are less important. That's an ethic of principle. . . . Likewise, the people who say "You must simply be true to God" . . . and "let the heavens fall" . . . really say that because of a conviction about Providence, trusting that if the heavens fall God has another better set of heavens ready, which is part of the process, so even that is not thumbing your nose at results. It's trusting God who gave the rules to know more about the results than we know. So I am increasingly convinced that the debate between the effectiveness ethic and the principle ethic is a false debate'

reasoning tends to be on the short side. It tends to advocate for visible, measurable, achievable results. The strongest argument against consequential reasoning is that what seems to be gained in the short term may well be reckoned a loss in the long term. Few things look more dated today than the consequentialist reasoning of two generations ago, assuming as it does that communism and fascism will be with us always. When Isaac Watts looks at the cross and says 'My richest gain I count but loss, | And pour contempt on all my pride', he is re-evaluating his ethics in view of the eternal perspective presented by the crucifixion of Jesus. A commitment to non-violence is serious, but requires a much longer time perspective than consequentialist reasoning is generally inclined towards. It assumes that the character of God will prevail over time, and certainly eschatologically, even if it appears to be defeated in the interim. In the words of the Letter to the Hebrews, 'As it is, we do not yet see everything in subjection to [human beings], but we do see Jesus' (Hebrews 2.8–9). The eschatological is the only ultimately real. To sustain such an ethic requires patience, courage, temperance, faith, and hope, and thus pacifism is more appropriately associated with a virtue ethic than with a deontological one.

And the other term that seems to be missing from Niebuhr's ethics is ecclesiology.[19] The units in which he deals are the sinful individual soul and the balanced body politic—moral man and immoral society. But if the Holy Spirit, along with Christ, is to be taken seriously in a fully Trinitarian ethic, account has to be taken of the primary form in which the Holy Spirit is made known—the church. Politics for Christians must begin, if they are to be real and serious, with the reality disclosed and made possible in Christ—forgiveness of sins and everlasting life—and the power named and experienced in the church—the Holy Spirit. If politics is about the possible, and about power, Christ and the Holy Spirit are the places where Christians go to discover the meaning of the possible and the meaning of power. Niebuhr does not seem to have a notion of church that is distinct but not secluded from the political world, embodying a reality that is distinct from and thus vital to the realm of

---

(J. H. Yoder, *Christian Attitudes to War, Peace, and Revolution: A Companion to Bainton* (Elkhart, IN: Goshen, 1983), 436–7).

[19] Michael Cartwright notes that Niebuhr's *An Interpretation of Christian Ethics* (New York: Harper Brothers, 1935) ends with this description of the two greatest evils for Christians: 'the impiety of making themselves God and the cruelty of seeing their fellow men as devils because they are involved in the same pretension' (*Interpretation*, 213). Cartwright notes, 'This is as close as Reinhold Niebuhr came to offering an explicit ecclesiology, but what we have is really Niebuhr's account of how 'prophetic religion' can keep the remnant of Western civilization afloat' (*Practices*, 32).

justice and power, looking to the coming of a peace the world cannot give. Baptism, for Niebuhr, neither addresses sin nor creates a new society.

Thus what is missing from Niebuhr's Christian realism is the Trinitarian God. Jesus defines little and changes nothing, and the Holy Spirit is deprived of power and of a community through which to exercise its gifts. The nature of Niebuhr's theology is to make the Trinity invisible in the cause of keeping the 'real' in view. This may be serious politics, but it can hardly be the foundation of serious theology.

6

Reinhold Niebuhr's 'Outsider Ecclesiology'

Wendy Dackson

INTRODUCTION

On 31 August 2008, a female reader's letter to agony aunt Mariella Frostrup appeared in the London *Observer Magazine*. The young woman's difficulty stemmed from her boyfriend's deepening commitment to Christian faith, a devotion which she did not share. The enquirer said that she believed her partner felt 'under pressure from his Bible study group to get married', and asked 'Can this relationship work?'

Frostrup's cautious reply to the writer indicates an incautious scepticism about the Christian religion. The first of her two most important insights concerning this dilemma expresses an admiration for the 'best manifestation' of Christianity: 'an aspirational moral code which many would argue has yet to be replaced by an improved formula'. Immediately, however, she levels a more devastating critique against what she presumes is the difficulty, saying that 'in its exaggerated, fervent, born-again form, it becomes much less benign and arguably downright aggressive'. She believes that 'religion' (and she makes little distinction between Christianity and religion more generally) 'teaches tolerance, but, in practice, the born-again variety isn't much celebrated for that virtue'. Scattered throughout the column are indications that Christian faith requires a near-fatalistic belief that everything is 'in God's hands', or a dedication to a (probably misguided and naive) 'life of good deeds', and that religious devotion is based on 'outdated mythology'. Without saying it, Frostrup has portrayed the enquirer's partner as a gullible young man, in need of an infallible institution to make his decisions for him; to provide him with the security of knowing that, in an uncertain world, at least his place in eternity would be certain; and to give him a sense of moral superiority over others.

There is nothing new in these objections to and criticisms of the Christian faith. Certainly, Reinhold Niebuhr was aware of them, whilst he himself levelled even more devastating criticisms of the Christian religion, and of the institutional Church. Niebuhr himself was no 'outsider' to Christianity. Indeed, as a prominent pastor, theologian, and seminary professor, he bene-fited from the Church's place in society. Nonetheless, understanding between Christians, corporately and individually, and the cultural context (as well as different Christian denominations), was a feature of his work from early on in his career. Even from his 'insider' position, Reinhold Niebuhr attempted to see the Church as those outside its membership might do—especially in its less attractive manifestations.

Ecclesiology is one of the weaker aspects of Niebuhr's thinking. He fre-quently collapses the ideas of 'Church', 'Christianity', and the aggregate of believers into one another in sometimes confusing ways. I will demonstrate in this essay that his theological outlook, which has come to be known as Christian Realism, gave him an awareness of the way those who stood outside the Church might view the institution, its beliefs and actions, and the individuals with whom they had daily contact in the wider social environ-ment, and by doing so, indicates an 'outsider ecclesiology' which describes the Church from the standpoint of those who are not its members. His ability to engage with respect those whose convictions and assumptions were very different from his own is not surprising from a man whose concerns were summed up in the following question: 'Can we deal with these differences in terms which will enhance understanding and not create misunderstanding?'[1]

Niebuhr's Christian Realism is an excellent method for proceeding in dialogue with non-Christians, in a way that respects other world-views, yet does not lose its integrity as a distinctively Christian form of discourse. According to Robin Lovin, Christian Realism does not indicate that morality is impossible apart from God, and it does not always 'speak explicitly of God'.[2] Rather, its basis in the Christian tradition does not make it inaccessible as public discourse, because the 'expanded attention it pays to the social and religious dimensions of experience, suggests a particularly complex view of the human good'.[3] It does not make definitive prescriptions or specific moral claims; rather it 'provides an explanation of how moral language is mean-ingful'.[4]

---

[1] Reinhold Niebuhr, *The Godly and the Ungodly: Essays on the Religious and Secular Dimensions of Modern Life* (London: Faber & Faber, 1959), 97.
[2] Robin Lovin, *Reinhold Niebuhr and Christian Realism* (Cambridge: Cambridge University Press, 1995), 33, 67.
[3] Ibid. 119.   [4] Ibid. 24.

Lovin indicates that: '[W]hat Christian Realism chiefly shares with the natural law tradition is the conviction that right action is action that conforms to human nature. The good person will act in ways that develop the capacities human beings have, rather than defying them.'[5] And it does so in the specific, concrete political and social situations in which people find themselves.[6]

Nonetheless, Lovin claims that

Niebuhr realized that Christianity survives in human history not as a set of clear and distinct ideas, but as a locus of possibilities that always transcends more immediate forms of thought and action. That which is clear and distinctive in human life has its day and disappears. What endures must have a measure of flexibility and ambiguity that is adaptable to the incoherences of real experiences.[7]

This ambiguity and flexibility are hallmarks of Niebuhr's dialectical approach, whereby he comes to theological definitions through the process of creating tensions and conflicts, and coming to understanding by testing the limits of a concept by stating what is excluded as much as what is included. There is little attention given to definitions and verbal formulae.[8] Here, I am looking at how a clearer understanding of Niebuhr's concept of 'Church' may be arrived at by means of examining the objections he believes non-Christians may raise concerning the tenets of the Christian faith, the actions of the institutions and individuals which make up the Church, and the interactions that believers and their communities have in and with the world.

WHAT IS THE CHURCH?

There are very few definitions of 'Church' in Niebuhr's writings, and even fewer expansions of that idea. A reader will be hard-pressed to find as much as a chapter on the nature of the Church in Niebuhr's work, let alone how that essence is lived out in responsible action, either towards its members or towards a wider society. This is the main difficulty in pinning down a well-elaborated ecclesiology in the thought of Reinhold Niebuhr.

Some of Niebuhr's statements on the essence of the Church are quite ordinary. One of the most fulsome assertions he makes is the following: 'The church is the body of Christ and Christ is the revelation of the living God, the creator, judge and redeemer of all nations. Such a fellowship can

[5] Ibid. 16.   [6] Ibid. 33.   [7] Ibid. 31.   [8] Ibid. 3.

never be completely at home in any nation or perfectly conform to national purposes and ambitions.'[9]

To refer to the Church this way is to use a standard biblical metaphor (albeit mixed with 'fellowship'). It sets the Church apart from complete identification with any national or cultural group, in part by making the *Church* the judge. This is deeply problematic, as to task the Church with sitting in judgment on the nations (indeed, all human endeavour) means that the Church is in a moral position to do so—and must itself be above judgment, and have the capacity to see as God sees. This is an obvious impossibility, and within a few pages, Niebuhr modifies his own position. He indicates that this fellowship is under the judgment of Christ.[10] More modestly, he claims that 'man's contrition is the foundation of the church. But God's grace is its completion.'[11] This is more in keeping with a realist view of the Church—neither individuals in their various capacities as Christians in the world, nor the whole company of the faithful together, have the right or ability to judge or to claim a view of the human situation that is not conditioned by their place and time, or their particular interests and advantages.

Nonetheless Niebuhr contributed to the report of the Oxford Conference of 1937, which stated, 'The Church is not, and can never be, the Church of a local community. The Church in any particular locality is part of a universal community, and is known to be such.'[12]

This is in tension with the understanding of the conference that the 'Church as an institution is subject to sociological forces and pressures and may succumb to the prejudices and illusions of the age'.[13] A year later, Niebuhr defined the Church as the

place in human society where men are disturbed by the word of the eternal God, which stands as a judgment upon human aspirations. . . . The Church is the place in human society where the Kingdom of God impinges upon all human enterprises through the divine word, and where the grace of God is made available to those who have accepted His judgment.[14]

---

[9] Reinhold Niebuhr, *Beyond Tragedy: Essays on the Christian Interpretation of History* (London: Nisbet, 1938), 84.

[10] Ibid. 86–7.

[11] Ibid. 61.

[12] J. H. Oldham (ed.), *The Churches Survey their Task: The Report of the Conference at Oxford, July 1937, on Church, Society and State* (London: George Allen & Unwin, 1937), 31–2. Niebuhr was a major contributor to the sections of the report which significantly addressed the church. The conference's great rallying cry was 'Let the Church be the Church'—all of which makes it more puzzling that a strong ecclesiology did not feature significantly in Niebuhr's later work.

[13] Ibid. 36–7.

[14] Niebuhr, *Beyond Tragedy*, 62.

This does not confuse the Church with the Kingdom; for Niebuhr, to do so would be a heresy (as he claims Augustine of Hippo to have been responsible for the Roman Catholic heresy of making that confusion[15]).

Niebuhr is reasonably clear that the Church is a human, contingent cultural institution that is subject to the same vanities and corruptions of any other institution.[16] Indeed, he is little concerned with the Church as a communion of saints transcending time, and including those who have gone before. Less still is he concerned with those 'whose faith is known to God alone', and are in some manner Christians despite standing aloof from the community of the faithful. The Church which he describes is the historic and visible Church, comprised of those who attend the worship and teaching for which it is organized.

But this makes it difficult to see how, without resorting to a theology of a 'mystical body' (something Niebuhr seems reluctant to do) which unites the various historical churches over space and time, transcending cultural and national boundaries, claims can be made for the universality of the Church. The difference could be seen in Niebuhr's insistence that the 'history of Christianity is the history of the truth of Christ contending against the truth as men see it';[17] fully aware that each Christian, and each local community, only has a partial grasp of 'the truth of Christ', and simultaneously are influenced by the 'truth as men see it'. This is rescued eschatologically in the doctrine of the resurrection, which 'Implies that eternal significance belongs to the whole unity of an historical realization in so far as it has brought all particularities into the harmony of the whole. Consummation is thus conceived not as absorption into the divine but as loving fellowship with God.'[18]

In history, the Church lives out this eschatological vision by living as a 'society organized for the specific purposes of worship, teaching, preaching, and the pastoral ministry', which makes it a different thing from other sorts of human association.[19] Religion, particularly the Christian religion, is a 'sense of the absolute', but not to be 'imagined in terms of man's own highest ethical aspirations'.[20] The task of the Church is to encourage this sense of the absolute and eternal beyond the human self, but not to set down absolute and eternal laws and pronouncements.

[15] Ibid. 121.
[16] Ibid. 38.
[17] Reinhold Niebuhr, *The Nature and Destiny of Man*, ii: *Human Destiny* (London: Nisbet, 1943), 49.
[18] Niebuhr, *Beyond Tragedy*, 307.
[19] Oldham, *The Churches Survey their Task*, 44–5.
[20] Reinhold Niebuhr, *Moral Man and Immoral Society* (New York: Touchstone, 1932), 52.

The question then arises as to whether the Church Niebuhr envisions can do anything at all, apart from the spiritual and ethical development of its members. He warns that we must not restrict our thinking to what the 'Church can do in its corporate capacity';[21] but include its capacity to influence society through its members in their role as Christian citizens who have the responsibility not to stand aloof from secular society. Rather, they are to acknowledge that they have a dual citizenship between the divine and secular societies, and are to influence the latter 'from within'.

The Church as an institution, has

no right to lay down a social programme, because it is not its business to establish a system of any kind. A system means a law, that is an attempt to establish timeless and abstract norms for the guidance of actual life. All legalistic systems ignore the person of the agent in his actual situation.[22]

Yet, this is precisely what the Church has done in times past, and as a result brought the wrath of society down upon itself. On the other hand, when the Church does not 'do something', it is criticized in equal, if not greater, measure.

Niebuhr's critical vision of the Church has tied its hands in terms of its effectiveness in preaching the gospel, which can only be done 'with power by a Church which takes its share of the burden of these [social and political] situations', and 'cannot therefore evade the responsibility of seeking to establish peace and achieve perfect justice'.[23] It must take concrete action, but it has no right and expertise to do so. In Niebuhr's ecclesiology, the Church is charged with conflicting responsibilities, but the essence of the Church is so ill-defined that it is impossible to tell if its being supports its doing.

THE OUTSIDER VIEW

As noted earlier, the Church is in something of a no-win situation in terms of possible objections raised by outsiders. Although it would be ridiculous to say that Niebuhr was in any way 'outside' the Church, a careful reading of his work indicates that he could see why non-Christians could object to the Church and its teachings. Indeed, those who observe the Church—whether in its official structures and representatives, or through daily contact with 'ordinary' Christians—may have a clearer idea of what they mean by the word

[21] Oldham, *The Churches Survey their Task*, 45.
[22] Ibid. 39.   [23] Ibid. 36.

'Church' than Niebuhr has given from his 'insider' position. I think that Niebuhr articulates his understanding of what the Church looks like from the outside more clearly than he is able to do from his position within the Church. Niebuhr provides an 'outsider ecclesiology' that raises important questions for Christian mission and the place of the Church in society.

The great contribution of this 'outsider ecclesiology' is that it points to the failures of the historic and concrete Church that render it unattractive to those who refuse its teaching and ministry. There are two primary difficulties, and although each is more associated with one aspect of the Church (the institution or the aggregate of believers), they are not mutually exclusive. The first of these failures is more associated with the institutional Church, and that is the failure of *arrogance*. The second is the failure of *foolishness*, which is more an attribute of the Church as the aggregate of individual Christians in their unofficial representation of the Church in their social, economic, and political interactions.

The first of these, the historical arrogance of the Church, is primarily associated with the institutional Church in its relation to the state or nation in which it is situated. In some instances, it is possible to conflate the ideas of Church and State, and to cite examples of when the Church is in collusion with the self-interests of the nation. This compromises the prophetic element of religion and its responsibility to correct and challenge political leaders and citizens alike. A particularly telling phrase Niebuhr uses in speaking of this collusion is that Christianity has, historically, 'played the court chaplain to the pride of nations', thus betraying its prophetic task of opposing the 'self-glorification of nations'.[24] The Church, then, is no better than the State, as both become the 'vehicle of collective egotism', allowing 'truth to be made the servant of sinful arrogance'.[25]

The arrogance of the Church (and of its official representatives, such as bishops or theologians) stems from its historically privileged status in society. Niebuhr is particularly critical of the political and economic power that the Roman Catholic Church has had through much of Christian history, and which he seems convinced it continued to hold (or believe itself to do) well into the twentieth century. He uses the metaphor of the Tower of Babel to represent constructions of human pride concerning the Church's ability to bring all of society together and to create the kingdom of God on earth, that great Augustinian heresy mentioned above, and yet was blind to the fact that it had not really done so: 'Roman Catholic Christianity, the traditional

---

[24] Reinhold Niebuhr, *The Nature and Destiny of Man*, i: *Human Nature: A Christian Interpretation* (London: Nisbet, 1941), 229.

[25] Ibid. 230–1.

instrument of the feudal Tower of Babel, refuses to the very last to admit that the civilisation which it has built is something less than a Christian civilisation.'[26]

As an instrument of the Tower of Babel, perhaps even that tower itself, the Roman Catholic Church committed what for Niebuhr is a cardinal sin: it failed to see its own limitations, and indeed it showed a 'pretentious disregard for its own limitations...by those groups who have compounded partial insights and particular interests with eternal and universal values'.[27] The 'rigorous searching of hearts' which would 'prevent prophets from mixing the prejudices of communities and the desires of kings with the counsels of God, and offering the compound as the word of the Lord'[28] had not been exercised.

Claims to have established the Kingdom of God on earth, and to be the governors or custodians of that kingdom, with a view of the human condition which transcended time and place, were thus premature; an absolutism in doctrine and discipline was enforced before its time. As Niebuhr maintains, religious absolutism may lead to heroic action, but it is 'a dangerous guide in immediate and concrete situations'.[29] Thus, the Church was prone to losing touch with the situation of real people, and aided and abetted a less-than-Christian feudal situation of economic and class injustice—the converse of the social ideals of the Kingdom of God.[30] To maintain the illusion that the Kingdom had indeed been established and that the Church was its manifestation, the Church had to use secular and earthly power (sometimes coercive power) to maintain its sovereign position in society. This was often a covert form of power (such as threat of excommunication), but it also involved using the force of the state, especially violent force (such as in the Crusades or the suppression and expulsion of Jews from Catholic countries). The cross, the symbol of Christian salvation for the Church, because of the Church's use of coercive power, is polluted beyond recognition:

Practically nothing can purify the symbol of Christ as the image of God in the imagination of the Jew from the taint with which ages of Christian oppression in the name of Christ tainted it. This is not merely an historic matter. We are reminded daily of the penchant of anti-semitic and semi-fascist groups, claiming the name of Christ for their campaigns of hatred.[31]

---

[26] Niebuhr, *Beyond Tragedy*, 33.
[27] Ibid. 32.
[28] Ibid. 83.
[29] Niebuhr, *Moral Man and Immoral Society*, 199.
[30] Ibid. 160.
[31] Niebuhr, *The Godly and the Ungodly*, 108.

This is not a mere wilful rejection of Christ or the gospel. It is, instead, an expression of 'resentment against the unjustified use of Christ as a "cover" for the historical relativities of culture and civilization in which it happens to be involved. It is not the Christ but "my Christ" who arouses this fury.'[32]

Without keeping these egregious historic injustices in mind, and without showing contrition for them, the Church has no right to 'preach to an age which we call secular', as these make a significant contribution to the discredited state of Christian faith in contemporary society.[33] If the Church is the representative of Christ on earth, the secular society will demand that the church actually *be* the suffering servant, who 'does not impose goodness upon the world by his power. Rather he suffers, being powerless, from the injustices of the powerful. He suffers most particularly from the sins of the righteous who do not understand how full of unrighteousness is all human righteousness.'[34]

Instead, those who have not historically shared the social and political position of the Church have not seen the 'suffering servant', but the one who causes the suffering. Niebuhr indicates that it is those who reject the Church because of the suffering (through religious persecution, spiritual bullying, or economic inequity) who are the ones who see the true nature of the 'Christian' society over which the church presumes to preside, when he asks,

Who is better able to understand the true character of a civilisation than those who suffer most from its limitations? Who is better able to state the social ideal in unqualified terms than those who have experienced the bankruptcy of old social realities in their own lives? Who will have more creative vigor in destroying the old and building the new than those in whose lives hunger, vengeance and holy dreams have compounded a tempestuous passion?[35]

Although Niebuhr is particularly critical of the place of Roman Catholicism in Christian history, and of its often too-close relationship with secular power, he is at least ecumenical in his assessment of the Church's role in perpetuating social injustices. He claims that liberal Protestantism has also been 'the religion of the privileged classes of Western civilisation', and has contributed to a 'civilisation reeking with social injustice', and understands that non-Christians are justified in their cynicism concerning Christianity more generally.[36]

---

[32] Reinhold Niebuhr, *The Nature and Destiny of Man,* ii: *Human Destiny,* 232.
[33] Oldham, *The Churches Survey their Task,* 36.
[34] Niebuhr, *Beyond Tragedy,* 181.
[35] Niebuhr, *Moral Man and Immoral Society,* 157.
[36] Ibid. 80.

It has been, according to Niebuhr, too easy for the institutional Church to forget that it is a very human creation and thus its representatives are subject to the same human failings as any other persons, sacred or secular. He says that

The pride of a bishop, the pretensions of a theologian, the will-to-power of a pious business man, and the spiritual arrogance of the church itself are not mere incidental defects, not merely 'venial' sins. They represent the basic drive of self-love, operating upon whatever new level of grace has pitched the new life.[37]

The difficulty is that pious individuals, and the institution of the Church itself, rarely recognize the drive of self-love which prompts them to protect their positions so fiercely.

The arrogance and lack of self-awareness of the Church (and its representatives) have been the cause, in Niebuhr's mind, of its mishandling of power, leading to gross historic misdeeds and inaction in the cause of social justice. Those who stand outside the Church, if they have either observed it closely or been the objects of its unjust actions, have not seen the 'body of Christ' in the role of the 'suffering servant'. If they have seen the Church as the (prematurely established and proclaimed) 'Kingdom of God', it is a kingdom against which they would rather plot a revolution than be its loyal and willing subjects. Unfortunately, through much of Christian history, they have not had a great deal of choice in the matter.

A large part of the problem has arisen from the identification of the Church with secular power—both in the Catholicism of medieval feudalism and in the Protestant sanctioning of the rising capitalism of the sixteenth century and beyond. In feudal Catholicism, the Church was almost synonymous with social power, and maintaining the status quo. However, despite a Christian society that included a somewhat more nuanced distinction of power between secular and ecclesiastical individuals, there was still the Christian sanction for the social order. Instead of seeing this as a sharper delineation between the temporal and the eternal, Niebuhr understood that 'on occasion the pious Protestant is as certain that his civilisation (capitalism) is God's peculiar civilisation as the Catholic was of feudalism.'[38] The socio-economic class became 'the community of most significant loyalty'.[39] This is a particularly easy state of affairs when a class of people can point to the temporal benefits they enjoy, and claim that they do so because God has blessed them and that their material situation is a sign of their being recipients of divine election and favour. Economic power, combined with 'religious dogmatism not only

[37] Niebuhr, *The Nature and Destiny of Man*, ii: *Human Destiny*, 141–2.
[38] Niebuhr, *Beyond Tragedy*, 124.
[39] Niebuhr, *Moral Man and Immoral Society*, 153.

accentuated intolerance and bigotry but also sanctioned the social hierar-chy'.[40] Furthermore, the institutional churches and those who most benefited from them fell into the same trap that Niebuhr understood Israel to have done: to understand themselves as 'uniquely commissioned by God' and to seek 'falsely to derive a special security from this mission'.[41] For those who were on the disadvantaged side of the 'way things were', it is little wonder that the Christian Church, in any of its incarnations, was often not seen as an attractive institution. Religious authority, especially when it sanctioned the status quo (intellectual as well as economic) as the will of God, inadvertently invites rather than suppresses revolt:

If modern civilization represents a bourgeois revolt against feudalism, modern culture represents the revolt of new thought, informed by modern science, against a culture in which religious authority had fixed premature and too narrow limits for the expan-sion of science, and had sought to restrain the curiosity of the human mind from inquiring into 'secondary causes'. The culture which venerated science in place of religion, worshipped natural causation in the place of God, and regarded the cool prudence of bourgeois man as morally more normative than Christian love, has proved itself to be less profound than it appeared to be in the seventeenth and eighteenth centuries.[42]

For Niebuhr, intellectual, as well as economic, religious, and racial, domina-tion led to some of the less fortunate exercises of power by institutionalized churches. When 'the religious man achieves power, whether inside or outside the church, he is in danger of claiming divine sanction for the very human and frequently sinful actions, which he takes and must take. Cursed be the man that trusteth in the man's church.'[43]

As problematic as the institutional church has been to those who resist it, individual Christians in their interactions with the wider society also pose a difficulty. This difficulty is manifested primarily in the form of naivety, or, to use Niebuhr's word, 'foolishness', which has two aspects. The first of these, in contrast to the institutional church, is not simply a wilful use of coercive power that individual Christians (alone or collectively) exercise that is prob-lematic. Rather, an unrealistic view of the world as it is, keeps them from applying their religious principles to the social, political, and economic situations in which they find themselves. The second is a failure to compre-hend that the pervasive character of sinful self-love is not only the province of

---

[40] Niebuhr, *Beyond Tragedy*, 233.
[41] Niebuhr, *The Nature and Destiny of Man*, ii: *Human Nature*, 29.
[42] Reinhold Niebuhr, *The Children of Light and the Children of Darkness: A Vindication of Democracy and a Critique of its Traditional Defenders* (London: Nisbet, 1945), 17.
[43] Niebuhr, *Beyond Tragedy*, 122.

the 'children of darkness', but that of the 'children of light' as well. Niebuhr is highly critical of this naivety, rooted as it is in traditional moralism, as it 'may point to any hedonistic doctrine as the creed of the children of darkness, because it has no real escape from egoism. But since it thinks it has, it illustrates the stupidity of the children of light, rather than the malice of the children of darkness.'[44]

It is not that individual Christians wish to perpetrate injustice and inequality—indeed, Niebuhr argues that democracy itself is dependent on the efforts of 'children of light'. But these have often been 'foolish children of light'.[45] However, Niebuhr claimed that it was a Christian duty to

Do everything in their power to create a more just ordering of economic life, by attempting to secure for all who are their neighbours such opportunities as are necessary for their full development as persons in body, mind and spirit. The responsibility of the Church is to insist on the true relationship of spiritual and economic goods.[46]

The difficulty lies in being sure that there is solid knowledge of what the economic and material goods of the society actually *are*. The 1937 Oxford Conference required that Christians listen to those who had expertise in their respective secular fields (whether or not those experts were themselves Christians), before they could exercise their 'double duty—both to bear witness to their faith within the existing economic order, and also to test all economic institutions in the light of their understanding of God's will'.[47] Failure to do so was a common shortcoming, which the Church is still not free from, and which brings the criticism of a naïve arrogance against the Church and its members.

However, seeking to improve the economic well-being of others, whether as individual Christians or as the institutional church, is still a suspect activity for Niebuhr. If it is mere philanthropic charity, it can be seen as an exercise of power which has a predatory aspect:

The man of power, though humane impulse may awaken in him, always remains something of the beast of prey...His philanthropy is a perfect illustration of the curious compound of the brutal and the moral which we find in all human behaviour; for his generosity is at once a display of his power and an expression of his pity.[48]

Philanthropy is suspect when it is used by the Church, as it has the ability to do short-term good by doing longer term harm, keeping people in need and

---

[44] Niebuhr, *The Children of Light and the Children of Darkness*, 27.
[45] Ibid. 15.
[46] Oldham, *The Churches Survey their Task*, 87. This was from the report to the conference on the Church's relation to the economic order, of which Niebuhr was the author.
[47] Ibid. 89.
[48] Niebuhr, *Moral Man and Immoral Society*, 13–14.

maintaining unjust social structures. The claim to have overcome the 'bestial' aspect of human nature is obviously false—and the passage of time and the refinements of civilization do not overcome socio-economic inequalities. They just make them slightly more acceptable to sensitive souls:

It might be added that not only the second and subsequent generations but the women of the mighty man fall particularly under [this] judgment. Every 'lady bountiful' who takes established injustice for granted but seeks to deodorise it with incidental philanthropies and acts of kindness, which are meant to display power as much as pity; every act of aristocratic condescension by which the traditional reputa-tion of the generosity of the 'gentle' has become established, falls under [this] judgment. The noble are not called in the Kingdom of God, at least not many of them, because they are lacking in inner honesty.[49]

Partly, this has to do with the stubbornness of both the institution and individual Church members in the insistence that the Church does not need to adapt to its historic and cultural circumstances. Niebuhr names this as 'one of the most potent causes of historical evil'.[50] Institutions and customs must be able to adapt to changing circumstances, even while holding on to what they believe are eternal truths and universal principles; the Church has been particularly bad at doing so, and individual Christians have not been much better. It is difficult because people fail to understand that they cannot be both historical and unconditioned at the same time, even if they are able to indicate something beyond their own historical and cultural situation.[51] For Niebuhr, authentic Christianity acknowledges the ambiguity indicated here. However, he understands the 'outsider' view that Christians, both individually and corporately, often fail to acknowledge their own partial and conditioned perceptions, yet force them on those they would like to 'evangelize'. The Christian intuition that the temporal and the eternal are connected is not to be denied—but it is suspect when Christian individuals and institutions claim an eternal viewpoint that is unconditioned by the temporal.

So, it is principally on these grounds—Christian arrogance, and Christian foolishness—that Niebuhr constructs a view of the Church that attempts to be sympathetic to an outsider critique, and attempts to understand why, histori-cally and in his own time, the Church could be held in suspicion and even contempt by those who say 'no thank you' to its ministries. Interestingly, despite using the Pauline metaphor of 'body of Christ' for the Church, Niebuhr nonetheless does not equate rejection of the historic Church with

---

[49] Niebuhr, *Beyond Tragedy*, 207.
[50] Reinhold Niebuhr, *Faith and History: A Comparison of Christian and Modern Views of History* (London: Nisbet, 1949), 12.
[51] Niebuhr, *The Nature and Destiny of Man*, ii: *Human Destiny*, 63.

rejection of the Christian message or of Christ himself. On the contrary, he suggests that rejection of the Church is rejecting a *false* version of Christianity, one in which the Christian hope is already fulfilled (or fulfillable) in temporal, secular terms.

Although Niebuhr never indicates that it is *right* to reject the Church, or that other systems of belief are equal or even superior to what he sees as authentic Christianity, throughout his writing, he attempts to empathize with those who hold other views. Whether or not he can be judged as having succeeded, the attempt in itself is remarkable, given the influence he had during his lifetime and after, especially in the United States and Britain—two nations which, according to Niebuhr, were strongly prone to a naïve Christian triumphalism, and guilty of exactly the kind of arrogance and foolishness against which he wrote and spoke so forcefully. Whether Niebuhr himself thought that the historic, temporal Church offered a remedy for human sin, individual or corporate, remains an open question. It is, however, evident to me that the historic, temporal church, in its conditioned situation, is largely unable to offer a remedy for its *own* sins.

SUMMARY

So, what was the Church for Reinhold Niebuhr? During my earliest years of Sunday School, boredom, plus a propensity for mixing up words, led me to remember one clause in the Apostles' Creed as 'the communion of sins and the forgiveness of saints'. That does not seem to me too far from one of Niebuhr's fullest descriptions of the Church:

> The church is created not by the righteousness of the Pharisee but the contrition of the publican; not by the achievement of pure goodness but by the recognition of the sinfulness of all human goodness. This contrition is the fruit of faith in the transcendent God who cannot be identified by any human goodness.[52]

Although 'outsiders' may not be able to articulate the nature of the Church in these terms, they can see its behaviour throughout history as something quite different—something that claims goodness and righteousness, yet does not acknowledge its own sinfulness or need for contrition. Although Niebuhr was in no way an 'outsider' to institutionalized Christianity, he was able at least to attempt an 'outsider' view of the Church, in an effort to understand the difficulties faced by Christian faith in having a positive influence on the

---

[52] Niebuhr, *Beyond Tragedy*, 60.

structures of society. It is less the fault of those who remain outside, when it is a matter of conscientious objection to ecclesial hypocrisy, than it is of the Church for inauthentic and irresponsible exercise of its authority. Before non-Christians can, in good conscience, accept the Church as a good thing, they must first be able to see it as the 'suffering servant', rather than as a ruler of the universe whose time has not yet come. Although Niebuhr offers few prescriptive remedies that the Church could take to improve this negative 'outsider' view, it does seem that his work is a rich vein that could be mined for a deeper theology of mission in the twenty-first century.

7

Niebuhr, Liturgy, and Public Theology

Stephen Platten

Reinhold Niebuhr's name is rarely, if ever, associated with the liturgy. Liturgy is rarely, if ever, associated with public theology, and what do we mean by *public theology* anyway? Is it a new phenomenon generated only in response to modern or even post-modern pluralist societies? Robert Taft, the liturgical theologian, suggests otherwise. He quotes Socrates the Byzantine historian:

> The Arians . . . held their assemblies outside the city. So each week, whenever there was a feast . . . on which it was customary to hold a synaxis in the churches, they congregated in public squares within the city gates and sang antiphonally odes composed in accord with the Arian belief. And they did this during the greater part of the night . . . John [Chrysostom], concerned lest some of the more simple faithful be drawn away by such odes, set up some of his own people in opposition to them, so that they too, by devoting themselves to nocturnal hymnody, might obscure the effect of the Arians and confirm his own faithful in the profession of their own faith.[1]

Earlier on in the paper in which Robert Taft uses this quotation, he notes:

> We are accustomed to viewing liturgy as something done in church . . . Things were not so in late-Antique Constantinople, when little symbolic or theological impact was assigned to the Byzantine church building . . . It deals, rather, with what took place *outside the church* [his italics], in the processions and services along the principal streets of the capital.[2]

Such stational liturgies were not new, of course, nor were they confined to Constantinople. We know this from the nun Egeria writing of Jerusalem in the fourth century. Indeed some New Testament critics, following the assumption that the gospels are 'passion narratives with an extended introduction', argue that the passion narratives in their present form probably issue from stational liturgies in *first-century* Jerusalem. However we view such theories, it is

---

[1] The Byzantine historian Socrates (d. after 430), quoted by Robert Taft, SJ in *Liturgy in Old Constantinople: Glimpses of a Lost World* (London: Alcuin Club, 2008), 4.

[2] Ibid. 3.

certainly the case that liturgy was a public event even from the very earliest years of the Christian faith.

The Lucan accounts of the earliest Christian community in the Acts of the Apostles confirm this. In Acts 2:41–2 we read: 'So those who received Peter's word were baptised, and there were added that day about three thousand souls. And they devoted themselves to the apostles' teaching and fellowship, to the breaking of bread and prayers.'

Even allowing for hyperbole and journalese, the public setting and significance of the gospel is clear, issuing here in a new form of liturgical life. Moreover, the setting is deliberately and spectacularly global; earlier in chapter 2 the implied reference back to Babel with the multitude of languages places religion in a global setting. A similar social outcome to that recorded here in the Pentecost narrative is assumed in the summary verses which describe the life of the embryonic Christian community (Acts 4:32 ff.). Peter's preaching is later set within a more deliberate context of public theologizing which is similarly implicitly liturgical. Indeed, his speeches can be placed alongside Paul's sermon on the Areopagus, reported later (Acts 17:22). Paul, referring to the altar to an unknown god, sets worship of Christ within and beyond the confines of already existing Greek civic religion just as Peter before him had addressed his fellow Jews celebrating their own public festival (Deut 16:9–12). Jesus' ministry too is undeniably public.

All this stands in clear continuity with Christianity's Jewish roots. It emerges from a longer tradition of prophetic or public religion. Amos, Hosea, and the later prophets were concerned about Israel's reversion to Canaanite public cults and liturgies. Israel's survival required religious purity which directed loyalty to the state. Jesus' encounter with the Pharisees over tribute money stands in this tradition. Indeed, other evidence implies similar public and corporate (that is, not just individualized pietistic) engagement. Apocalyptic literature (both Daniel and the Revelation to St John for example) is clearly politically motivated, with the cult never far away. Paul's nuanced advocacy of quietism in Romans 13, Luke's apparent desire to mollify the Roman authorities, the early severe persecutions of the Church—all this and further evidence suggests that the Church through its liturgy and its life directly engaged with politics. At the very least it suggests that the Church was perceived to offer a political challenge.[3] Early Christianity was therefore akin neither to a private world of individuals nor to an exclusive and inner-directed 'gnostic' sect. Christianity emerged on the scene

---

[3] See, e.g., the essays in Richard A. Horsley's edited volumes: *Paul and Politics: Ekklesia, Israel, Imperium, Interpretation* (London and New York: Continuum, 2000) and *Paul and Empire: Religion and Power in Roman Imperial Society* (London and New York: Continuum, 1997). See also Wayne A. Meeks *The First Urban Christians: The Social Worlds of the Apostle Paul* (New Haven, CT: Yale University Press, 1984).

in a *public* manner which will have required the beginnings of a theology similarly directed. This makes it clear that *public theology* is intrinsic to Christianity from its inception.

Indeed many of these examples imply conflict or competition with another public liturgy—be it Arian, Roman, or indeed some form of 'Athenian democracy' of the polis, as implied by the setting of the speech on the Areopagus. William Cavanaugh and other contemporary theologians would argue that a comparable rival 'liturgy' is there still in the form of a civil religion implied through the operation of the modern nation-state.[4]

The late twentieth century saw a re-emergence of these same issues. It has been classically rehearsed in the works of Martin Marty,[5] to which we shall return. Marty was concerned to clarify the role and nature of 'civil religion' in the United States. In debate with Robert Bellah, Marty coined the term 'public church' for civil religion. This *public church* engages in *public theology*, which he defined as an attempt 'to interpret the life of a people in the light of a transcendent reference'.[6] This engagement goes well beyond the realm of the self-consciously Christian communities and relates to society more widely. Thus it attempts to order 'civil, social and political life from a theological point of view'.[7] Such engagements one can argue require a liturgical expression to manifest and support them.

Although Marty's reference point is ostensibly the United States, much of his analysis can be applied more broadly, adjusting it of course to the relative degrees in which Christianity is 'established' or independent of the state in different cultures and polities. Marty argues that both in 'the academy' and in society more widely religion has often been defined as a private matter, thus excluding it from many areas of life. This has partly resulted from the use of spatial metaphors which require religion and other 'areas' of experience to be differentiated. Instead Marty uses an analysis developed by Michael Oakeshott when he writes of 'modes of experience'. So Marty writes: 'Oakeshott bids one think of the world as a continuous, pluralistic conversation, a whole, offering an experience of a world.'[8] On this basis Marty establishes the nature

---

[4] William T. Cavanaugh, *Theopolitical Imagination: Discovering the Liturgy as a Political Act in an Age of Global Consumerism* London: T. and T. Clark, 2002), 31. See also 'Killing for the Telephone Company: Why the Nation–State is Not the Keeper of the Common Good', *Modern Theology*, 20/2 (Apr. 2004), 243–74.

[5] Cf. Martin Marty, *The Public Church* (New York: Crossroad Press, 1981).

[6] Ibid. 16.

[7] Ibid.

[8] Martin Marty, 'Religion: A Private Affair, in Public Affairs', Public lecture to the Center for the Study of Religion and American Culture, Oct. 1992, <www.illuminos.com/mem/selectPapers/religionPublicPrivate.html>.

and significance of public theology. While this terminology is of recent coinage, it is clear nevertheless that much theological discourse established before Marty's definitions were fully refined falls into the realm of public theology. That is effectively where we began, in fifth-century Byzantium, fourth-century Jerusalem, and the embryonic apostolic and sub-apostolic churches of the New Testament.

Nick Spencer has crystallized what public theology might mean in a recent article in a popular journal:

The nature of Christian 'public witness', and in particular whether it takes place within, without or against the public authorities, depends *not* on what the population thinks—whether people are 'Christian' or churchgoing, for example—but rather on whether it embodies values, a concept of the good, that the public recognises and assents to.[9]

In that sense, then, all Christian discourse should be patient of translation into 'public theology'. This is the point at which Reinhold Niebuhr enters on to the scene. We can begin now to relate two points of the title of this chapter; liturgy will have to wait a little longer. On the basis of Marty's definition, Reinhold Niebuhr is classically a public theologian.[10]

Interestingly enough, Niebuhr's role as a public theologian emerges most clearly in his work on social ethics, before the publication of his most major theological treatise. In his early works Niebuhr effectively establishes the principles which Marty later expounds. Having been formed in the crucible of Liberal Protestantism, Niebuhr moved gradually away from that tradition, although he reacted too to the neo-orthodoxy of Karl Barth. He did sympathize with Barth's attack on immanentist theologians since he believed that they undermined the transcendence of God. It was that very transcendence which for Niebuhr helped sharpen the 'Christian realism' for which he became famous: divine transcendence reminds humanity of its fallibility. Barth's dogmatic theology rooted in revelation, however, ran counter to Niebuhr's emphasis upon the historical, the rational, and the experiential. Niebuhr was very clear about the cultural determinants of human consciousness. For him, Barth's insistence on revelation as the only foundation for theological discourse and his parallel rejection of natural theology were unacceptable. Niebuhr was also critical of the determinism of Marxism although he was significantly influenced by it as a tool of social and economic

---

[9] Nick Spencer, 'A Private Affair', *Third Way*, Jun. 2008, 29.

[10] See Daniel M. Bell, Jr, 'State and Civil Society', in Peter Scott and William T. Cavanaugh (eds.), *The Blackwell Companion to Political Theology* (Oxford: Blackwell, 2004), 432. Bell sees Niebuhr as the classical exemplification of public theology in the twentieth century.

analysis. His time as a pastor in Detroit amidst the automobile factories was formative here. So, for example, he writes out of that experience:

We went through one of the big automobile factories today . . . We all want the things which the factory produces and none of us is sensitive enough to care how much in human values the efficiency of the modern factory costs. Beside the brutal facts of modern industrial life, how futile are all our homiletical spoutings. The church is undoubtedly cultivating graces and preserving spiritual amenities in the more pro-tected areas of society. But it isn't changing the essential facts of modern industrial civilisation by a hair's breadth. It isn't even thinking about them.[11]

This precisely captures Marty's definition of public theology which is less concerned with 'saving faith' and more concerned with 'ordering faith'. 'Saving faith' might refer to the ways in which an individual is reconciled to God but is indicative of a theology that does so without reference to our participation in wider social, cultural, or political modes of existence. By contrast, a theological understanding of 'ordering faith' helps to offer a critique to society and even refashion it. Both, of course, are essential, but the above quotation takes us a stage further in Niebuhr's own thought, for it was such insights that helped form his critique of already existing Christian social ethics. Neither the Liberal Protestant tradition nor a pietistic focus upon individual ethics would suffice. Niebuhr was a strong critic of Protestant individualism: 'Protestantism's present impotence in qualifying the economic and social life of the nation is due not so much to the pusillanimity of the clerical leaders as to its individualistic traditions.'[12] This is where a critical use of Marxism with its analysis of social forces was one of Niebuhr's essential tools. This critique of individualism emerges most sharply in Niebuhr's *Moral Man and Immoral Society*. In this book Niebuhr is determined to press home the need for a Christian social ethic. He is clear that a focus uniquely upon the individual cannot achieve this.

It may be that Niebuhr makes the modern assumption identified by both Marty and Cavanaugh: the religious and secular are seen as two entirely separate spheres.[13] The state is concerned with what is properly 'public' whereas religion is relegated to being a matter of individual conscience within the private realm. The Church is thus privatized and is no longer seen as having a distinctly public function. Hidden, then, is the sense of rivalry between different public liturgies which we have encountered in the New Testament and in the sub-apostolic period—the church now has no public

---

[11] Reinhold Niebuhr, *Leaves from the Notebook of a Tamed Cynic* (San Francisco: Harper and Row, 1929), 78–9.
[12] *Leaves*, 96.
[13] Cavanaugh, *Theopolitical Imagination*, 31.

role and the state disavows possessing a rival, albeit secularized, 'liturgical' function. Niebuhr is intent on bridging what he presumes to be a divide between a privatized church and public life but he does not do this by asserting the claim to truth of the church but seeks to develop a Christian social ethic that will be intelligible within and to a democratic state.[14] Following from this is the related distinction in Niebuhr's mind between Catholic sacramental theology, which touches on the magical, and a more rational Christian *realist* vision, which saw the Church, with its account of human sinfulness, as being necessary to moderate the pride of public institutions.

Niebuhr thus moves the church away from a concern with the merely private and individual and reasserts its prophetic and social role. Niebuhr does not deny the significance of the individual and indeed elsewhere devotes space to it,[15] but he argues that any morality that is purely individual is impotent. This means that a Christian's engagement with politics is unavoidable. He states this with some irony: 'The real problem for the Christian is not how anyone as good as he can participate in unethical political activity but how anyone as sinful as he can dare to set himself as a judge of his fellow man.'[16] A similar insight led to one of Niebuhr's most famous aphorisms, on this occasion about democracy: 'Man's capacity for justice makes democracy possible; but man's inclination to injustice makes democracy necessary.'[17] Niebuhr is keen to sharpen the distinctive issues that need to be taken into account in developing an effective social ethic. Issues of individual ethics often contrast with those undergirding a social ethic. So, at root, Niebuhr argues that the individual will almost invariably behave more morally than will society. A social ethic is necessary because individualistic ethical motivation alone is insufficient. For society is not an aggregate of individuals but a body. Bodies, as wholes, behave differently from the separate individuals from which they are constituted.

This social ethic is essentially lived out in such a manner as to undermine institutional injustice. Niebuhr thus writes of national egotism and of the impossibility of nations being able to aspire to social knowledge and conscience. He notes that even social peace is little more than a *Pax Romana*, hiding its will-to-power under the veil of its will-to-peace. The 'will-to-live becomes the will-to-power' and ultimately the 'will-to-power of competing

[14] William T. Cavanaugh, 'Church', in *Blackwell Companion*, 400–1.
[15] Reinhold Niebuhr, *The Nature and Destiny of Man*, i (London: Nisbet, 1941), ch. 3, pp. 57–8.
[16] Reinhold Niebuhr in *Christianity and Society*, Spring 1938, page number unknown.
[17] Reinhold Niebuhr, *The Children of Light and the Children of Darkness* (London: Nisbet, 1945).

national groups is the cause of the international anarchy which the moral
sense of mankind has thus far vainly striven to overcome'.[18] The key to
Niebuhr's social ethical thought is the dialectic of love and justice. Justice
embodies but never completely fulfils the requirements of love. Love widens
the idea and application of justice, but it cannot be substituted for the
institution of justice. It is the perfect love seen in Christ which grounds this.
Niebuhr is summed up by William Werpehowski thus:

How can anyone deny that Niebuhr's is the quintessential example of a political ethic
of free responsibility? His vision, one might say, never rests in uncritical contentment.
Justice may be realized in human societies with no positive limit to it set in advance.
Yet all achievements fall short and are judged by the law of love, since they are all
tainted by sin . . . and so forth.[19]

This makes abundantly clear the reasons for seeing Niebuhr as a classic
example of a *public theologian*. Niebuhr is clear that theology must be dialectic
in its response to the world and to the nature of our humanity. Without a
clear anthropological and cultural analysis it is impossible to relate God to the
created order and to human society. For these reasons Niebuhr did not see
himself primarily as a theologian, but first and foremost as a Christian social
thinker.

*   *   *   *   *

Undoubtedly Niebuhr's anthropological starting point did not lead him to
engage at depth with ecclesiological issues. This means that there are few
sustained reflections on the significance of liturgy and worship in his work.
There are certainly frequent references to preaching; Niebuhr was himself a
powerful orator both in the pulpit and in the lecture theatre. Niebuhr and
liturgy, however, are rarely placed alongside each other. Nonetheless, recent
developments in liturgical theology suggest that Niebuhr's theological and
ethical analysis of humanity ought to be brought into conjunction with the
liturgical tradition. Increasingly the formative and transformative nature of
the liturgy is being stressed.[20] The Eucharist re-presents the central mystery of
the Christian faith—the passion, death, and resurrection of Jesus Christ.
In this re-presentation people are taken into the mystery and this forms
both their being and their living. Niebuhr's writing does not approach
theology from this direction and his reflections upon liturgy often tend to
reflect the Liberal Protestant world in which he was nurtured. He was thus
weak on ecclesiology and therefore also on the doxological roots of theology.

[18] Reinhold Niebuhr, *Moral Man and Immoral Society* (New York: Scribner's, 1932), 18–19.
[19] William Werpehowski, 'Reinhold Niebuhr', in *Blackwell Companion*, 188.
[20] Cf. *Transforming Worship*, Church of England General Synod. 2007. GS1651 London.

At this point, then, we shall respond to some of the critical reflections of his most recent theological detractors. We may then analyse some of his own references to the liturgy before seeing how his ethical and theological analysis might be brought into a clearer liturgical conjunction as an integral part of a public theology. As we have seen, this conjunction was part of the Christian tradition from its earliest days.

One of Niebuhr's sharpest recent critics is Stanley Hauerwas. Hauerwas is clear that the key role of the Church is 'to be the Church'. It is to witness to the gospel of Jesus Christ and so Christology itself stands at the centre. The Christian is not there to engage with the state; that, Hauerwas believes, is one of the key flaws in Niebuhr's work. The gospel, and Christology in particular, are compromised by the political, cultural, and anthropological world with which Niebuhr engages. Hauerwas roots his analysis in a strong ecclesiology which is partly dependent upon the work of John Howard Yoder. Yoder is clear that the Christian Church cannot disavow all political respon- sibility. Some engagement with the state and thus with politics remains essential, but Yoder's resistance remains passive. Almost certainly Niebuhr would have seen Yoder's non-violent, passive resistance as colluding with such coercion. Here we can see the tension between the two approaches most vividly. Yoder may be reprimanded for colluding with coercion, Niebuhr for not taking the Church sufficiently seriously as a body bearing witness itself and challenging the values of the state.

There is a sharp point of contention here. Both Yoder and Hauerwas are keen to develop a proper ecclesiological basis for their theological ethics. This requires the Church to set itself apart and model a life of holiness which takes its point of departure from Christology. Such setting itself apart and embrac- ing non-violence begins with the Christian Church living key elements in- cluding forgiveness and reconciliation. Only by learning how to live through such practices can we as a people come to see the violence, often present in our lives, that would otherwise go unnoticed.[21] There is, then, a proper self- consciousness with which the Church needs to engage.

The criticism is thus that Niebuhr failed to take these elements of the Church's witness seriously enough. How therefore can the Church respond effectively as a witnessing community and not simply as a pressure group aimed at resisting or attacking political policies head on? By taking the state as a given and then offering a critique, the Church may appear to accept the basis of society as a democracy (in the case of the United States) and attempt simply to amend its modus operandi through political means. Hauerwas sees

[21] Stanley Hauerwas, *Dispatches from the Front* (Durham, NC: Duke University Press, 1994), 130.

this as compromising the challenge of the gospel. The gospel is embodied in a people—the Church—who exemplify a more excellent form of social existence. In an interesting analysis, William Werpehowski offers a critical approach which seeks out the strengths and weaknesses of both theological enterprises. So, he argues that Niebuhr arrives at his position 'because he tends not to place the resurrection of Jesus Christ in history, even though historical Christian faith presupposes it'. Later Werpehowski notes:

My analysis suggests that without considered attention to concrete practices in a church that witnesses to a new life promised and present in the risen Christ, and without an integrally related attention to what God is doing in the world in calling political agencies to repentance and transformation beyond their narrower faiths, political freedom is bereft.[22]

Although Werpehowski does not spell it out, the performance of the liturgy must be at the heart of this but so must an engagement with the relativities of the world. Indeed this returns us to the very beginning of our reflections where we saw how in apostolic, sub-apostolic, and Patristic times the liturgy stood central to what we might now call a *public theology*. Liturgy, worship, and prayer mark off the Christian Church from other human agencies and so are crucial to any public living and proclaiming of the gospel. This has been ignored by many liturgical theologians as well as systematicians. Bernd Wannenwetsch offers an interesting analysis of this linkage of liturgy and public life which mirrors something of the critique of Hauerwas and Yoder alongside that of Niebuhr noted earlier. He sees three models for the relationship between worship and politics: first, religion is *counter-cultural*—the Augustinian tradition is the clear example here; second, as an *ideal type* religion sets out a pattern for the ordering of society—here William Temple is cited; finally, the Church *paradigmatically* lives the gospel, witnessing to the redemptive pattern which God establishes in Jesus—this model includes Hauerwas and Yoder. Within this analysis, Niebuhr would fit most obviously within the Augustinian tradition, following that tradition through its Lutheran trajectory. Wannenwetsch argues for a different approach where 'liturgical experience spills over in a complex and manifold way'.[23] This would allow for a development of the Augustinian tradition which does not too easily baptize the values of democratic society, but which develops Niebuhr's social ethical critique and allows it to be deployed more effectively through the liturgy as public theology. In other words, it does not simply afford the public realm an autonomy distinct from all theology.

[22] Werpehowski, 'Reinhold Niebuhr', 192.
[23] Bernd Wannenwetsch, 'Liturgy', in *Blackwell Companion*, 87–8.

This sort of pattern has been commended by Edward Foley, who specifically mentions Niebuhr in this context. Foley's argument is that worship can itself be public theology if: it is grounded in the public ministry of Jesus; it is at least a public event; it is enacted for the sake of the world. Foley argues that churches are engaged in a ritual form of worship whether they like it or not and therefore that requires of them some care in what they rehearse theologically in that worship. So we must be clear about what we are intending to articulate in the liturgy. It must be anchored in the tradition; it must be congruent with the rest of a community's public life; it must be engaged in a mutually critical public dialogue. This final point stands four-square within the Niebuhrian tradition. Foley notes that Niebuhr largely saw apologetics and social ethics as sufficient, but also sees a seed for further development in Niebuhr's own work, and notably in his Gifford Lectures, which set out his theological anthropology most fully.[24] Foley refers specifically to Niebuhr's 'distinctions between the vitalistic and the rational as a way to underscore the importance of symbolic mediation for the good not just of a church but of a republic'.[25] We shall return to this later.

*   *   *   *   *

At certain points Niebuhr does refer to the liturgy. However, the majority of references by Niebuhr to worship focus upon preaching. There are extant recordings of Niebuhr lecturing and preaching and the effect is electrifying. Richard Fox, Niebuhr's biographer, captures this emphasis sharply when he writes:

His own ecclesiology, sketchy as it was, remained fundamentally Protestant in its stress on symbolism. There was no real presence of God in the sacrament, but a symbolic representation of God's presence. The church was a community of grace, but grace was mediated more through the word that was preached than through the eucharist that was broken and shared. Niebuhr's grace was verbal, active—a grace that confronted the believer and challenged even the Church itself. A sacramental Church was too liable to passivity, self-satisfaction, too prone to believe itself sanctified. Beginning with his Detroit pastorate Niebuhr therefore stressed the Jewish prophetic 'roots of Christianity.'[26]

This is very clear from entries in his stylized diary of those early years. He writes of his attendance at a funeral in a Roman Catholic church in a manner which is both critical of his own tradition and of the mass:

[24] Edward Foley, Capuchin, 'Engaging the Liturgy of the World: Worship as Public Theology', *Studia Liturgica*, 38/1 (2008), 35.
[25] Ibid. 47–8.
[26] Richard Fox, 'The Living of Christian Realism', in Richard Harries (ed.), *Reinhold Niebuhr and the Issues of Our Time* (London: Mowbray, 1986), 20–1.

I don't think the mass is so satisfying as a well conducted Protestant funeral service . . . But it is certainly immeasurably superior to the average Protestant service with its banalities and sentimentalities. Religion is poetry . . . [however,] one must not forget that the truth is not only vivified but also corrupted by the poetic symbol for it is only one step from a vivid symbol to the touch of magic. The priest does, after all, deal with magic.[27]

Here Niebuhr's analysis is unsophisticated. The use of the term 'magic' is unfortunate. He rejects what he calls magic for a more subtle appreciation of God's presence in the 'workaday world'. He is faltering after a deeper sense of the sacramental than his own tradition often offers, but he is wary and even suspicious of Catholic sacramentalism as he understands it. As an Anglophile (married to an English woman), he knew Anglicanism well and was appreciative of a patterned and more formal liturgical usage: 'The idea that a formless service is more spontaneous and therefore more religious than a formal one is disproved in my own experience.'[28] Nevertheless, here (as elsewhere) he does not develop this idea by exploring the significance of a formal liturgy nor of the sacramental tradition. Later, indeed, he reveals his own Protestantism in his response to the controversy over the Church of England's 'deposited' (and so non-authorized) Prayer Book of 1927:

Here is the Episcopal Church which many of us have counted blessed because it was the one bridge over the chasm which separates Catholicism and Protestantism—but the chasm is now revealed as too wide for any bridge. Cooperation with the Catholic demands connivance with religious practices which reduce religion to magic. No wonder the Protestant laymen in Parliament threw the revised prayer book out. How can anyone in the year of our Lord 1927 be seriously exercised over the problems of the 'real presence' in the Eucharist?[29]

This encapsulates Niebuhr's rather naive understanding of sacramentality. Elsewhere, however, he reflects upon this argument and makes a tentative link between the moral life and worship:

Religion is a reaction to life's mysteries and a reference before the infinitudes of the universe. Without ethical experience the infinite is never defined in ethical terms, but the soul which is reverent and morally vital at the same time learns how to apprehend the infinite in terms of holiness and worship a God who transcends both our knowledge and our conscience.[30]

Here is a much clearer hint towards a sacramental embracing of the principles of his ethical theory and the need to express these through the liturgy. There is a mystifying dysfunction between these various reflections. There appears to

[27] *Leaves*, 32–3.   [28] Ibid. 61.   [29] Ibid. 156.   [30] Ibid. 55.

be a proper seeking after a sacramental sense; Niebuhr is engaged by the poetic, and his own writing, preaching and prayer indicate a real sensitivity not only to the power of words, but to a deeper sense of glimpsing God in the material things of everyday experience. His Protestant formation, however, frightens him away from what he feels inevitably will direct the Church towards a 'magical' understanding of liturgy, worship, and theology. Perhaps, by exploring this tension we can develop a clearer sense of how Niebuhr's social ethical critique may be used more directly in liturgy as public theology.

Edward Foley points to Niebuhr's exploration of the polarities of vitalism and rationalism. By vitalism Niebuhr appears to mean the basic natural life force in humanity, which can then be constrained by rational thought. This vitalism is present most explicitly in his Gifford Lectures, but it appears elsewhere in his specifically ethical writings where Niebuhr balances the influence of romanticism and utilitarian rationalism in producing his own framework of 'prophetic religion'.[31] This is where Niebuhr is directly critical of the Liberal Protestant tradition in which he was nurtured. This tradition abandoned the proper theological elements of the mythical symbolism at the heart of the gospel which helped interpret the nature of our humanity with all its aspirations and fallibilities. It attempted to remove these elements separating history and theology and transposing Jesus so that he became instead the good man who walked the shores of the Sea of Galilee; he simply exemplified human goodness. But by so limiting both Jesus and the Christian religion, the transcendent is excluded. Alongside this, the power of evil, the will-to-power, and the coercive elements within human society are played down or ignored thus producing an inappropriate 'ideal' which ignores human fallibility and so subverts the fallibility which is central to Niebuhr's Christian realism.

In his Gifford Lectures, exploring the two polarities of vitalism and rationalism, Niebuhr notes the vitality present in all creatures but identifies the specific nature of human vitalism through focusing on our self-transcendence. It is the way that this vitalism works within us that defines human creativity. God is the source of this vitality as well as of order and rationality. Niebuhr reviews a number of developments within modernity, including the protest of the Romantics against rationalism,[32] and both the contribution and deficiencies of Marxism. He is clear that it is impossible to resolve fully the

---

[31] See for example, Reinhold Niebuhr, *An Interpretation of Christian Ethics* (London: SCM Press, 1936), 213 ff.

[32] For a reference to this in a specifically Christian context, see Stephen Platten, 'One Intellectual Breeze: Coleridge and a new Apologetic', *Theology*, 111/863 (Sept./Oct. 2008), 323–35.

tension between vitality and form, between vitalism and rationalism.[33] Even so, it is from this tension that his social theory grows, embracing the cultural and anthropological but allowing for the vitality which is God-given to free us from a sterile rationalism. From this emerges a symbolic mediation which embraces the patterns set out in Christian orthodox thought; the work of Christ is not exhausted in a Liberal Protestant picture of Jesus as 'the good man' nor indeed in attempts to root all in rediscovering the historical Jesus. The pattern of salvation in Christ transcends a purely rationalistic framework.

Ironically it appears that in his own living out of the Christian gospel Niebuhr was unable to engage with how this understanding might have an immediate relationship with liturgy and worship. The roots of this may lie in his own declared rejection of the term theologian for his work. As he energetically embraced the world, he was steered away from any self-conscious reflection upon the nature of the Church. For many this remains the most refreshing and distinguishing feature of Niebuhr's undoubted theological contribution, despite his own protestations. As a theologian he almost certainly influenced politics on both sides of the Atlantic more than any other twentieth-century Christian writer. Ironically, however, this seems to have constrained him liturgically. The liturgy remained for him largely an exercise for the church community except inasmuch as it was the platform for prophetic preaching.

Liturgy is, however, not a purely ecclesial community event. It is a public event and at certain moments Niebuhr recognized this, as we have seen. What he did not respond to was the performative nature of the liturgy and thus its place within a developed public theology. The performative element of the liturgy means its capacity to be formative and transformative of the wider community. This comes as a result of the liturgical event itself and through the potentially transformative power of the community of faith, constituted by that event.

There may be ways in which public liturgies—occasional offices, processions, memorials, inductions of new ministers, 'ways of the cross'—can be made to impinge on society at different levels. The main argument, however, lies deeper. The liturgy is the means by which the Church receives itself from beyond. It creates a medium which can literally embody Niebuhr's critical insights and so can also be transformative in its public interactions. Liturgy within a clear ecclesiological framework can make Niebuhr's critique still more potent. Niebuhr's refreshing ability to look outward from the Church, challenging society, meant that his ecclesiology was virtually non-existent. We

---

[33] Cf. Niebuhr, *The Nature and Destiny of Man*, i, esp. pp. 27–56.

see this in the naive way in which he understands sacramentality as a form of 'magic' and yet at the same time hints at some form of sacramentality by rooting the gospel in the things of everyday life. In this sense he was not a theologian, at least not an ecclesial theologian, as he himself declared. He was, however, undoubtedly a public theologian, assuming, that is, that public theology can be strengthened through a further key liturgical insight. The Eucharist is the key performative Christian liturgy and is unitive in bringing together not only humanity and God but also in bringing humanity itself together in solidarity. In doing this the Eucharist also transgresses international boundaries and subverts the national will-to-power and rivalry or subsequent rivalry which Niebuhr so clearly identified. By embracing this theological insight, Niebuhr's theology effectively can be enriched, strengthening the Church and giving a clearer sense of ecclesiology.[34]

As Foley argues, the liturgy itself is or ought to be a crucial element within any public theology. The message is clear for the Church. What message do we broadcast through our liturgy? Does it measure up to those images with which we began, in fourth-century Byzantium, at the Areopagus or indeed in Jesus' own ministry? Hauerwas's and Yoder's critique of Reinhold Niebuhr may miss the mark overall. Nevertheless, that critique may hit its target in encouraging a more adequate ecclesiology rooted in a performative liturgy which will focus Niebuhr's theological anthropology and not only through the preached word, but actually within corporate worship itself. The Eucharist re-presents the central mystery of the Christian faith—the passion, death, and resurrection of Jesus Christ. It was the impact of that mystery that ultimately shaped Niebuhr's social ethics. How can the liturgy reflect Niebuhr's critique performatively? That is, how can the Church as a community formed by its worship live out in its daily life that performative challenge?

---

[34] Cavanaugh, *Theopolitical Imagination*, 49–50.

8

Falling Far Short

Taking Sin Seriously

Martyn Percy

The landscape of contemporary religious belief is often a puzzling vista to contemplate, and one of the more baffling features of modernity is the relatively rapid dissolution of the doctrine of sin. As David Lodge remarks in his novel *How Far Can You Go?*, it seems as though hell disappeared in the 1960s, and that nobody noticed.[1] And if there is no hell, then there is nothing—such as sin—that can really take us there. Hell therefore becomes an abstract concept; something to gaze on and ponder in literature and art, perhaps puzzle over in primitive religion, but only to ultimately rejoice in our deliverance from such a manipulative and fear-inducing theological construction of reality.

In this brief chapter, I propose to sketch lightly the contours of the difficulties churches currently face, in our modern secular society, of talking about sin. Implied within this, of course, comes a complementary struggle: how to talk about salvation and redemption, but in terms other than those that reflect our zeitgeist, namely greater spiritual fulfilment and personal development. The focus is the grammar and doctrine of sin: pondering its absence in public space, some of the consequences of that absenteeism, and how Reinhold Niebuhr's insights contained within the two volumes of *The Nature and Destiny of Man* might help us to reflect on this situation.

The term 'secular' is of course a contested one; in this chapter I use it to denote late modern societies in which belief is no longer hegemonic. The connections between Christian vision and social flourishing are of course particularly thick in the writings of Reinhold Niebuhr, who illuminates some of the emergent tensions in late modern society. This can be seen in his

---

[1] D. Lodge, *How Far Can You Go?* (London: Penguin Books, 1980). See also Martin E. Marty, 'Hell Disappeared. Non-one Noticed: A Civic Argument', *Harvard Theological Review*, 78 (1985), 391–8.

changing position in relation to Roosevelt's 'New Deal'—the term given to a series of economic programmes he initiated between 1933 and 1936 with the goals of giving work (*relief*) to the unemployed, *reform* of business and financial practices, and *recovery* of the economy of the United States during the great Depression. Concerned with the harsh realities of life for working-class labourers, Niebuhr was initially critical of the New Deal, fearing that any attempt at a gradual transition from capitalism to socialism could only create instabilities that would lead to a fascist backlash. But by the 1940s, a political pragmatism had crept into his arguments. As Ronald H. Stone puts it, in Niebuhr's revised view, '[c]oncrete human needs and lives take priority over conceptual schemes for a new society or over dreams that may comfort one but produce no results in political action'.[2]

Niebuhr, perhaps inevitably, developed a Christian critique of the inequality he had witnessed: and it partly gave rise to the new Niebuhrian realism that addressed the countervailing power relations between capital, labour, and government. Echoing Augustine, Niebuhr's writings (especially in *The Nature and Destiny of Man*, 1941–3, volumes 1 and 2) began to argue that sin is any word or deed or thought against the eternal law. Correspondingly, the injustice of structures—be they social, commercial, or governmental—needed to be challenged. The sins of modernity were bound to be more subtle forms of oppression that had found their ways into the polities and praxis of society, as a direct result of gradual processes of secularization.

This brings us, neatly enough, to the problem of sin in modern society: if hell did indeed disappear in the 1960s—and no-one noticed—what has happened to sin, trespassing, and transgression in late modernity? Even the mention of the word seems faintly problematic. Setting aside Advent or Lent as periods of penitence and holy preparation at the beginning of the twenty-first century (at least in developed countries) seems almost risibly counter-cultural. Few Christians (let alone agnostic members of the public) appreciate churches that dwell on sin and moral shortcomings too much. In our therapeutically attuned culture, the very concept has been somewhat down-graded. Sin may induce guilt and shame. Such concepts, we are frequently assured, are paralysing and unhealthy.

Indeed, a recent local survey of children's attitudes to sin suggested that the concept is becoming rather outmoded.[3] Even the children from quite religious families struggled to explain what sin was. One child said biting his sister was 'bad'; another, that jumping on the sofa was 'naughty'. And from

---

[2]   Ronald H. Stone, *Reinhold Niebuhr: Prophet to Politicians* (Nashville: Abingdon, 1972), 234.
[3]   Ann Richardson (ed.), *Through the Eyes of Children* (London: Church House Publishing, 2009).

their schools, including those that are Church of England, the children seemed to have learnt that the great evils of the day are global warming, pollution, and bullying. And the answers to these vices? Take more care of the world; and be nice to other people.

Yet a culture that is mainly formed out of desire and achievement may find itself in the grip of a subtle temptation. Namely, to confuse sin with imperfection; with what we lack as people, and on how to achieve greater fulfilment. Falling short, in other words: but not by much. To be sure, it is often helpful to be conscious of sins of omission and negligence. Indeed, there are many popular definitions of sin to be found in Christian paperback books that simply conceive of sin as some kind of shortfall. Yet a society that plays down the idea of serious personal and social sin, and even apparently unfashionable concepts such as original sin, does so at its peril. For in ignoring the dark side of human nature, there is a risk of collapsing into a falsely optimistic and even utopian world-view that then struggles to cope with the reality of evil when it strikes. Rather than accepting sin as commonplace, modern societies often presume to regard the state as exceptional, and even as a private matter.

I suspect that one aspect of the problem may lie in language. Sin is a short, simple word—almost too easy and quick to utter. The very accessibility of the word has arguably played a part in the weakening of its power. Our older and arguably denser religious vocabulary preferred the word 'trespass': 'forgive us our trespasses as we forgive those who trespass against us'. The word captures something active; the idea that lines have been crossed; that some of the things we say, do, and think are actually offensive, and grieve God. Cranmer's majestic collect for purity in the *Book of Common Prayer* understood that a great deal of sin is concealed inside us. Yet to God, all hearts are open—replete with their miscible emotions and motives. And all our desires are known too, with no secrets hidden. All of them are seen by the one who is returning. Yet the prayer continues in petition, 'cleanse the thoughts of our hartes by the inspiration of thy Holy Spirit'.

A second aspect of the problem lies with churches themselves, some of which have unintentionally colluded with the demotion of the concept as a meaningful part of public discourse. The word has been attached to a select range of vices, which though they may be serious and potentially harmful (or corrupting), has lessened the range and scope of the concept more generally. Too much attention focused on sexuality, for example, exacerbates the heightened sense that some kinds of relationships are always 'right' and others always 'wrong'. This then robs the Church of the possibility of talking critically and empathetically of the need for confession and absolution in *all* relations of loving intimacy. True enough, some relationships are invariably wrong: those that are abusive, selfish, and exploitative, for example. But other forms of relationship that struggle for recognition and affirmation in modernity may be the portent and bearer of many virtues, and not be sinful in the ways that appear to be immediate and obvious. Correspondingly, the very idea of sin might be something that needs to be rescued from fundamentalists and other Christian groups that have appropriated it in order to focus on a relatively narrow range of personal and social vices. Only when society faces and names the fuller range of thoughts and actions that grieve God can culture be truly challenged, and humanity gently ushered into a more restorative notion of flourishing and relationality.

A third aspect of the problem may lie in the subtle yet insidious ways in which churches and faith communities have been seduced into colluding with consumerism. Robert Bellah notes that in America there are over 220 million religions—'one for each of us'.[4] The very possibility of such choice (over and against obligation) puts the survival of the community of memory at risk, as it is replaced by 'empathetic sharing' by loosely associated individuals and networks. Religion becomes a 'quasi-therapeutic' activity amongst self-selecting individuals who opt into a particular group for a chosen period. Under such conditions, faith can quickly become privatized and lacking in the kind of continuity that lends itself to wisdom; the property of a sect that sees itself as engaged with but apart from society. Such groups are ill placed to offer a gentler, more nuanced voice to counter the 'more vigorous forms of radical religious individualism, with their dramatic claims of self-realization, or the resurgent religious conservatism that spells out clear, if simple, answers in an increasingly bewildering world'.[5]

A fourth and final aspect to mention is that in falling far short of the vision of catholicity—both social and ecclesial—churches have not been slow to attract spiritual consumers, hunting for meaning and fulfilment. As Peter Schmiechen perceptively points out, the emphasis on pragmatism (or technique) and consumerism in American Christianity creates a range of problems:

one is that the techniques can be borrowed from general organizational theory and marketing strategies and have no goal other than meeting people's needs as a way of expanding membership. This opens the door to the great debate over what are legitimate and illegitimate needs for religious communities to meet. While Jesus Christ does in fact meet our heartfelt and deepest needs, in America the gospel too often has become a technique for self-improvement and personal happiness...[6]

---

[4] R. Bellah, *Habits of the Heart: Individualism and Commitment in American Life* (Berkeley: University of California Press, 1985), 113 ff.

[5] Ibid. 114 ff.

[6] Peter Schmiechen, *Saving Power: Theories of Atonement and Forms of the Church* (Grand Rapids, MI: Eerdmans, 2005), 364–5, n. 5.

Such 'user-friendly' forms of religion abound in America, and increasingly in other developed nations too. Schmiechen has in mind church-growth movements like Willow Creek, and also the writings of Rick Warren.[7] The common thread is the promotion of religion as something that will solve problems and improve the lives of individuals. The highly successful publications of Rick Warren appear to place the emphasis on God's purposes for the individual. However, nagging questions remain. Are churches and individuals being asked really to give their lives over to God's purposes? Or, is it the case that God's alleged purposes are simply a veneer of techniques to enhance the quest for meaning and success?

To be sure, it is easy enough to survey contemporary life in most developed countries, and join in Ezekiel's ancient lament for a nation:

In those days they shall no longer say: 'The Fathers have eaten sour grapes, and the children's teeth are set on edge'. But every one shall die for his own sin; each man who eats sour grapes, his teeth shall be set on edge . . . Behold all souls are mine; the soul of the father as well as the soul of the son is mine: and the soul that sins shall die.[8]

To take one example here of what a latter-day Ezekiel might have in mind, consider the consequences of unfettered consumerism in late-modern capitalist societies, which are perhaps all too well known. Children, exposed to relentless advertising for their foods of choice (rather than what might be good for them, less preferable, but arguably more obligatory), eschew vegetables, fruit, and balanced diets in favour of snacks and foods that are high in fats, resulting in obesity. Further exposure to commodities may lead to children knowing what they want to have (i.e. acquisitions), but not what they want to be (i.e. vocations, careers, etc.), with the latter simply being the means of obtaining the former. Here of course, we may discover that less is more; that by reducing choice we enhance our enjoyment of ourselves and one another. But to appreciate this, unfettered capitalism has to be checked and challenged as not only unwise, but also probably sinful too. The illusion of endless choice turns our gaze away from the other to the self. So, even the innocent 'gap years' (i.e. between school and college) have begun to suffer from apparent commodification, increasingly becoming 'off the peg' consumer items that are now more like touristic rites of passage rather than a means for constructive engagement with the needs of developing countries. No-one is suggesting, of course, that children and young adults are now no longer

[7] See Rick Warren, *The Purpose-Driven Church: Growth Without Compromising Your Message and Mission* (Grand Rapid, MI: Zondervan, 1995).
[8] Ezekiel 18:1–4.

moral. However, the problem is more subtle than that, for there seems to be no compass.[9] Morality is obscured by consumerism. The master narratives that would inform moral horizons and provide depth and density in content have been quietly left to one side. The consequence of religion becoming a private matter—and with no accompanying common 'grammar of sin'—is that individualism and expressivism flourish at the expense of the social and collective. When it becomes impossible to talk about sin seriously, the scope for discussing goodness is also diminished.

How then might Reinhold Niebuhr help us to think through this? For Niebuhr, one of the most important insights into the modern doctrine of sin was that the truth is 'hidden from them' (Luke 18:34), and they (i.e. human beings) constantly 'delight in their own good' (Isaiah 66:3). Thus,

Man is insecure and involved in natural contingency; he seeks to overcome his insecurity by a will-to-power which overreaches the limits of human creatureliness. Man is ignorant and involved in the limitations of a finite mind; but he pretends that he is not limited. He assumes that he can gradually transcend finite limitations until his mind becomes identical with the universal mind. All of his intellectual pursuits therefore become infected with the sin of pride. Man's pride and will-to-power destroy the harmony of creation.[10]

Correspondingly, sin is both passive and active. It is passive in the sense that it is often a subtle form of subtraction: ignorance of ignorance. The fathers who ate sour grapes could not know what they were doing; nor could they know of the consequences. Niebuhr argues that because we are ignorant of so much (for example, we cannot know the future); we are also often unaware or ignorant of the very limitations that might accompany such ignorance. Sin is also, however, active: the will-to-power. Here, sin is partly conceived of as the effort to obscure individual and collective blindness, but only by overestimating the degree of sight; and, in Niebuhr's thinking, this simply obscures humanity's insecurity—by stretching power beyond its limits.

Pride, then, becomes an important key for Niebuhr in understanding the nature of the human condition and its problematic dimensions. For Niebuhr, the insecurity of the ego, and the grasping after power to make itself more secure, is a fundamental issue, since it leads to the quest for sufficient power to guarantee security. Linked to this is intellectual pride. For Niebuhr, every ruling oligarchy in history has found its ideological pretensions as important a bulwark

[9] See Francis Davis Elizabeth Paulhus and Andrew Bradstock, *Moral, But No Compass: Government, Church and the Future of Welfare* (Cambridge: Von Hügel Institute and Matthew James Publishing, 2007).

[10] R. Niebuhr, *The Nature and Destiny of Man*, i (London: Nisbet, 1941), 190 ff. The question of gender raised by his use of exclusive language is one to which I will return shortly.

of authority as its own policing power. So, intellectual pride is a pretension that all human knowledge is actually truer than it really is or can be. Here, Niebuhr has Marxism and other ideological frameworks in mind: the modernist meta-narratives of communism, fascism, and (to a lesser extent) social democracy that form credulously complete templates through which individuals are supposed to construct lives and their meaning. Niebuhr sees an all too present danger with such political and social systems: erroneous moral pride and self-righteousness. Goodness becomes something that is personal, social, and temporal; but is now no longer unconditional: 'The whole history of racial, national, religious and other social struggles is a commentary on the objective wickedness and social miseries which result from self-righteousness.'[11]

But in case one begins to detect some kind of competition (or even war) for the supremacy of types of knowledge in modernity, or the restoration of (mythic) Christendom over and against modernity, Niebuhr is actually no less critical of the kind of spiritual pride that might assume to out-narrate and dominate the intellectual arrogance he targets: 'As soon as the Christian assumes that he is, by virtue of possessing this revelation, more righteous, because more contrite, than other men, he increases the sin of self-righteous-ness and makes the forms of a religion of contrition the tool of his pride.'[12]

The sin of pride, then, is a complex one to contemplate. It is rooted in insecurity (and the will-to-power response). But it can also lead to the self-deification of social groups: humanity and divinity can be easily conflated. The chosen people, nation, or individual can all arise out the 'collective egotism' that imagines itself to be godly. And even here, the churches can be vehicles for this kind of collective egotism. A contemporary example of this danger is offered by the biblical scholar Itumeleng Mosala. Writing on the subject of South African theology, he warns that 'we can see a biblical hermeneutics of liberation for black theology as liberating neither because it is black nor on the grounds that it is biblical. Rather, it is a *tool of struggle* in the ongoing human project of liberation.'[13] In matters of social justice and human endeavour, there is a constant danger of uncritically identifying God with a particular human goal, so that what begins as an important and necessary social movement becomes idolatrous. When this happens, Niebuhr sees such developments as the invasion of the spirit by something less than the Holy Spirit: indeed, nothing less than the demonic.[14]

[11] R. Niebuhr, *The Nature and Destiny of Man*, i (London: Nisbet, 1941), 212.
[12] Ibid. 214.
[13] Itumeleng J. Mosala, *Biblical Hermeneutics and Black Theology in South* Africa (Grand Rapids, MI: Eerdmans, 1989), 9.
[14] R. Niebuhr, *The Nature and Destiny of Man*, ii (London: Nisbet, 1943), 115.

It is worth pausing at this point in order to reflect a little more on Niebuhr's insights into the human condition. Whilst some might class his observations as caricaturing—and with the temporal and contextual limits of the mid-twentieth century to bear in mind also, since it must not be forgotten that he is writing at the very heights of power for both fascism and communism—the prescience with which he analyses the individual and collective challenges to humanity continue to have significant resonance. For Niebuhr, human beings are simultaneously bound and free; limited and limitless. This leads directly to the anxiety he narrates in *The Nature and Destiny of Man*: an anxiety that establishes the precondition for the escape into falsehood. Thus, there is an in-built temptation for individuals and groups to overstep limitations (which, Niebuhr holds, is a sin: 'trespassing'), which resides in human nature:

The ambition of man to be something is always partly prompted by the fear of meaning-lessness which threatens him by reason of the contingent character of his existence. His creativity is therefore always corrupted by some effort to overcome contingency by raising precisely what is contingent to absolute and unlimited dimensions.[15]

Arguably, the critique of the human condition and the excavation of the concept of sin is at its deepest in Niebuhr's writings when he turns his attention to the subject of sensuality. Here, he sees the inordinate focus on the sensual in late-modern societies as a destruction of the harmony within self. Various 'sins of excess' arise from this: human beings, having lost the true centre of their lives, are no longer able to maintain their own will as the centre of themselves. With absorption and distraction come disorientation and de-centring: humanity becomes lost in its own attempt at meaning-making. This prompts Niebuhr to pose a question: 'Is sensuality...a form of idolatry which makes the self God; or is it an alternative idolatry in which the self, conscious of the inadequacy of its self-worship, seeks escape by finding some other god?'[16]

He answers his own question by suggesting that sensuality is always an extension of self-love to the point where it defeats its own ends. It also represents some kind of attempt to escape the 'prison' of the self by finding a god in a process or person outside the self. And it can also be seen as some kind of endeavour to escape from the confusion which sin has created, into some form of subconscious existence. Underpinning these kinds of observations, perhaps naturally enough, is Niebuhr's theological realism that refuses to relinquish a doctrine of original sin. For Niebuhr, sin is inevitable in the human situation itself. The self lacks the faith and the will to subject itself to

---

[15] R. Niebuhr, *The Nature and Destiny of Man*, i (London: Nisbet, 1941), 198.
[16] Ibid. 248.

God. There is an inevitable (empirically derived) tendency towards self-love which derives in turn from the primordial sin of a lack of trust in God.

Niebuhr's argument about the sinful tendency towards self-love has led feminists to critique what they perceive to be the male-centred nature of his theology. Daphne Hampson puts it this way

> I am not faulting Niebuhr's analysis. It is surely illuminating. I am simply saying that it is a description of what is a peculiarly male temptation. His analysis reminds me of the discussion of the outlook of boys by Carol Gilligan (a Harvard development psychologist) in her best selling book *In a Different Voice.* Jake, an eleven year old, with great self-confidence and sense of his own importance, sees the world as though he were in the centre of it. Christian theology, written by men, has well understood their problem. Indeed, these myths and stories about pride and fall, have been formulated because they correspond to a truth. William Temple, whom Niebuhr does not quote, puts it neatly: 'Sin has "I" in the middle.' What I want to say however is that this is inadequate as a description of woman. My criticism is of Niebuhr's equation of male with human.[17]

For Hampson, a much wider understanding of sin is required than an excess of self-love. This is necessary, she argues, because so many women are brought up to empty themselves out in the service of others. For women in this position, the true sin is not an excess of self but a profound denial of self, an inability to give oneself one's due. Hampson's argument is helpful because it draws attention to the diversity of human experience in our modern western society, and to the concurrent need for a range of different understandings of sin in order to facilitate human flourishing. A similar insight into the psychological and social complexity of our modern society leads Oliver O'Donovan to argue for the inadequacy of Niebuhr's understanding of sin on slightly different grounds:

> A single protological concept such as 'pride' cannot to service as a complete phenomenology of sin, which will always be diversified. As Aristotle observed, sin is always multiple... There is scope, certainly, for seeing the pride of the primal sin worked out in the will-to-power; but an exclusive focus on power will restrict our observations too narrowly... Individual power-holders may indeed be corrupted by power; but they may be corrupted by weakness, too, and by indolence, compassion, or stupidity, or by not having to take responsibility and by being protected from it by others.[18]

O'Donovan takes Hampson's argument one step further, arguing that even those who have grown up at the centre of their own universes can still find

---

[17] Daphne Hampson, 'Reinhold Niebuhr on Sin: A Critique', in Richard Harries (ed.), *Reinhold Niebuhr and the Issues of Our Time* (London: Mowbray, 1986), 47.

[18] Oliver O'Donovan, *The Ways of Judgement* (Grand Rapids, MI: Eerdman, 2005), 80–1.

themselves corrupted by a whole range of influences. People are multi-faceted, and while they may well exercise huge and potentially corrupting power in some aspects of their lives, they will undoubtedly experience huge weakness or neediness in other matters. They are as likely to be corrupted by an excess of compassion or by sheer fallibility or ignorance as they are through the characteristic that Niebuhr identifies as pride. O'Donovan's analysis is helpful because it moves away from Hampson's straightforward account of gender, into the recognition that sin operates in all kinds of subtle ways, within individuals and corporately within the complex web of human relations. Niebuhr's notion of the will-to-power and Hampson's insights into gender are important parts of the picture, but they do not account for the whole. As the Radical Orthodoxy theologian William T. Cavanaugh argues, 'sin is scattering into mutual enmity—both between God and humanity and among humans'.[19] Taking Niebuhr's fundamental insight into sin as basically sound, there is an obvious need to note his own historicity, and to continue the dialogue with contemporary society, correcting those areas of his theology which fall short.

What, then, is the Christian response to this? For Niebuhr, the true theological realism that addresses sinful nature lies in the realm of grace. It is only baptism (the reproductive system at the heart of Christian practice) that can help humanity on its way. As Paul states succinctly in the Epistle to the Galatians (2:20), 'it is no longer I that live, but Christ who lives in me'. Christians are born of the Spirit, and in grace they find the sanctification and justification ultimately to overcome the sin that is indelibly a part of our human nature. Niebuhr comments that

the new self is the Christ of intention, not of achievement. It is the self only by faith, in the sense that its dominant purpose and intention are set in the direction of Christ as the norm. It is the self only by grace, in the sense that the divine mercy 'imputes' the perfection of Christ and accents the self's intentions for its achievements.[20]

As with baptism, so with the rest of Christian life: through death to the self there is birth, and it is there that we ultimately find new life, and the true promise of freedom that delivers our natures from slavery to sin.

Charles Taylor argues that the Church has colluded in removing this emphasis on renunciation, and the newfound freedom to which it leads, from our newly secular society. He believes that for true and deep forms of

---

[19] William T. Cavanaugh, 'The City: Beyond Secular Parodies', in John Milbank, Catherine Pickstock, and Graham Ward (eds.), *Radical Orthodoxy* (London: Routledge, 1999), 184.
[20] *The Nature and Destiny of Man*, ii. 118.

social flourishing to take place, religion (or more particularly, the Church) might have to rediscover its nerve:

> [The] Reformation has helped to produce . . . today's secular world, where renunciation is not just viewed with suspicion—to a certain degree that is always healthy and necessary—but is off the radar altogether, just a form of madness or self-mutilation. We end up with a narrower, more homogeneous world of conformity to a hedonic principle. The Church was rather meant to be the place in which human beings, in all their difference and disparate itineraries, come together: and in this regard, we are obviously falling far short.[21]

Falling far short? This seems a curious and resonant phrase with which Taylor chooses to conclude his magnum opus. He means by this, I suppose, the loss of catholicity from the churches; the omnipresent seduction afforded by creeping denominationalism that allows churches and faiths to individualize, specialize, and homogenize in a consumerist culture (and thereby compete), but surely at the expense of pursuing a much richer and larger vision that might be rooted in a deep fusion of sociality and transcendence. Such a vision is beyond the temporal aspects of simply being 'established', or for that matter, of concordats; or indeed of alternative models of ecclesial polity that are communitarian, sectarian, and disestablished. It is, rather, a hope that the Church can be broadly and deeply incorporative within its given social context, providing the necessary shape, ethos, and purpose for life that enables true flourishing, and enables the horizons for social flourishing to be elevated beyond our collective interest. Put another way, the Church can be the place that orders the world in a way that makes common sense; but without losing the humility that must accompany worship and mystery. Recognizing the huge diversity of human agendas that form our modern society, and therefore also the diversity of potential forms of sin, Taylor regards the Church as the place that retains the grammar that can still lead people into a healthy state of repentance, and that can thereby enable people to knit together a healthier society.

   To conclude, it is my contention that one of the unintended by-products of secularization has been the gradual dissolution of the doctrine and grammar of sin from public life. This has reduced the capacity of more developed societies to reflect on human nature, whereby 'sin' becomes something that is mostly narrated as mere imperfection rather than being something much deeper, darker, denser, and more destructive in our collective and individual lives. Churches have unintentionally colluded with this movement, and have bound up sin by nominating a contentious and narrow range of personal

---

[21] *The Nature and Destiny of Man*, ii. 772.

vices, which do little to help societies and individuals reflect on the nature and destiny of humanity in terms of sinfulness. Niebuhr's work, as we have seen all too briefly in this chapter, has the capacity to help transform our understanding of sin and human nature, thereby enabling society to begin to engage with the complex and reticulate forces that both bind and blind our vision, which ultimately impairs our freedom and destiny.

Niebuhr achieves this through a well-grounded psychological understanding of sin, but one which is not merely individualist. There is also recognition of the institutional and collective nature of sin, which also throws some light on how secularization has subtly impeded the contribution that the grammar and doctrine of sin might make to public life and social space. For example, his discussion of sensuality, briefly discussed earlier, is a far more promising place to augment a discussion of sexual practice in contemporary society. By locating his reflections in the realm of the sensual, Niebuhr helps us to see that separation from God is not just a matter of personal choice; it is also the subtle and insidious cultural forces (often unchallenged) that bind us. Pride and self-love, both of which spring from anxiety and insecurity, together with an investment in knowledge which exceeds its natural limits, and a whole host of complex societal pressures on our increasingly diverse communities, combine to form a powerful alloy in which the cultural basis for many of our assumptions and much of our reasoning can be said to be intrinsically sinful. We, like Niebuhr himself, are blinded by the spirit of the age.

That said, Niebuhr does not see the situation as one without hope. There is always the recognition of higher possibilities, and specifically the availability of grace that not only redeems, but also calls humanity to fulfil the possibilities of life. Our situation, therefore, in Niebuhrian terms, is something like this. There is the possibility of freedom, and the fulfilment of our God-given vocations: but this requires us to submit our wills and hopes to the higher destiny that God has for us. In service, there is perfect freedom. In the midst of this, humanity has to face the limitations and corruptions of all entities in all historical realizations. History cannot succeed in fulfilling this aim of itself. History therefore points beyond itself to God, who alone can fulfil the destiny of humanity:

The mercy of God, which strangely fulfils and yet contradicts the divine judgement, points to the incompleteness of all historic good, the corruption of evil in all historic achievements and the incompleteness of every historic system of meaning without the eternal mercy which knows how to destroy evil by taking it into itself.[22]

The death that flows from sin, then, is 'swallowed up in victory' (I Cor. 15:54). Yet we live in complex times. In the midst of our late-modern societies,

---

[22] *The Nature and Destiny of Man*, ii. 212.

riddled as they are with pride, an abundance (or even excess) of knowledge, sensuality, and consumerism, it is easy to lose sight of the prescient vision that Reinhold Niebuhr points us towards: one in which society faces and names a fuller range of thoughts, conditions, and actions which are understood to grieve God. Only when this takes place can culture be truly challenged, and humanity slowly restored to the image of its maker. As Charles Taylor remarks:

There is now something higher in one's life . . . a dimension of longing and striving which one can't ignore . . . Evil is capturing this for something less than, other than God. This is a tremendously powerful temptation. It is constitutive of human life as we know it that it has felt and succumbed to this temptation. Modes of life are built around this succumbing. The untransformed is endowed with some higher, even numinous power. So the self-feeling of power becomes pride, *philotimo*; but also the wild frenzy of killing, or sex, can be endowed with the numinous . . . This is the fallen condition . . .[23]

Yet this fallen condition is not without hope. However, for the churches and societies to fall less short requires more than merely aiming higher. It means taking sin seriously; engaging constructively and humbly with the grammar and doctrine of sin, which otherwise continues to quietly shape the life, practice, and ethos of individuals, communities, and nations. Niebuhr would doubtless agree with Taylor's assertion that 'God's pedagogy' in the midst of this conundrum never ends. That pedagogy, which might do so much to reform our nature and reshape our destiny, 'turns on deepening our sense of the mysteries of sin and atonement; it never properly 'ends' at all: there is no era of satisfied graduates, who can look down condescendingly on the imperfect grasp of their less advanced predecessors'.[24] Anything less than this is falling far short.

---

[23] Charles Taylor, *A Secular Age* (Cambridge, MA: Belknap Press/Harvard University Press, 2007), 668.

[24] Ibid. 851, n. 72.

9

Distinguishing Hope from Utopian Aspiration

Revisiting Reinhold Niebuhr

Ian Markham

It is important to distinguish between hope for a different future and an unrealistic utopian aspiration. The former can be a major motivation for change, while the latter leads to disillusionment and misguided policy implementation. However, how exactly do we identify the differences between hope and utopia? To what extent has the recent past confused these two? And at a moment in history of deep economic turmoil, how best do we strive for hope and not lapse into utopian wishful thinking?

In this chapter, I shall place John Gray in conversation with Reinhold Niebuhr. In *Black Mass: Apocalyptic Religion and the Death of Utopia*, John Gray argues that Christianity provides much of the impetus for the utopian tendencies in the political discourse that dominates Britain and America. Gray believes the best example of this was the so-called 'neoconservative' confidence in liberal democracy and the attempt to use force to create a democratic Iraq.

Reinhold Niebuhr understood all too clearly the danger of a utopian propensity shaping political discourse. So having summarized the principles out of which Reinhold Niebuhr shapes his outlook, I shall identify three principles embedded in Niebuhr's thought that can both challenge all utopian aspirations and help us understand more clearly the nature of hope.

These principles are then applied to our current economic predicament. Having sketched, briefly, the reasons for our current difficulties (much of which vindicates Niebuhr's analysis), I argue that a Niebuhrian approach can help us navigate this crisis.

I

John Gray's thoughtful study of the utopian tendencies in political discourse starts with religion. In *Black Mass: Apocalyptic Religion and the Death of Utopia*, Gray begins with Christian eschatological expectations. It was Jesus who came as an apocalyptic prophet. This was the religion that saw time as taking a linear form moving slowly to a climax at an endpoint in the future.

Gray is right to emphasize that Augustine of Hippo modified this picture in a significant way. The city of God and the city of humanity intertwine in complex ways, such that we always have to live with ambiguity in the present. However, plenty of Christian groups have not accepted the Augustinian picture. And the religious impulse of utopia that can be realized on earth has given birth to many secular equivalents.

Gray's definition of a utopian project is interesting. Gray writes,

A project is utopian if there are no circumstances under which it can be realized. All the dreams of a society from which coercion and power have been for ever removed—Marxist or anarchist, liberal or technocratic—are utopian in the strong sense that they can never be achieved because they break down on the enduring contradictions of human needs. A project can also be utopian without being unrealizable under any circumstances—it is enough if it can be known to be impossible under any circumstances that can be brought about or foreseen.[1]

For Gray, a utopian project is one that cannot be realized. The definition stresses the need for practical steps to realize a project. Now there is a difficulty with this definition—mainly his failure to distinguish more clearly 'hope' from a 'utopian project'—a point I shall return to later in this chapter. However, for now, we shall use this definition and explore the details of Gray's argument.

The left, explains Gray, has an abundance of visions of the world where justice is brought about by government edict. For much of the twentieth century, it was Karl Marx who provided this vision of the world. Advocating the use of force to overturn an unjust economic structure, Marx predicted the emergence of a social order, where economic equality would prevail. Gray explains that the problem with any central planning of a nation's economy is knowledge. However, as Gray then writes,

the utopian quality of Marx's ideal does not come only from the impossible demands it makes on the knowledge of the planners. It arises even more from the clash between

[1] John Gray, *Black Mass: Apocalyptic Religion and the Death of Utopia* (London: Penguin, 2008), 28.

the ideal of harmony and the diversity of human values. Central planning involves an enormous concentration of power, without—as Lenin made clear in his 'scientific' definition of proletarian dictatorship—any institutional checks.[2]

No doubt as a result of the present global economic crisis there are plenty of neo-Marxists who are ready to revisit their *Das Kapital*. However, the utopian quality of the Soviet project has been widely recognized. The more interesting part of Gray's argument is the way in which he sees the utopian becoming part of the discourse of the mainstream (and in British and American politics—the discourse of the political right).

Gray documents the steps. When Francis Fukuyama declared that the end of communism marked the end of history, we had a utopian impulse becoming part of the mainstream political discourse. Free-market, liberal, democratic capitalism was now the best social order for society. Although Margaret Thatcher was never persuaded by the Fukuyama thesis, she did believe in the project of exporting 'democracy' around the world. Gray explains:

The neo-liberal world-view that Thatcher accepted by the end of the 1980s was a successor-ideology to Marxism. Ideological thinking tends to adopt a one-size-fits-all approach to society, and so it was at the end of the eighties, when the close of the Cold War gave neo-liberal ideas a catastrophic boost. Led by Thatcher, western governments told the countries of the former Soviet bloc that if they wanted prosperity they had to import the free market.[3]

The emergence of the neoconservative movement in the United States was an attempt to create a political approach free from any collectivist propensity. Patrick Moynihan, Norman Podhoretz, Albert Wohlstetter, and William Kristol put together the project that persuaded many of the key figures in the administration of President George W. Bush. Under the shadow of a Muslim apocalyptic, utopian movement that attacked the United States on September 11, 2001, a program emerged that saw the invasion of Iraq as a key stepping stone into creating a democratic state at the heart of the Middle East. Gray believes that this 'neocon' 'religious' vision deliberately distorted the intelligence data and embarked on a utopian project of creating an Islamic Shia democratic state.

Thus we have Gray's argument. And there is much that is right in his book. The western religious impulse that periods of great uncertainty are a prelude to the emergence of a transformed and positive age has been replayed endlessly in our political and social discourse. From Hitler's Third Reich to the Marxist communist vision, we are still under the spell of the apocalyptic

---

[2] Ibid. 73.   [3] Ibid. 117.

hope of a thousand years' reign being born through the violence and struggle of a particular time. The propensity for movements to arise that offer an alternative narrative (often identifying a conspiracy opposed to the vision), which is grounded in certain intrinsic certainties, is a real part of the dynamics in the public square. The significance of certainty within these worldviews is important. Gray explains this certainty within many utopian movements as imitating the certainties embedded in science. The attraction of creationism is that it creates the chimera of scientific certainty for a religious text. So, Gray goes on to point out:

> Yet creationism is hardly more ridiculous than Social Darwinism, dialectical materi-alism or the theory that as societies become more modern they become more free or peaceful. These secular creeds are more unreasonable than any traditional faith, if only because they make a more elaborate show of being rational.[4]

However, although there is much of value in Gray's stimulating argument, we do need to be a little more nuanced in our critique. Gray's definition of 'utopian' stresses the practical—it is a vision that is unrealizable. In an important passage, Gray attempts to disentangle utopianism from idealism. The charge of being utopian has been made against countless causes; it was utopian to believe that slavery and segregation would end; it was utopian to believe that apartheid could end; and it is utopian to believe that we can manage economic growth to avoid its damaging environmental side-effects. Now Gray concedes the question and explains:

> How do we know when a project is unrealizable? Some of the greatest human advances were once believed to be impossible. The campaign to abolish slavery that began in the early nineteenth century was opposed on the ground that slavery will always be with us. Yet it was fortunately successful. . . . Does this not show the value of the utopian imagination? I think not. To seek to end slavery was not to pursue an unrealizable goal. Many societies have lacked slavery, and to abolish the institution was only to achieve a state of affairs others have taken for granted.[5]

However, this provokes the obvious question: precisely and in what ways was the vision of a democratic Iraq unobtainable? One could respond to Gray and point out that as with slavery, totalitarian regimes are not universal—there are plenty of democratic countries. And there is nothing intrinsically impossible about a Muslim democratic nation (see Indonesia and Turkey). Furthermore, at the point of writing this essay, the surge is succeeding and

---

[4] John Gray, *Black Mass: Apocalyptic Religion and the Death of Utopia* (London: Penguin, 2008), 293.
[5] Ibid.

Iraq is on the cusp of starting a new election,[6] so perhaps it might still be obtainable.

This is the point at which we need to revisit Reinhold Niebuhr. Niebuhr, himself, flirted with such a utopian ideology (namely Marxism) as he coped with the challenges of the auto-industry in Detroit. However, Niebuhr both anticipated and saw the ways in which regimes used Marx to create societies that were ugly and unproductive. And out of this experience, Niebuhr formed a theological worldview that embraced the complexity of the real of the real world. It is to Reinhold Niebuhr that we turn next.

II

It is worth pausing and acknowledging how Reinhold Niebuhr is always worth reading. He is especially worth reading at a time when a Marxist analysis is, once again, a temptation and various countries are at war. His project is easy to misunderstand and oversimplify. So let us start by understanding the project with some care.

As Durkin has shown, Niebuhr makes considerable use of certain theological myths around which his entire ethical system is built.[7] Although Lehmann is right to emphasize the position of Christology, this is not central.[8] Although Minnema can point to Niebuhr's Gifford Lectures as clear evidence that the understanding of the human person is important, this is still not central.[9] Instead, as Tillich was the first to point out, Niebuhr's 'system' (insofar as the ever changing Niebuhr had one) is built around the four primary myths of Creation, Fall, Atonement, and Parousia. This biblical religion, as Niebuhr calls it, or these primary myths, explain the deepest human needs and wants. They provide an analysis and solution to the situation of the human creature. So Niebuhr writes,

Man does not know himself truly except as he knows himself confronted by God. Only in that confrontation does he become aware of his full stature and freedom and of the evil in him. It is for this reason that Biblical faith is of such importance for the proper understanding of man, and why it is necessary to correct the interpretations of human

---

[6] See 'This Time, Iraqis Hear and See Candidates', *New York Times*, 7 Jan. 2009, A5.

[7] Kenneth Durkin, *Reinhold Niebuhr* (Harrisburg, PA: Morehead, 1989).

[8] For Lehmann, see C. Kegley and R. Bretall (eds.), *Reinhold Niebuhr: His Religious, Social, and Political Thought* (New York: Macmillan, 1961), 251f.

[9] T. Minnema, *The Social Ethics of Reinhold Niebuhr* (Amsterdam: Kampen, 1958).

nature which underestimate his stature, depreciate his physical existence and fail to deal realistically with the evil in human nature, in terms of Biblical faith.[10]

Self-knowledge is made possible by an appropriate understanding of the significance of these myths. Put simply, the Niebuhrian method is that one should suggest policies compatible with the insights about humanity derived from biblical religion.

The ultimate ethical reference-point for Niebuhr is the law of love, supremely expressed in the Cross of Christ. It is a standard which is both in and beyond history. This must be the ultimate point of reference against which all other historical systems should be judged. This is his first criticism of Natural Law. Niebuhr believed the law of love is reduced to a sort of addendum in Natural Law theories. His second criticism is that he believed Natural Law systems are intrinsically inflexible: 'But Catholic theory assumes that the requirements of natural law are absolute and inflexible, being contained in the reason which the creature shares with God.'[11] Not only is it historically impossible that any culture and age could provide the standard by which all human nature in every age should be judged, but this sort of claim undermines the law of love. Natural Law, for Niebuhr, is virtually synonymous with legalism. And Niebuhr believes that love can provide a standard against both legalism and relativism.

The actual policy recommendations Niebuhr proceeded to make show considerable sophistication. His sensitivity to the irrational potential for evil within humanity meant that he became a clear advocate of democracy.[12] His awareness of the social power structures made him an uncompromising critic of pacifism.[13] He is misunderstood as a prophet of sin and doom; in fact Niebuhr believed that once armed with the insights of biblical religion, one would avoid illusory utopian solutions, and start to construct genuinely hopeful and realistic options.

So emerging from his Niebuhrian system is a deep commitment to hope and realism, grounded in biblical religion, which avoids a utopian tendency. This is the point at which we need to apply the Niebuhrian critique to the utopian critique set out by Gray. And there are three insights that need to be taken seriously.

---

[10] Reinhold Niebuhr, *The Nature and Destiny of Man*, i (London: Nisbet, 1941), 140f.

[11] Reinhold Niebuhr, *Faith and History* (London: Nisbet, 1949), 211.

[12] Reinhold Niebuhr, *The Children of Light and the Children of Darkness* (London: Nisbet, 1945).

[13] See Reinhold Niebuhr, *Moral Man and Immoral Society* (London: Mowbray, 1963). For an interesting discussion, see R. Harries in R. Harries (ed.), *Reinhold Niebuhr and the Issues of Our Time.* (London: Mowbray, 1986), 105.

First, we have *a sense of the limits to the political.* Reinhold Niebuhr took the Fall seriously. His anthropology recognizes a fundamental limitation. So Niebuhr explains that the human is 'a child of nature, subject to its vicissitudes, compelled by its necessities, driven by its impulses, and confined within the brevity of years which nature permits'; at the same time he is 'a transcendent spirit who stands outside of nature, life, himself, his reason, and his world'.[14]

The political realm needs to work with the human reality. Humans are limited in so many ways (necessities, impulses, and brevity of years), yet simultaneously they are not determined by those limitations. In addition, humans have destructive propensities that express themselves in a variety of different ways. And Niebuhr's picture of the individual is appropriately complicated on the social level. As Niebuhr argued in *Moral Man and Immoral Society,* organizations, especially nations, have a distinctive dynamic of their own. While the individual can have moral impulses, the social whole can end up operating in distinctively ambiguous ways.

Niebuhr's anthropology provides the best answer to 'why can't we all just get along?' By virtue of our location in creation as finite creatures with a limited temporal perspective, this was always going to be difficult. However, add to the picture the Fall, and we find we have particular human tendencies that can make cooperation difficult. Complicate the picture further by the intrinsic ambiguity of organizations, and we can see why all utopian visions are doomed to fail.

At the heart of Gray's argument is the claim that political discourse becomes utopian when it is unrealistic. Within a Niebuhrian perspective, a more accurate way of stating the problem is that political discourse becomes utopian when it fails to recognize the complex nature of the person and, especially, the ways in which humanity as a group can thwart progress. The problem in Iraq, perhaps, was less the utopian vision, but more the failure of implementation—a failure grounded in the view of humanity.

Second, we have the *imperative of humility as we construct an understanding of the present in the light of an ever-changing future.* For Niebuhr, a key expression of a religious disposition is humility. In his discussion of toleration, Niebuhr contrasts a religious attitude to religious diversity with a Catholic (where there is a quest for a return to a unitary culture) and a secular one (where religion is denied). Niebuhr has a vision of a religious disposition that retains deep commitment, while recognizing our historical contingency shapes everything (including our religious beliefs). It is a call for

---

[14] Niebuhr, *The Nature and Destiny of Man*, i. 3.

a humility grounded in the way that God has made the world. So Niebuhr writes:

Religious humility is in perfect accord with the presuppositions of a free society. Profound religion must recognize the difference between divine majesty and human creatureliness; between the unconditioned character of the divine and the conditioned character of all human enterprise. According to the Christian faith, the pride which seeks to hide the conditioned and finite character of all human endeavor is the very quintessence of sin. Religious faith ought therefore to be a constant fount of humility; for it ought to encourage men to moderate their natural pride, and to achieve some decent consciousness of the relativity of their own statement of even the most ultimate truth. It ought to teach them that their religion is most certainly true if it recognizes the element of error and sin, of finiteness and contingency, which creeps into the statement of even the sublimest truth.[15]

It is as if God does not want us to assume that we have arrived at the perfect solution to any given problem. We are made by God to be located in community—to see the world from a certain perspective. We are inevitably limited. Given this reality, we are forced always to recognize that our understanding of the world is partial. It forces on us a sense of humility, which should force us to recognize the importance of community and conversation. Community and conversation become important because our limited perspective needs the perspective of others to form an understanding of the world that is more likely to be true.

So once again Gray is right that the utopian 'neocon' project was grounded in hubris. There were voices that stressed the challenge of the post-Iraq situation; but these voices were not invited to the table. And at this point, Niebuhr's analysis accords exactly with Gray. Any program needs to be shaped by a range of voices so the complexity of the world is reflected in the conversation. What Gray identifies as a key feature of a 'utopian' project, Niebuhr would frame as the lack of humility.

Third, we have *the paradox of hope*. One of the most interesting Niebuhrian themes emerges around his discussion of the Sermon the Mount. For Niebuhr, the love command, for example, is an impossible possibility. It is deliberately paradoxical. The implication of the paradox is this. We should recognize in the Sermon on the Mount a hope—a hope of a world that is different. We should invite that hope to serve as a constant pressure on the present. The United States should not rest content with large numbers lacking health insurance, a growing prison population, and a public school system in the urban centers that is failing the young. However, we should simultaneously

---

[15] Niebuhr, *The Children of Light and the Children of Darkness*, 94.

recognize that challenges, problems, and difficulties are an inevitable part of our social life. This does not mean that we resign ourselves to fatalism, but rather strive to realize the hope, while recognizing that it is always, ultimately, unobtainable.

This is where Niebuhr has the advantage over Gray. Gray is unconvincing in his distinction between 'idealism' and 'utopian'. Niebuhr has a clearer sense of the challenge. For Niebuhr, we are constantly invited to put into conversation our vision of the world differently ordered (rightly ordered) with the realities of persons and organizations. Hope is the commitment to a different world; the realism means that we know that the political is always imperfect. We strive constantly for transformation, but know it will at best be incremental movement.

For Gray, the utopian propensity was seen in American and British foreign policy, especially around Iraq. However, as we have placed Gray in conversation with Niebuhr, we have seen that Niebuhr works with all of Gray's concerns, but does so in a way that is more illuminating. Indeed the principles around this theme which have been derived from Niebuhr's writing can be applied to issues beyond the war in Iraq. As we shall now see.

III

Taking these three insights—the limits of the political, the importance of humility, and the paradox of hope—into the final section of this essay, we can now reflect on the implications for our current crisis and moment in history.

It is puzzling how we got here. On the economic front, the Clinton–Blair years seem to have found the solution to the 'boom and bust' years. From the perspective of the early 1990s, as we looked into the future, an expectation emerged of steady economic growth and low inflation. We are still not entirely sure why this unraveled; in particular, it is deeply unclear why it suddenly unraveled with such a calamitous impact on the banking system in October 2008. Insofar as a narrative is emerging, it includes the following features, which, interestingly, seem to vindicate a Niebuhrian analysis.[16]

The key feature is the housing market in the United States. The legitimate goal of encouraging home ownership, coupled with low interest rates (due to the lack of inflationary pressures in the economy), led to a range of mortgage

---

[16] What follows is heavily dependent on a presentation made by economists and housing specialists at the Trinity Roundtable, organized by the Center for the Study of the Presidency in Washington, DC, November 2008.

products. In itself this should have been manageable. However, some of these mortgage products were problematic: the 'low-start' interest rates (say three years at a significantly reduced rate) were very attractive to a number of low-income households. However, the expected rate after the initial three years was then much higher than the household could afford.

For those selling these mortgages, the fateful assumption was that housing values, which had risen dramatically during the 1980s and 1990s, would continue to rise indefinitely. The presumption was that as the higher rate took effect the mortgage holder would be able to refinance and move to a new mortgage product (with the added benefit of fees being collected by the mortgage broker).

Looking back, one can see that this assumption was very misguided. For decades, the housing market of the United States has tended to increase only with the inflation rate of the country. The 1980s and 1990s were atypical and probably fed by the stimulation of the market with these new innovative mortgage products.

The sheer quantity of these distinctive mortgage products was staggering. And as they were bundled and resold around the world countless financial institutions were affected. As inflationary pressures grew in the economy, the interest rates increased. And the option of refinancing these 'low start' mortgages was not available. Suddenly, the whole edifice started to unravel very quickly. It started with families losing their homes. Unable to pay the increased interest rates, the financial institutions moved in to repossess the property. With the increased supply of properties, the value of the housing market started to fall quickly. Financial institutions found themselves holding worthless mortgages.

So the financial institutions were suddenly vulnerable in ways that hitherto were unknown. However, the falling value of housing was having a further impact. Countless consumers had used the equity in their home to finance the consumer-led boom. As this disappeared, so did the consumption. As the consumption disappeared, a recession loomed. Products and services were no longer required. Companies started to cut back, employees were asked to leave, and demand in the economy for goods and services started to fall further.

This in summary is the widely accepted narrative. And it is classically Niebuhrian. We have a legitimate aspiration—a person owning his or her own home is a good end. We have human 'greed' as financial institutions create products and persuade those least able to appreciate the risks to buy these 'low start' mortgages. (One tragic dimension to all this was the sheer number of people who converted a perfectly good thirty-year fixed-income mortgage into one of these low-start products.) So we have a good aspiration that goes wrong, coupled with human fallibility—two classic Niebuhrian themes.

The way forward is perhaps the hardest aspect. This is an entirely new situation for economists. The conventional wisdom is that we need to work at the most fundamental level of all. It is often pointed out that capitalism is an act of faith. It depends on consumer confidence, especially in the financial institutions. Given the lack of consumer confidence in the banks, governments are now frantically seeking to underwrite and reignite confidence in the financial institutions. Given the lack of demand in the economy, governments are now frantically seeking to provide the demand to create the economic growth necessary for employment and wealth.

So having noted the ways in which a Niebuhrian analysis helps us understand what has happened, can a Niebuhrian perspective (especially in the two ways identified above) help us find the way forward? I want to suggest that perhaps it can. And perhaps the most important way is to manage 'utopian' expectations. With Barack Obama, the utopian temptation is not in the realm of foreign policy but domestically. This time, it will be government programs that make a difference. From a Niebuhrian perspective, the need is for an approach to the public square that takes a Christian anthropology seriously (thereby working within the limits of the political) and is characterized by some humility, yet continues to recognize the importance of hope.

Such an approach to the public square would involve the following: First, there is the careful management of expectations, with a clear recognition that ambiguous unforeseen consequences are inevitable. It is important that we avoid talk that implies 'we have arrived'. So talk of the 'end of history' or the 'end of boom and bust' is an act of hubris. We need to recognize the reality built into creation. We are small finite, located creatures. Our knowledge of the world is also partial and partly reflects the limited perspective that we have been given. The world is complicated. Good actions have unforeseeable expectations. Humans find ingenious ways of misbehaving that can have calamitous consequences. All this means that we act with limited knowledge making decisions that progress issues incrementally and always have a downside in the long run. We might wish that God had made the creation differently: so we are not so located and partial and that the bigger picture (the God's-eye perspective) might be easier to see. But this is not how the world is. And to imagine that we are not so constrained is the fundamental sin of hubris—indeed the sin of Lucifer.

Expectations need to be managed so that we all appreciate that the challenge of living is a constant participation in challenge, struggle, and hope. Any program that delivers constructive change will generate new difficulties. Our political discourse needs to recognize this reality. Most decisions are 60:40;

they are not 80:20. We weigh options—many of which are difficult and all with foreseeable problems—and seek to manage the outcome.

Second, hope is an ever-present pressure on the moment. Perhaps even now a better ordered society, with a democratic impulse, can emerge in Iraq. It must not be utopian—it will not be a heaven on earth. But it can and should be so ordered so that minorities are protected. This is hope. We should certainly trust that the Palestinians and Israel reach an understanding that is a distinct improvement on the present. From a Niebuhrian point of view, we are constantly invited to be dissatisfied with the present, yet not allowing ourselves to expect a complete solution that will eliminate every conceivable difficulty.

Third, all government programs recognize the dangers of abuse, inefficiency, and becoming an end in themselves. The conventional wisdom is probably correct. Government action is the only way to create confidence in our financial institutions; and government action is the only way to generate significant demand in the economy. And after all, there is plenty that needs to be done—infrastructure needs to repaired and enhanced. However, in the same way that the 'free market' in mortgages led to abuse, so one can expect that these government programs will be abused. As an initiative is passed in the Congress, there will be countless actions and decisions at the level of the states and government agencies, which will exploit the initiative. Once we recognize the reality of a Christian anthropology, so we should expect and aspire to manage (i.e. regulate) the inevitable risk of abuse.

Fourth, our political discourse needs to be characterized by humility. The only way humanity can progress in this world is to work together. At the level of information, we need the perspectives of others to help us understand the complexity of this world. At the level of initiative, we need others to help regulate potential abuse and correct it as the unforeseeable happens. A primary biblical theme is the centrality of community—first the nation and then the church. The illusion of the individual making all the decisions without reference to others is constantly challenged by our Scriptures, which call us to recognize our mutual interdependence.

Traditionally, Christians believe that it will take a divine action to bring about a utopian society. Therefore, it is important that we surrender utopian talk that implies that human agency can bring about a complete solution to this or that difficulty. Instead, as we take Reinhold Niebuhr's analysis seriously, we should move to a different vision of the present. It is incremental; it takes seriously the law of unforeseen difficulties emerging from a good initiative; and it encourages a culture of discourse where are different perspectives are held with humility.

10

Reinhold Niebuhr and the Political Possibility of Forgiveness

Nigel Biggar

The question of how the ethic of Jesus can find political expression is one that has long perplexed the Christian Church. At one end of the spectrum of responses lie Christian pacifists, who hold that Jesus means 'non-violence' and that either Christians must eschew government or government must (somehow) eschew violence. Here the influence of Jesus upon political life is considered to be ideally complete. (Whether or not government, and therefore political life, could actually survive such influence is, of course, a moot point.)

Close to the opposite end of the spectrum sits Martin Luther. Instructed by the Peasants' War in the horrors of anarchy, Luther was deeply convinced of the necessity of government and of its use of the temporal 'sword' to maintain order in the face of the fact that in this world 'the wicked always outnumber the good'.[1] He did not think this affirmation of governmental coercion to be unchristian, however, since it is entailed by love for the neighbour.[2] Further, he implied that Christian belief and faith can and should qualify the manner in which force is used. Minimally, the conviction that the public use of force is divinely authorized to serve the good of others fills 'a man's heart with courage and boldness' and so makes 'the fist more powerful'.[3] If this is not quite how Christian love is usually expected to inform the use of force, nor is it the sum of

---

I wish to acknowledge, with gratitude, the support of the McDonald Agape Foundation in the preparation of this essay.

[1] Martin Luther, 'Temporal Authority: To What Extent it Should be Obeyed' (1523), in *Luther's Works*, American edition, vol. 45, 'Christian in Society, II', ed. Walther I. Brandt (Philadelphia: Fortress Press, 1962), 91. To say that Luther was convinced of the need for government to curb wickedness is not to say that he considered this to be its only function. According to Bernd Wannenwetsch, Luther held that government is also necessary for human flourishing, not just by ensuring the good of security, but also by ordering social life harmoniously ('Luther's Moral Theology', in Donald K. McKim (ed.), *The Cambridge Companion to Martin Luther* (Cambridge: Cambridge University Press, 2003), 130).

[2] Ibid. 97–8.   [3] Ibid. 93.

Luther's views of the matter. He also suggested that a Christian prince will not use force to domineer or to pursue selfish ends;[4] and that he will go beyond the duty to punish rebels and offer them an opportunity to come to terms.[5]

Luther did not, therefore, consider the spiritual 'realm', in which the individual is addressed and shaped by the Gospel, to be absolutely separate from the temporal 'realm', in which public officers must use coercion to enforce law.[6] As he saw it, Christian love can and should shape the necessary public use of force. Nevertheless, that love has more and less distinctive forms; and Luther did not envisage the public expression of Christian love in its most distinctive form as patient forbearance in the face of injury. As he saw it, this has room to operate only in cases where Christians do not carry official responsibility for maintaining public order, and where their forbearance does not diminish it—for example, when they themselves are being oppressed by a tyrannical government.[7] In Luther's eyes, then, the scope for an evangelical qualification of political life is quite restricted.

Since Reinhold Niebuhr was brought up in circles that were partly Lutheran,[8] one might expect his social ethic to bear Luther's impression. It need not, of course, for not everyone chooses to maintain original ties. Niebuhr, however, does; although what he maintains, he also changes. The very title of what is arguably his most famous book, *Moral Man and Immoral Society* (1932), echoes Luther's realistic distinction between the 'realm' of the Gospel and the 'realm' of political life. Niebuhr's distinction, however, elaborates and qualifies Luther's. According to the latter, what limits the political operation of evangelical love is the need for public authorities to use (maybe lethal) force to maintain law, order, and peace, and the need for that force to be applied resolutely (with a powerful 'fist'). Niebuhr's distinction, however, is drawn somewhat differently.

---

[4] Luther, 'Temporal Authority', 118.

[5] Martin Luther, 'Against the Robbing and Murdering Hordes of Peasants' (1525), in *Luther's Works*, American edition, vol. 46, 'Christian in Society, III', ed. Robert C. Schultz (Philadelphia: Fortress Press, 1967), 52. The implication here that Christian government will be qualified by the exercise of a certain mercy, does not square with the statement in 'An Open Letter on the Harsh Book against the Peasants' (1525) that Scriptural passages that speak of mercy apply only to the kingdom of God and to Christians, and not to the kingdom of the world, which is the realm of strict duty (*Luther's Works*, American edition, vol. 46, 'Christian in Society, III', ed. Robert C. Schultz (Philadelphia: Fortress Press, 1967), 70).

[6] Thus Wannenwetsch, 'Luther's Moral Theology', 123, 127, 132.

[7] Martin Luther, 'Whether Soldiers, Too, Can be Saved' (1526), in *Luther's Works*, American edition, vol. 46, 'Christian in Society, III', ed. Robert C. Schultz (Philadelphia: Fortress Press, 1967), 108.

[8] Niebuhr was raised in the Evangelical Synod, an American version of the Prussian Union Church, which combined both Lutheran and Reformed theologies and liturgies (Richard Fox, *Reinhold Niebuhr: A Biography* (New York: Pantheon, 1985), 4–5). I have Robin Lovin to thank for drawing my attention to this.

He understands Christian love[9] in typically Lutheran terms as entirely unselfish and disinterested,[10] rising in 'sublime naivete'[11] above the mean calculations of prudence[12] and in 'sublime madness' above immediate enmities.[13] What constrains its operation is not primarily sin and the need to curb it, however, but rather the creaturely fact that 'moral attitudes always develop most sensitively in person-to-person relationships',[14] and the creaturely limitation of human imagination,[15] which together hinder the outward expansion of sympathy. Altruistic impulses[16] can transcend egoistic ones more effectively in relation to near neighbours than to distant ones,[17] since it is easier for human creatures to develop sympathy for those with whom they can more readily identify. Consequently, love has greater scope in interpersonal relations than in social ones, and in social relations between proximate groups than in those between remote ones.[18] A further consequence is that social relations are ordered less by love than by justice.[19] And more often than not such justice will be more formal than real, comprising an expedient balance of competing interests that rests on a measure of unjust coercion by the dominant group: 'Politics will, to the end of history, be an area where conscience and power meet, where the ethical and coercive factors of human life will interpenetrate and work out their tentative and uneasy compromises'.[20]

However, '[a]ny justice which is only justice soon degenerates into something less than justice. It must be saved by something which is more than justice.'[21] Accordingly, Niebuhr does allow that (the Christian) religion's ideal of love can leaven social justice to a limited extent, preventing it from being 'purely political'[22] and restraining even the use of violence. This it does partly through the loving appreciation of the transcendent worth of all life[23] and partly through the spiritual disciplining of resentment.[24] This latter is achieved by placing the moral agent 'under the scrutiny of [God's] omniscient

---

[9] Throughout *Moral Man and Immoral Society* Niebuhr talks about 'religious love' when he means primarily Christian love.

[10] Reinhold Niebuhr, *Moral Man and Immoral Society* (New York: Scribner's, 1960), 263, 265–6.

[11] Ibid. 53.

[12] Ibid. 57, 257, 263, 265–6.

[13] Ibid. 255.

[14] Ibid. 53.

[15] Ibid. 6, 72–3.

[16] Niebuhr affirms that human beings 'are endowed by nature with both selfish *and unselfish* impulses' (ibid. 25). The italics are mine.

[17] Ibid. 28, 53–4. For Niebuhr, social justice invariably comprises both political and ethical elements—both the expedient balancing of interests and (Kantian) rational consistency or fairness (ibid. 29).

[18] Ibid., pp. xi–xii.   [19] Ibid. 257.   [20] Ibid. 4, 6, 16, 20.

[21] Ibid. 258.   [22] Ibid. 80.   [23] Ibid. 255.   [24] Ibid. 248.

eye',[25] which issues in his contrite acknowledgement that the enemy's moral frailty is also his own.[26]

Three years later, in *An Interpretation of Christian Ethics* (1935), Niebuhr basically confirmed this view of love's role in political life, albeit with a positive shift in the weight of emphasis from its limitations to its possibilities. The Kingdom of God's moral ideal of love and vicarious suffering is, he tells us, 'really possible, and lead[s] to new actualities in given moments in history'.[27] It is 'involved in every moral aspiration and achievement'[28]—specifically in all approximations of justice.[29] Indeed, there is 'a dynamic relationship' between love and justice,[30] the latter needing refinement by the former, which is the fruit of moral and spiritual disciplines.[31] The regulative principle of justice—equality—echoes the law of neighbour-love;[32] and 'imaginative justice' goes beyond equality to a consideration of the special needs of the life of the other.[33] In the specific case of corrective justice, love reduces the element of vengeance and increases that of reform.[34]

Nevertheless, love cannot be realized in history in its pure form, but only approximately:

[Jesus'] Kingdom of God is always a possibility in history, because its heights of pure love are organically related to the experience of love in all human life, but it is also an impossibility in history and always beyond historical achievement. Men living in nature and in the body will never be capable of the sublimation of egoism and the attainment of sacrificial passion, the complete disinterestedness which the ethic of Jesus demands.[35]

Forgiveness—'the demand that the evil in the other shall be borne without vindictiveness because the evil in the self is known'—is the crown of the ideal of love.[36] However, genuine forgiveness of enemies requires the contrite recognition of one's own sinfulness and the acceptance of mutual responsibility for the sin of the accused, and this is the achievement only of rare individuals and is beyond the capacities of collective man.[37] Further, forgiveness of the enemy should not be made to take the place of action for justice, including punishment.[38] So, while forgiveness can qualify punishment, 'in the absolute sense' it is impossible.[39]

It is true that these accounts of the political expression of Christian love belong to the middle of Niebuhr's career: *Moral Man and Immoral Society* and *An Interpretation of Christian Ethics* were published when he was forty and

[25] Niebuhr, *Moral Man and Immoral Society*, 51, 60.
[26] Ibid. 254–5.
[27] Reinhold Niebuhr, *An Interpretation of Christian Ethics* (New York: Seabury Press, 1979), 36.
[28] Ibid. 63.   [29] Ibid. 85.   [30] Ibid. 87.   [31] Ibid. 123, 132.
[32] Ibid. 65, 90.   [33] Ibid. 66.   [34] Ibid. 67.   [35] Ibid. 19.
[36] Ibid. 137.   [37] Ibid. 67.   [38] Ibid. 140–1.   [39] Ibid. 141.

forty-three years old, respectively. Nevertheless, they remain the most systematic presentations of his view of this matter that he made, and subsequent writings in the 1940s and 1950s echo them.[40] Take, for one example, his 1950 article, 'Justice and Love', where he tells us—*pace* 'moralistic Christianity'— that consistent selflessness is not possible,[41] that justice requires discriminate judgements between claims of the self and claims of the other,[42] and that '[i]nsofar as justice admits the claims of the self, it is something less than love',[43] but that, nevertheless, 'it cannot exist without love and remain justice. For without the "grace" of love, justice always degenerates into something less than justice.'[44]

Like Luther, Reinhold Niebuhr recognized that historical political life is bound to involve coercion, because peace and justice require it; and that the scope for Christian love to find political expression is quite limited. Niebuhr's Lutheranism, however, was informed by Marxism; so, unlike Luther, he was aware that what passes for 'peace' and 'justice' invariably involves a balancing of nakedly political interests, in which dominant power unjustly calls the shots. Moreover, while unswerving in his conviction that love is an ideal that is a political 'impossibility', he had a more elaborate—and a more positive— appreciation of the ways in which this impossibility can yet become (approximately) possible. The ideal of love presupposes a certain equality among human creatures that inspires justice; it moves justice to go beyond equal treatment to attend to the special needs of particular neighbours; and, combined with contrition, it disciplines resentment, curbs vengeance, restrains violence, and orders punishment in the direction of the reformation of the enemy. Nevertheless, Niebuhr remained convinced that forgiveness, which is 'the crown of the ideal of love', remains beyond the reach of political expression, since social injustice merits opposition and perhaps punishment:

The victim of injustice cannot cease from contending against his oppressors, even if he has a religious sense of the relativity of all social positions and a contrite recognition of the sin in his own heart. Only a religion full of romantic illusions could seek to

---

[40] For example, according to 'Love your Enemies' (1942) and 'The Bombing of Germany' (1943), love and the use of violent force are compatible (*Love and Justice: Selections from the Shorter Writings of Reinhold Niebuhr*, ed. D. B. Robertson (Cleveland and New York: Meridian, 1967), 218–19, 221, 222–3); according to 'Is There another Way?' (1955), justice is the servant of love and yet it involves 'an equilibrium of power' (ibid. 300); according to 'Proposal to Billy Graham' (1956), 'the calculations of justice' are foreign to Christian ethics (ibid. 157); according to 'What Resources can the Christian Church Offer to Meet the Crisis in Race Relations?' (1956), 'There seems to be nothing in the Christian ethics about prudence, and prudence is what is demanded in such critical situations as this one' (ibid. 154).

[41] Reinhold Niebuhr, 'Love and Justice', in *Love and Justice*, 27.

[42] Ibid. 28.   [43] Ibid.   [44] Ibid.

persuade the Negro to gain justice from the white man merely by forgiving him. As long as men are involved in the conflicts of nature and sin they must seek according to best available moral insights to contend for what they believe to be right. And that will mean that they will contend against other men. Short of the transmutation of the world into the Kingdom of God, men will always confront enemies . . .[45]

It is my view that this underestimates the possibility of the political manifestation of forgiveness. If Niebuhr granted love greater political expression than Luther, then I would grant it even further expression than Niebuhr. I do not think that forgiveness is incompatible with active opposition to injustice, with enmity toward oppressors, or even with punishment of them. That is to say, forgiveness, if properly understood, does not deal with conflict—and the injustice that inspires it—simply by pretending that they are of no importance and passing them over. Rather, it takes the persistent reality of conflict seriously, and yet qualifies it in ways that mitigate it and that might eventually overcome it. It can be both realistic and Christian. Let me explain.[46]

Talk about forgiveness is often confused by a tendency to conflate two moments that ought to be distinguished. This leads many Christians to hold on biblical and theological grounds that victims are bound to forgive their oppressors unilaterally and unconditionally, without waiting for any sign of repentance.[47] This is, I think, not only psychologically unrealistic but also morally dubious. That is why others hold on philosophical and psychological grounds that the victim's forgiveness must be conditional upon the perpetrator's repentance, if it is to be morally responsible.[48] And yet that raises (at

[45] Niebuhr, *An Interpretation of Christian Ethics*, 140–1.

[46] The analysis of forgiveness that follows here comprises a modified version of the first section of my article 'Forgiving Enemies in Ireland', *Journal of Religious Ethics*, 36/4 (Dec. 2008), 560–4.

[47] See, for example, Paul Fiddes, *Past Event and Present Salvation: The Christian idea of Atonement* (London: Darton, Longman, and Todd, 1989), 176–7; and L. Gregory Jones, *Embodying Forgiveness: A Theological Analysis* (Grand Rapids, MI: Eerdman, 1995), 21, 102, 121, 144, 146, 160–1. Fiddes appeals to the cases of Zacchaeus (Luke 19:1–10) and the prostitute who anointed Jesus' feet with ointment (Luke 7:36–50) in support of his view that, according to a Christian understanding, forgiveness should precede repentance: 'When Jesus asks for hospitality from Zacchaeus, the notorious tax collector of the Jericho area, he does not first require him to return what he has gained through fraud and extortion, though this is the happy outcome. He accepts from a prostitute the intimate act of her anointing his feet and wiping them with her hair, without first establishing whether she has given up her trade, and pronounces the forgiveness of God without further enquiry' (*Past Event and Present Salvation*, 177). Alternatively, one might say that Jesus' asking for hospitality amounted to an act of compassionate forbearance rather than one of absolving forgiveness; and that he did not need to ask first whether the prostitute had repented, since her tears made it implicitly clear that she had.

[48] Richard Swinburne, *Responsibility and Atonement* (Oxford: Clarendon Press, 1989), 81–6, 148–9.

least for Christians) the question, 'What about the initiating grace and creative generosity so characteristic of Jesus' forgiveness?'

It seems to me that both sides are half-correct, for each champions a different moment of forgiveness, one of them unilateral and initial and the other conditional and final. I call these, respectively, 'compassion' and 'absolution'. Yet both sides are also half-wrong, since each champions one moment to the exclusion of the other; whereas in fact a Christian process of reconciliation should incorporate them both.

The first moment of forgiveness, 'compassion', is where the victim allows her feelings of resentment to be moderated by a measure of sympathy for the perpetrator. Whence the sympathy? In part it arises from the acknowledgement of the authority of certain truths: the truth that the victim herself is no stranger to the psychic powers that drive human beings to abuse each other; the truth that some individuals, for reasons that remain hidden in the mysterious interpenetration of history and the human will, are less well equipped than others to resist common pressures; the truth that some are fated to find themselves trapped in situations where only an extraordinary moral heroism could save them from doing terrible evil. Even victims have responsibilities; and one of them is to acknowledge truths like these even in the midst of the maelstrom of pain and resentment.

Openness to the truth, however, is not the only matrix of sympathy and the only force for moderation. There is also the commitment to rebuild rather than destroy—to reconciliation rather than vengeance. Now, reconciliation should mean different things according to the nature of the relationship between victim and perpetrator. In the paradigmatic case of interpersonal relationships between family members or friends it will mean the restoration of intimacy, signaled typically by the act of embrace. In the case of political relationships between political dissidents and their informers or of *génocidaires* and surviving victims, however, it will usually mean something analogous and weaker—say a readiness to coexist in the same city or neighbourhood or street.[49] But whatever kind of reconciliation is appropriate, victims should prefer it to the sheer wreaking of 'vengeance'—that is to say, action whose overriding intention is to inflict harm and which takes no care to moderate the harm inflicted.

Why should victims prefer reconciliation? At least, because of a proper care for their own souls—or, if you like, for the shaping of their moral and

---

[49] For further discussion of the relationship between political 'reconciliation' and its interpersonal paradigm, see Nigel Biggar, 'Conclusion', in Biggar (ed.), *Burying the Past: Making Peace and Doing Justice after Civil Conflict* (Washington, DC: Georgetown University Press, 2003), 314–17.

spiritual characters; since to devote oneself to vengeance is to drink a poison that embitters and tyrannizes. The point is arrestingly made in Peter Shaffer's play, *The Gift of the Gorgon.* Here, Edward Damson, hot-blooded playwright of Slavo-Celtic parents, champions the cleansing, cathartic virtue of the passion for revenge. Liberal forbearance and tolerance, in his eyes, is 'just giving up with a shrug—as if you never really cared about the wrong in the first place... *Avoidance*, that's all it is!'.[50] But to this Helen, his wife and cool English daughter of a classics don, retorts:

> You go on about passion, Edward. But have you never realised that there are many, many kinds—including a passion to kill our own passion when it's wrong?... The truest, hardest most adult passion is not just stamping and geeing ourselves up. It's refusing to be led by rage when we most want to be... No other being in the universe can change itself by conscious will: it is *our privilege alone.* To take out inch by inch this spear in our sides that goads us on and on to bloodshed—and still make sure it doesn't take our guts with it.[51]

At the very end of the play Helen wins the argument by showing that it is forgiveness, not revenge, that requires the greater strength and realizes humanity. But there is one cliff-hanging moment when, enraged by a macabre trick that Edward has played on her, Helen sways on the brink of plunging into vengeance. What pulls her back are the bald words of her stepson, Philip: 'The truth is', he says, 'you must forgive him or die'.[52] That is to say, she must forgive or forever be enslaved by bitterness.

Another, real-life expression of this prudential wisdom comes from the lips of the daughter of one of three women taken from the Spanish village of Poyales del Hoyo on the night of 29 December 1936 and murdered by Falangists at the roadside. Interviewed sixty-six years later, she said: 'This thing has stayed in my mind all my life. I have never forgotten. I am reliving it now, as we stand here. All the killers were from the village... I can pardon, but I cannot forget. We have to pardon them or it makes us just like them.'[53]

Vengeance does grave moral and spiritual damage to the one who wreaks it. That is one good reason why victims should steer clear of it. Another is that vengeance is—by common definition—excessive.[54] It does not strive to

---

[50] Peter Shaffer, *The Gift of the Gorgon* (London: Viking, 1993), 16.

[51] Ibid. 60–1.

[52] Ibid. 92.

[53] Giles Tremlett, *Ghosts of Spain: Travels through a Country's Hidden Past* (London: Faber and Faber, 2006), 13–14.

[54] I am aware that some argue for the moral rehabilitation of vengeance as an appropriate response to grave and malicious injury (e.g., Willa Boesak, *God's Wrathful Children: Political Oppression and Christian Ethics* (Grand Rapids, MI: Eerdmans, 1995); Willa Boesak, 'Truth, Justice, and Reconciliation', in H. Russel Botman and Robin M. Petersen (eds.), *To Remember and*

proportion its retribution to the wrong done. Its driving ambition is to make the wrongdoer—together with his family or his village or his race or his country—*suffer*. As a consequence, vengeance has the effect of multiplying injustice, as wrongdoers are made to suffer more than they deserve and suffering is inflicted on innocents who do not deserve it at all.

Whatever the way in which it moderates resentment—whether through the confession of human solidarity in sin-as-moral-weakness or through the commitment to reconciliation—forgiveness-as-compassion is unilateral and unconditional. It does not need the green light of the perpetrator's repentance in order to proceed. It is entirely the responsibility of the victim to acknowledge the truths of solidarity-in-sin and to commit herself to reconciliation rather than revenge.

However, compassion is just the first moment of forgiveness. The second is 'absolution'. This is the moment when, paradigmatically, the victim addresses the perpetrator and says, 'I forgive you. The trust that was broken is now restored. Our future will no longer be haunted by our past.' Forgiveness-as-absolution should not be granted unilaterally and unconditionally. To proffer trust to someone who has shown himself to be untrustworthy and who is unrepentant about it is, at very least, foolish. But it is also careless of the wrongdoer, for it robs him of the salutary stimulus to reflect, learn, and grow, which the punitive withholding of trust constitutes. Even worse, it degrades him by implying that what he does is of no consequence.[55] Out of respect and care for the wrongdoer, then, forgiveness-as-absolution should wait for signs of his genuine repentance—all the while looking upon him with the eyes of forgiveness-as-compassion.

It might be thought odd, even inappropriate, to use the word 'forgiveness' to refer to compassion. Why not speak simply of an initial moment of compassion, and reserve 'forgiveness' for the concluding moment of absolution? The reason is that we *do* not so reserve it. It is not uncommon to hear victims say that they have 'forgiven' their oppressors, when what is meant is not at all that they have been reconciled with them, but rather that, in spite of the absence of any apology or reparation, they have nevertheless managed to

---

to Heal: Theological and Psychological Reflections on Truth and Reconciliation (Cape Town: Hutman and Rousseau, 1996); and Martha Minow, *Between Vengeance and Forgiveness: Facing History after Genocide and Mass Violence* (Boston: Beacon, 1998), 9–24). One may, of course, choose to use the word 'vengeance' to refer to proportionate retribution. My own sense, however, is that in common English usage 'vengeance' tends to connote something excessive and out of control; and that therefore to talk of 'vengeance' when one means something moderated and proportionate is to risk at least confusion and perhaps even serious misunderstanding.

[55] My thinking here follows Richard Swinburne (e.g., *Responsibility and Atonement*, 81–6, 148–9), except that what he takes to be the whole of forgiveness, I take to be just the second moment.

tame or transcend their anger toward them. It means that the victims' lives are no longer possessed by rage and hatred. This does not quite amount to the growth of compassion, although it is a major step in that direction. The main point, however, is that the victims' taming of anger and growth of compassion are both entirely subjective processes, which proceed independently of what the perpetrators do or do not do and which do not change the objective relationship between them. To refer to such processes as 'forgiveness' is appropriate, partly because it describes what actually happens and partly because it is good that it does so. Were it otherwise, the deliverance of victims from all-consuming rage would have to wait upon the perpetrators to repent; and in some cases, that would condemn them to vengeful obsession forever.

One major advantage of analyzing forgiveness into the two components of compassion and absolution is that it avoids presenting it as a rival to justice. According to this conception, the process of reconciliation contains not only initial compassion and final absolution, but between them also the contradiction of injustice by the expression of proportionate resentment and the meting out of proportionate punishment. Forgiveness-as-compassion qualifies but does not replace resentment; and it qualifies but need not replace punishment.[56] It makes them both media of communication intended to persuade the wrongdoer of the wrong he has done, to elicit his repentance, and so to enable forgiveness-as-absolution and consequent reconciliation. By ordering resentment and punishment toward reconciliation, it saves them from vengeance.

In sum, the ideal process of reconciliation—as I see it—consists of the following sequence of moments:

1. Victim: forgiveness-as-compassion (1): unilateral, unconditional, and redemptive;
2. Victim: condemnatory expression of resentment via communicative punishment (whose simplest form is withdrawal and estrangement), which is disciplined by and proportioned to reconciliation;
3. Wrongdoer: repentance;
4. Victim: forgiveness-as-absolution (2): conditional, and ushers in . . .
5. Mutual reconciliation.

---

[56] Insofar as the resentment of injustice finds any external expression—say, in the victim's mistrustful attitude and behaviour toward his wrongdoer—it is itself a kind of informal punishment. Forgiveness-as-compassion should not replace the punitive expression of proportionate resentment. However, insofar as the expression of this resentment succeeds in communicating to the wrongdoer that he has done wrong, and elicits from him sufficient apology and reparation as to restore trust, further, formal punishment is rendered unnecessary.

This integration of forgiveness with the hostile expression of resentment and meting out of punishment confers a further advantage; for it enables us to discern how forgiveness could find fitting political expression in circumstances where simple absolution would be breathtakingly naive and inappropriate—that is, in circumstances of deep enmity born of atrocious injustice from which there has been no repentance. And insofar as forgiveness is a defining feature of a Christian ethic of response to wrongdoing, this conception spares such an ethic from having to choose between relevance and plausibility.

For example, I take it for granted that, in response to the attacks of September 11, 2001, it would not have been heroic but ludicrous for the US government to have addressed al-Qaeda and said, 'We forgive you. We will not let what you have done sour our regard for you. We will continue to treat you as friends.' If such were the sum of forgiveness, then it could have no plausible place in America's reaction. If, however, forgiveness can take the form of compassion as well as absolution, then it could have two plausible roles. First, it could order the use of force toward the end of peace, and discipline it away from sheer vindictiveness. And second, it could move the US government to entertain the possibility that, though al-Qaeda's ill-disciplined resentment has festered out of all proportion, not all of its roots are simply malevolent and irrational, and that in the rank growth of its malice and falsehood there lie genuine grievances that deserve sympathetic attention. Thus conceived, forgiveness could have plausible political purchase.

Take another example. The setting is Northern Ireland, ten years after the signing of the Good Friday (or Belfast) Agreement, which marked the beginning of the end of the thirty years of political violence known as 'the Troubles'. During those years republican paramilitaries, most of them members of the (Provisional) Irish Republican Army (IRA)[57] were responsible for 55.7 per cent of the 3,268 political killings (as against the security forces' 10.7 percent), and for 24.7 percent of the killing of Catholics (as against the security forces' 20.5 per cent).[58] Irish republicans who were members of the IRA have now been elected as representatives of Sinn Féin to the province's legislative assembly, and some of them are ministers of government. On 4 December 2008 the BBC broadcast a current affairs panel discussion from Newry, Northern Ireland, in which the Sinn Féin Minister for Regional Development,

[57] Strictly speaking, it was the *Provisional* Irish Republican Army (PIRA) that carried out a campaign of violence during the Troubles. However, since they are widely referred to as the 'IRA', that is how I shall refer to them here.
[58] See Marie Smyth, 'Putting the Past in its Place', in Biggar (ed.), *Burying the Past*, 137–8, tables 7.3 and 7.4.

Conor Murphy, likened the British Army in Iraq and Afghanistan to the IRA and made some disparaging remarks about the police.[59] Murphy had been convicted in 1982 of membership of the IRA and for possessing explosives; and in 2005 he had publicly refused to express regret at the IRA's bombing of the Conservative Party's 1984 conference in Brighton, in which one MP, one regional party office-holder, and three wives were killed. In reaction to the television programme I received an email from a serious and thoughtful Christian, who had served in the Royal Ulster Constabulary for eleven years in the midst of the Troubles. Here follows an excerpt:

> Just last week here [in Northern Ireland] the BBC reported the conviction of a man in connection with a brutal double murder that took place a few years ago close to where I live. The victims were hacked and stabbed to death. The journalist was unable to report the court proceedings . . . much too horrible for the public to hear. Many of my former colleagues could report visiting the scenes of many terrorist atrocities. Many of us were physically sick, others suffered mental breakdowns. And some of the people who organised (and participated in) this carnage over many years are now shiny suited politicians in high office . . . You can see that these matters still mightily disturb me . . . It seems to me that we have ignored real wickedness—failed to call it what it really is. Indeed, we have rewarded it. So many were simply bought off. All in the name of political and pragmatic expediency. Long-term this will not work.

   It seems to me that it would be quite inappropriate to expect my correspondent—even as a Christian—to forgive the representative of an organization that has perpetrated brutal murders and has not repented of them. It seems to me quite proper that he should continue to resent the gross wrongdoing, and to distrust someone who has not repudiated it. On such an occasion forgiveness-as-absolution would not so much exceed the moral capacity of most individuals, as it would simply not make sense. Forgiveness-as-compassion, however, would make sense. It would be appropriate, I think, to expect my correspondent—at least as a Christian—to submit his resentment to moderation by recalling his own subjection to common historical fate and his own participation in common sinfulness; to wonder about the circumstances that encouraged the perpetrators to do the dreadful thing that they did, and about whether his own people were at all complicit in producing those circumstances; to remember the compassion of the God who, wearing the face of Jesus, looked down upon his killers and said, 'Father, forgive them, for they know not what they do' (Luke 23:34); and to look for the resurrection of the dead, the vindication of the innocent, and eschatological reconciliation with the penitent.

---

[59] The programme was 'Question Time', and it was broadcast on BBC 1 television.

If this is at all plausible, then there is more to be said about the political manifestation of love than Reinhold Niebuhr manages to utter. Niebuhr says more than Luther, but he still does not say quite enough. He recognizes that love can discipline resentment, curb vengeance, and order punishment toward the reformation of the wrongdoer. Yet he thinks that forgiveness aspires to overlook injustice and the conflict it generates, and to transcend punishment altogether; and for that reason he cannot see a place for it in political life. In this I think Niebuhr was mistaken. There *is* scope for love's 'crown'—forgiveness—to find political expression that is not glib, gauche, and ineffectual. We *can* speak of an initial moment of forgiveness-as-compassion that does not paper over bitter conflict, proportionate resentment, and the propriety of penitence-seeking punishment, but which can look them in the eye and govern them. Not all resentment is vengeful, as Joseph Butler—following St Paul—recognized; and so not all resentment is contrary to forgiveness.[60] Nor is all punishment. Forgiveness, therefore, can be more realistic than Niebuhr supposed. In which case, there is yet more that Jesus' ethic has to offer 'the burden-bearers of the world'[61] as they strive to negotiate just peace between violently contending parties.[62]

---

[60] Joseph Butler, 'Sermon VIII—Upon Resentment', in *Fifteen Sermons and a Dissertation upon Virtue*, intro. W. R. Matthews (London: G. Bell & Sons, 1953), 123. Butler cites St Paul in his Epistle to the Ephesians, where he writes, 'Be ye angry and sin not' (4.26). Niebuhr incorrectly assumes that resentment is self-interested and vindictive, and that it is therefore contrary to Jesus' injunction to forgive one's enemy (*An Interpretation of Christian Ethics*, 27–8).

[61] This nice phrase appears on a few occasions in *An Interpretation of Christian Ethics*—e.g., on p. 15.

[62] Ibid. 23, 31.

11

What Makes Us Think That God Wants Democracy?

Richard Harries

The nature of democracy, its strengths, weaknesses, and Christian justification, was a life-long interest for Niebuhr. He discussed it in a range of articles before the Second World War, in his 1932 book *Moral Man and Immoral Society*, and in his 1939 Gifford Lectures later published as *The Nature and Destiny of Man*. He returned to the subject again in 1969 with *The Democratic Experience*. It was, however, in *The Children of Light and the Children of Darkness*, published in 1944, that his thought on this subject received its most systematic formulation. It also contained his famous aphorism:

Man's capacity for justice makes democracy possible; but man's inclination to injustice makes democracy necessary.[1]

In 1944 he was gloomy about the prospects of democracy in a post-war world and wrote *The Children of Light and the Children of Darkness* to provide a stronger basis for it than it had hitherto had, and one which in the American context would help the revival of Americans for Democratic Action (the ADA), the leftish political movement in which he was a key member. 'It was a reassuring vision for a time of liberal rebuilding.'[2]

Niebuhr was sufficiently influenced by Marxist analysis to recognize that from one point of view the rise of liberal democracy was an expression of bourgeois interests breaking the stranglehold of a feudal order dominated by the aristocracy and the church. As he put it:

The most pathetic aspect of the bourgeois faith is that it regards its characteristic perspectives and convictions as universally valid and applicable, at the precise moment in history when they are being unmasked as the peculiar convictions of a special class which flourished in a special situation in western society.[3]

---

[1] *The Children of Light and the Children of Darkness* (London: Nisbet, 1945), p. vi.
[2] Richard Fox, *Reinhold Niebuhr: A Biography* (New York: Pantheon, 1985), 220.
[3] *The Children of Light and the Children of Darkness*, 91.

Yet he also believed that democracy expressed values of abiding validity. The freedom of subjects to choose their own governments and the equality associated with this, so that in the political order one counts for one, neither more nor less, was, he argued, fundamental to both a Christian and a secular view of existence. Moreover, this freedom, expressed in economic terms through the market, and in other ways, allowed creative possibilities for the future to emerge. Much that was wrong might come about as well, but taking this risk was better than blocking developments that might enhance human life and well-being.

MAN'S INCLINATION TO INJUSTICE MAKES DEMOCRACY NECESSARY

That justification of democracy, however, the Enlightenment one, was, in Niebuhr's view inadequate by itself, for it was based on an over-optimistic view of humanity which assumed that conflicts could always be resolved and progress achieved. Hence the subtitle of *The Children of Light and the Children of Darkness* is *A Vindication of Democracy and a Critique of its Traditional Defenders*. For Niebuhr the best vindication of democracy was based on an awareness of our tendency to oppress one another and the consequent need to control political power. Hobbes and Luther both had a realistic sense of the way human beings do violence to one another, and from this followed their call for strong government to stop people tearing themselves apart. What they failed to point out is that potentially the biggest oppressor of all is government itself, hence the paramount need to have some way of checking, balancing, and controlling it. From this springs the classical separation of powers into the executive, the legislature, and the judiciary, together with fixed elections and other mechanisms.

In Niebuhr's classic defence of liberal democracy the children of light are western thinkers of the Enlightenment and their followers in subsequent ages, who believed there was a capacity for altruism in human beings, who argued that real progress could be made in the human lot, and who thought that through education and reason most problems could be solved and most disputes settled. For Niebuhr this was all foolishness. The children of darkness are wiser, because they know the power of human egoism and the ineluctable tendency of human beings to expand their interests at the expense of others; but they are children of darkness because in their moral cynicism they act as though this is the only force at work. The only sound basis for democracy is one that takes our tendency to human aggrandizement at the expense of others realistically into account but which sets this in a moral framework provided by the children of light. So, as he put it:

The preservation of a democratic civilization requires the wisdom of the serpent and the harmlessness of the dove. The children of light must be armed with the wisdom of the children of darkness but remain free of their malice. They must know the power of self-interest in human society without giving it moral justification. They must have this wisdom in order that they may beguile, deflect, harness and restrain self-interest, individual and collective, for the sake of the community.[4]

Niebuhr argued that historically democracy was the joint achievement of Christian and secular thought, forms of Calvinism and Christian sects on the one hand and rationalists on the other. He also believed that Christianity contributes three insights of permanent validity. First, a basis for authority outside government itself, as expressed in the biblical notion that we are called to obey God rather than Caesar. Secondly, a non-instrumental view of human beings. All individuals are of value in themselves for themselves, and must never be treated simply as a cipher in a larger scheme of things. And, thirdly, an awareness of our human sin, whereby the ordinary struggle to survive is turned into a drive for prestige and power. This is the insight that liberal idealists totally failed to see.

He also believed that Marxists were guilty of the same naivete about human nature, for though they believed in the class struggle until a truly communist society came into being, they thought that in such a society all conflict would be resolved, because its basis in an unjust economic order would have been corrected. But they ignored the fact that economic power, however important, is not the only form of power, and the human will to power remains even in a society where economic inequalities have been done away with.

So western liberals, both secular and Christian, and Marxists, share an over-optimistic view of human nature. As Niebuhr put it: 'The facts about human nature which make a monopoly of power dangerous and a balance of power desirable are understood in neither theory but are understood from the standpoint of Christian faith.'[5]

Niebuhr's justification of democracy from that point of view is as pertinent today as it was then. But his classic aphorism has two parts to it, not only the statement that 'man's inclination to injustice makes democracy necessary', but that 'man's capacity for justice makes democracy possible'. The question

[4] *The Children of Light and the Children of Darkness*, 34.
[5] Reinhold Niebuhr, *Christian Realism and Political Problems* (London: Faber, 1954), 99.

I wish to consider is whether there is not a stronger Christian basis for the first part 'Man's capacity for justice makes democracy possible', than Niebuhr himself put forward.

MAN'S CAPACITY FOR JUSTICE MAKES DEMOCRACY POSSIBLE

This capacity for justice has three aspects to it: liberty, equality, and the social nature of human life.

Few would disagree that the first and most fundamental value of liberal democracy is individual freedom. This basic liberty includes a range of freedoms: freedom of speech, of worship, and of assembly, for example. But it certainly includes freedom to choose those by whom we will be governed.

We now take this so much for granted that we forget how new this is, and how until comparatively recently the Roman Catholic hierarchy in some countries opposed democracy. It is important to see why they might have done this. For if God is a Divine Ruler who has revealed his law to us, it is natural to think that this pattern should be reflected in human rulers, and obedience to their law. Hierarchy and obedience are as it were written into the very constitution of the universe. And this, in itself, can provide a very beautiful vision for the ordering of both the cosmos and society. So it is easy to see how democracy, in the sense of rule of the people, by the people, for the people, might be regarded as inimical to it.

C. S. Lewis, like Niebuhr, argued that we need democracy in our fallen, sinful state, because we can never trust human rulers. But, he argued, this is a concession. In a perfect unfallen world we would have hierarchy and obedience. He argued that our real hunger is for inequality. 'The man who has never wanted to kneel or bow is a prosaic barbarian', he wrote.[6] This desire for inequality, he argued, is reflected in the adulation we give to heroes and superstars, and why right-wing dictatorships can gain adherents. We do indeed need democracy in this world; nevertheless, 'there is no spiritual substance in flat equality'. We should recognize that 'under the necessary outer covering of legal equality, the whole hierarchical dance and

---

[6] C. S. Lewis, 'Equality', reprinted in the Canadian *C. S. Lewis Journal*, Summer 1990. It originally appeared in *The Spectator* in 1943. See also his *A Preface to Paradise Lost* (Oxford: Oxford University Press, 1942), ch. 11, where he is highly critical of the failure of modern critics to understand the proper role of hierarchy in Milton and other western thinkers.

harmony of our deep and joyously accepted spiritual inequalities should
be alive.'

However, we can hugely admire someone for her spiritual qualities without
this leading to either prostration or obedience. Rather, admiration leads to a
desire to learn from and be influenced by the person. Furthermore, it will
almost certainly be a characteristic of the person we admire that she precisely
does not want us to kneel and obey her. They will want us to gain our own
insights and find our own way. Nicholas Ferrar, who founded the religious
community at Little Gidding in the seventeenth century, based on his family,
wrote to his niece: 'I purpose and hope by God's grace to be to you not as a
master but as a partner and fellow student.' Such an attitude is rooted in a
faith that believes God has come amongst us in Jesus as brother and partner
in God.

Although Locke, one of the seminal thinkers for the development of
democracy was a Christian believer and his view of both government and
human rights is based on the reality of God, subsequent theorists have
detached the theological foundations of this and argued for the legitimacy
of Locke's views in themselves, irrespective of whether they are undergirded
by a creator in whose image we are made. Related to this is the fact that
despite the serious Christian faith of Locke and a good number of other
Enlightenment thinkers, many people persist in seeing the Enlightenment as a
secular achievement. We need to understand why this is so.

Kingship is the prime model for rule in the scriptures. If the Enlightenment
is seen in terms of the rejection of kingship, at least in its absolute form, then
it is easy to see how the emergence of democracy might be seen as primarily a
secular achievement. So it is necessary to probe the kingship model to see
what it does and does not imply.

The dominance of the kingship metaphor, at its best, allows for the
C. S. Lewis view that in heaven there is rule by a divine king who is totally
given over to our good but that we need democracy now because no human
ruler can be trusted. This was a view also expressed on BBC Radio 4 in a
'Thought for the Day' on 6 September 2008 by Joel Edwards, who speaks for a
good number of evangelicals, when he said that whilst here on earth 'God
does democracy'. But, 'In biblical terms God's ideal would be a theocracy in
which all aspects of human relationships come immediately under his rule
and sovereignty.' However, this is just the kind of contrast that we need to
question. For if democracy is just a temporary expedient, a concession to our
human weakness, due to be done away with when the rule of the perfect
Divine King is established, I wonder whether it provides a firm enough
foundation for a truly Christian polity?

A parallel can be made with another human institution, marriage. Jesus is reported to have said that in heaven there is neither marrying nor giving in marriage, but we are like the angels. Now it is true that there will be no need for procreation in heaven, one of the purposes of marriage. But this does not mean the end of deep and intimate relationships. There is no marrying or giving in marriage because in a sense everyone will be married to everyone else; there will be a deep and intimate communion within the body of Christ not only with Christ himself, but in him with all other members of the body. So whilst there is one aspect of marriage for which there is no continuing purpose in heaven there is another which finds its fulfilment there. Can we say the same about democracy?

In so far as democracy exists to check and stop the emergence of despotic rule, there is indeed no need for it in heaven, for there all is perfected. But there is another aspect of democracy, and that is the natural coming together of human beings to order their common life. This is the emphasis in democracy going back to the ancient Greeks and preserved in the Catholic if not always in the reformed tradition. If this is a fundamental feature of what it means to be a human being, and not just a concession to either finitude or sin, then perhaps like marriage it finds its proper fulfilment in heaven, in ways of course which we cannot now imagine.

Lewis and many others suggest that because God is the perfect king, who desires only the well being of his subjects, there is no need for any form of government other than that. But this is to misunderstand the relationship between divine and human activity, and to suggest that they are mutually exclusive accounts of human behaviour.

God has bestowed on us the awesome gift of freedom. He has taken the risk of putting things in our hands. If this gift of freedom is fundamental to God's intention for us, what indeed helps to define us as human beings, then it would seem odd that this is a gift only for this life, as though we have it now, and then it is taken away from us. A better approach is to say, not that it is taken away from us, but that in heaven, made perfect in a *milieu* of intimate communion with the Divine Presence, that freedom is exercised rightly.

Furthermore, heaven is a society, a communion of saints; but still a society. And, as Austin Farrer used to emphasize, the Divine Presence that fully enfolds us is met in and through that society; in and through the body of Christ, the communion of fellow believers.

It can also be pointed out that the image of kingship is not the only one suggested by the New Testament. Jesus said to his followers that in the Kingdom they will sit on thrones judging the twelve tribes of Israel. There was a period in the history of Israel when it was judges, rather than kings, that arbitrated and ordered the common life. So it may be that God without ceasing to be king delegates the ordering of the common life in heaven as he does on earth. His kingship in other words does not just consist of each individual before the throne, but human beings in communion with one another, sharing responsibility for their common life before the throne. God rules, in the sense that the whole body of Christ moves in perfect harmony with his purpose. But that body has a properly delegated function, shared responsibility for the common life.

All this is very speculative, but what it suggests is that there are elements in liberal democracy which are not just here for the interim, a concession to finitude and sin, but which, however impossible to picture, have their proper grounding and fulfilment in heaven. The reason for making such a suggestion is to counter the suspicion that democracy is really a secular achievement rooted in secular political philosophy. Furthermore, it may be that whilst the emphasis Niebuhr gave to 'man's inclination to injustice' was a necessary corrective and a permanent insight, he did not give a strong enough theological grounding to the Enlightenment stress on 'man's capacity for justice'. This is in part because his own emphasis is rooted in a Protestant understanding of the state as a concession to human sin, rather than the Catholic understanding that it is natural and right for human beings to come together to order their common life.

THE CRITIQUE OF OLIVER O'DONOVAN

I now consider what Oliver O'Donovan has written on democracy. I do so because he offers a learned and deeply challenging critique of the whole tradition of western thinking about the basis of democracy, including both aspects of Niebuhr's aphorism. His alternative approach is very wide ranging and it is possible here to consider only what he writes under the heading of 'legitimacy'. There is for O'Donovan a fundamental distinction between good government, which he is prepared to call liberal government, and liberal democracy. He describes, without arguing for, good government in the following terms:

This account has a number of elements, all to do with responsiveness to the real and felt needs of society: an elected parliament as a formal court of pleas; local representative organs with local autonomy; the admission of open and candid speech on all matters relating to the common good; the obligation of government to natural and divine law; the recognition of basic individual rights at law as a limiting constraint upon inequalities of social order; the independence of courts from executive interference; due forms of consultation and deliberation in preparing legislation and due process for promulgating it, and so on.[7]

For him the key question is how far this kind of good government is dependent on its legitimation through democratic elections. He suggests that election is neither a necessary nor a sufficient condition. There have been good governments without elections, and elections that that have resulted in unjust governments. He then considers three ways in which democratic elections might be considered integral. The first claims that democratic elections are implicit in the very idea of good liberal government, as it were the second stage of a developing idea. He rejects this on the grounds that in fact what we are left with is 'the humdrum practice of voting in elections'[8] which seems very far from the kind of grand claims made for liberal democracy about regenerating society. There is a very great deal wrong with western-style democracies at the moment, but when we are feeling disillusioned one of the pictures we need to bear in mind is that of black South Africans queuing for hours in order to cast their votes in a system that for the first time allowed their votes to count.

One aspect of the democratic idea that O'Donovan does not seem to consider is the gradual widening out of the franchise until it became universal. Previously excluded groups such as Roman Catholics, Jews, men without property, women as a whole, and then women below the age at which men were allowed to vote, over the course of a hundred years or so were enabled to share in the process of electing their government. The key moral idea here is that one counts for one, neither more, nor less. O'Donovan rightly bases his idea of equality on the equal dignity and worth of all human beings in the eyes of God, and rightly believes this has important political implications, like equality before the law. Whilst again, rightly, he is anxious to avoid any flat notion of equality which fails to take into account the different gifts and vocations which society needs for its flourishing, he seems strangely blind to the realization of the Christian idea of equality in the idea of one person one vote. If people are to be consulted about the government they want, then there can be no basis for denying that the perspective on life and views of every individual ought to be taken into account on an equal basis.

Secondly, there is the claim that liberal democracy ensures just government, and here he quotes Niebuhr. But, he argues, this:

Can only be that envisaged by the contractarian myth, which sees political authority as derived from a founding act of popular will. Otherwise we would not look to

---

[7] Oliver O'Donovan, *The Ways of Judgement* (Grand Rapids, MI: Eerdmans, 2005), 168.
[8] Ibid. 170.

democracy to achieve justice but to intra-governmental 'checks and balances.' The power of an electorate to dismiss and choose its rulers can only be a guarantee of good government, if good government is understood as that which rulers exercise under the authority of the popular will.[9]

Here we note in passing that in his chapter on 'The Powers of Government' he is concerned to stress the unity of governmental power, rather than its threefold expression in the executive, the legislature, and the judiciary. Whilst he does not deny the threefold dispensation, his stress on the rightness and inevitability of the unity of government is open to the charge that it weakens the effect of the separation of powers as a check and balance on the unbridled power of the executive.

More substantially, we have to note his deep hostility to the contractarian myth and to ask if this is really necessary. If the concern is to safeguard the fact that Government is ultimately given by and accountable to God, the contractarian myth does not necessarily rule that out. Furthermore, Christians regard themselves as accountable both to God and to one another within the body of Christ. When they come to the Sunday Eucharist they come accountable for the week just past not just before God but before one another. This sense of accountability before other human beings can be and ought to be even stronger in office holders in the church. So there is no incompatibility in saying that governments are accountable both to God and to the people who elect them. If the people who elect them find them wanting, then they have the right to look for a different government. That new government is also accountable to God, and from a theological point of view is given by God.

The fact is that while popular election by itself is not a guarantee of just government, it is one key element along with others, such as the separation of powers and human rights guaranteed by law, which helps prevent tyranny. The fact is that there is no way of guaranteeing good government. Democracies can and are manipulated in all kinds of ways, as we see at the moment in Russia and many other countries. The alliance of political power with big money, leading to control or heavy manipulation of the media, with weak processes of law for safeguarding human rights, is a sad reality. But it would be even sadder without the possibility of the electorate bringing in an alternative government *in extremis*.

The third claim which O'Donovan considers, the most modest one, is that elections guarantee that those who are elected are genuinely representative of the electorate. He argues, to the contrary, that election is no such guarantee, as we see in the case of the European institutions, for representation is primarily

---

[9] O'Donovan, *The Ways of Judgement*, 173.

a matter of the imagination. In the European Union, there are elections, but people feel very distant from the bodies to which they have elected people.

For O'Donovan representation is primarily a matter of the imagination. However, being able to envisage someone representing us assumes our willingness, that is, our free choice, to so imagine: in other words, free elections. It can also be pointed out that the European institutions are comparatively recent, and it could be that in the future people will feel more identified with them than they are now. They would be even less likely to do this if there were no elections.

So in the end O'Donovan comes to make a very limited claim indeed for liberal democracy.

The case for democracy is that it is specifically appropriate to western societies at this juncture. It is a moment in the Western tradition; it has its own ecological *niche*. This allows us no universal claims of the 'best regime' kind, nor does it permit the imperial view that the history of democracy is the history of progress. Yet, within its own terms it allows us to be positive about democracy's strengths. The best regime is precisely that regime that plays to the virtues and skills of those who are governed by it; and this one serves us well in demanding and developing certain virtues of bureaucratic and public discourse that the Western tradition has installed. It is our tradition; we are bred in it; we can, if we are sensible about it, make it work.[10]

The rejection of imperialist claims is welcome indeed; nevertheless, I believe this very limited claim is too modest. First, there is the question of the universal franchise, which I have argued is one inescapable implication of believing in the equal worth and dignity of every single individual human being. It is noticeable that a number of countries with traditional political regimes are now inching their way towards this, and some Muslim scholars argue that it is an essential development of two Islamic ideas. The first is the tradition of *ijtihad,* which allows for creative reinterpretations of traditional legal texts in response to modern needs. The second is the institution of the consultative assembly, *Majlis al-Shura.* It is well established that rulers should consult with their leading men and institutions. So it has been argued by Muslim scholars that a true consultative assembly would allow for full democracy.

Secondly, whilst the election of governments is no guarantee that the government so elected will act justly, for populations can be manipulated, it is one element, along with others, that seeks to act as a brake on tyrannous tendencies.

[10] Ibid. 178.

That said, there is one development that is no less crucial and in some respects more so than elections, and that is the guarantee of human rights by law. This is necessary in liberal democracies in order to protect minorities from the tyranny of the majority and to protect individuals from being harmed as a result of 'reasons of state', however rationally justified. In non-democratic societies, where women in particular may be severely disadvantaged, the entrenchment of human rights in law is an even more pressing priority than governments by election, though it is highly likely that the latter will lead to the establishment of the former, not least because women will have the vote.

I suggest that there are elements in liberal democracies that have a wider moral relevance than O'Donovan allows, and this question is discussed below.

DEMOCRACY AS A VISION OF WHAT SOCIETY SHOULD BECOME

Until the resurgence of Islam the major critique of liberal democracy was provided by Marxism. As Marx put it, democracy meant no more than 'the opportunity of deciding once in three or six years which member of the ruling class was to misrepresent the people'.[11] For Marxism the rise of democracy was simply the rise of rule by bourgeois interests, and these would rightly and inevitably be replaced by rule by working-class interests. However, you do not need to be a thoroughgoing Marxist to recognize the element of economic interest at work in political life. Niebuhr was certainly highly aware of that: but what is important to recognize is that with globalization economic power is even more powerful now than it was in his time. Behind the press, behind party funding, behind advertising, behind the organization that wins elections, sadly, even behind some legal judgments in court, lies money: the interests of finance and business. And in the modern world, with so much finance being on a global scale, the power of government to control the movement of money is much weaker.

Figures worldwide suggest that whatever improvements are being made in the lives of the poorest, this imbalance is in fact growing. This highlights two factors. First, the crucial importance of governments acting for the common good. In a world where economic power on a global scale reigns supreme, this

---

[11] Karl Marx, *The Paris Commune*.

will mean that political power needs to be used not just to facilitate business, but to enable the most marginalized to share in the full life of their society.

Secondly it highlights a distinction made by John de Gruchy between 'democracy as a *vision* of what society should become, and democracy as a *system* of government that seeks to enable the realization of that vision within particular contexts'.[12]

De Gruchy finds the foundation for a Christian understanding of democracy in the eighth-century BC prophets, with their vision of social equality, freedom, and justice and its development in five trajectories. First, in the messianic hope of true liberation for all people from all that oppresses; secondly, in the medieval championing of the common good and the development of trade guilds and other expressions of civil society; thirdly, in the Reformation concept of covenantal obligation, whereby human beings are called to accountable responsibility both to God and to one another; fourthly, the other more radical Reformation emphasis on individual freedom and the separation of church and state. Fifthly, in modern liberation theology, which seeks to overcome economic injustice and oppression.

This distinction between democracy as a vision and democracy as a system is an important one and it reminds us that democracy must always be seen as an ongoing project towards the realization of that vision. We note, from recent years, the civil rights movement and the different aspects of the struggle for equality for women, which has been part of that quest for full and equal participation by all members of society. The fact that modern Western politics is now so characterized by single-issue campaigns is no bad thing, for it is an indication of other groups, for example the disabled or children, struggling for their proper place.

Given the distinction between democracy as a vision and democracy as a system, is there anything in the system as it has so far been developed, *contra* Oliver O'Donovan, which is absolutely fundamental, and crucial to stand up for? Even given its present manifest flaws does the system safeguard some essential insights into what it is for us human beings to live in society? Or are we to say that this is the system that has developed in our society and a good number of others, but other systems may be just as good for rather different kinds of society?

The word democracy has been claimed by a good number of societies we would judge undemocratic. As T. S. Eliot wrote: 'When a term has become so universally sanctified as "democracy" now is, I begin to wonder whether it

---

[12] John de Gruchy, 'Democracy', in Adrian Hastings (ed.), *The Oxford Companion to Christian Thought* (Oxford: Oxford University Press, 2000), 157. See also John de Gruchy, *Christianity and Democracy* (Cambridge: Cambridge University Press, 1995).

means anything, in meaning too many things . . . If anybody ever attacked democracy, I might discover what the word meant.'[13]

I think meaning can be given to liberal democracy, and it is worth standing up for. One essential element in a liberal democracy, the rule of law and the right to a fair trial, all that we mean by habeas corpus, does not belong to democracy alone. It is essential to democracy, and where it fails, as in Iraq so far, democracy fails. But it is not unique to democracy. Islamic societies too insist on the rule of law. Of course, questions arise about how far the judiciary is independent from the executive. It is a mark of a democratic system that they are, but even in an Islamic society there is a measure of independence. But what about other features of liberal democracy in relation to Islam?

It has been suggested that what we should look for in the Muslim world are political systems that allow for government by consent. It is certainly important that we should not simply think of the imposition of secular Western liberal ideals on Islamic societies. Nevertheless, given this caution, I think we have to go further and argue that liberal democracies stand not only for government by consent, but they look to obtain that consent in a particular way, by universal franchise, and as mentioned above, there are some Muslim scholars who now argue for this. Another mark is the genuine separation of powers, with a truly independent judiciary safeguarding the rule of law against arbitrary decrees of government and the separation of the executive from the legislature.

These are not of course the only essential features. There is freedom of speech and the press, freedom of assembly, freedom to form political parties, freedom of worship. There is also, I would maintain, the acceptance of certain fundamental rights as well as these freedoms. Human rights are not simply an add-on to democracy but fundamental to it. This is because of what Alexis de Tocqueville called the despotism or tyranny of the majority. It is possible in a democracy for the majority view to be elected to government, and then for that government to oppress various minority interests. Those fundamental human interests need to be protected.

When it comes to social and economic rights, as opposed to political rights, their realization depends significantly on the state of development of that society. But the rights of individual people, of women, of gay and lesbian people and the disabled, and in particular their right to be protected from cruel and demeaning treatment, are fundamental and we cannot take the view that one society's attitude to them is just as good as another's.

---

[13] T. S. Eliot, *The Idea of a Christian Society and Other Writings* (London: Faber, 1982), 48.

There is a danger that if we start making value judgements that some things are better than others, we can slip over not only into arrogance, but into a crusade mentality. Some of President Bush's rhetoric before the Iraq war had something of this about it. What is necessary is the ability to make value judgements, to say, yes, liberal democracy does safeguard certain essentials about what it is for human beings to live in society and to stand up for these in peaceful ways, but always to be aware that democracy as we know it is very flawed, and even at its best it is only a proximate good, a project towards the realization of a vision. One of the great strengths of the whole of Niebuhr's writings, not least his prayers, was his ability to make clear judgements whilst at the same time avoiding any suggestion of moral superiority.

Democracy came out of the Enlightenment from the work of Christian as well as secular thinkers, and it expresses a Christian understanding of what it is to be a human being in society, a social being, who is at once made in the image of God and a violator of that image. Christianity has of course lived under a range of different kinds of government and democracy as we know it is open to the criticism today, as Eliot put it in the 1930s, that 'what we have is not democracy, but financial oligarchy'.[14] But all qualifications notwithstanding, it does stand for something. It does contain features that safeguard certain fundamental insights into a proper understanding of what it is to be a human being in society.

However, Niebuhr was conscious that democracy is the product of a long and painful history in America and Britain, in which various essential factors for the emergence of democracy were present. These were not yet there in a number of countries.

Democratic self-government is indeed an ultimate ideal of political community. But it is of the greatest importance that we realize that the resources for its effective functioning are not available to many nations.[15]

Again, although he saw democracy as the least bad political system we have so far evolved, he warned strongly against making it into an idol. He thought that Americans had developed an uncritical almost religious attitude towards it, which was dangerous.

If one may judge by the various official pronouncements and commencement speeches, Americans have only one religion: devotion to democracy . . . democracy is worth preserving. It is a worthy object of qualified loyalty. But is it a proper object of unqualified loyalty? Does not the very extravagance of our devotion prove that we live

---

[14] Ibid. 48.
[15] A point made in a number of articles, quoted by Charles C. Brown, *Niebuhr and his Age: Reinhold Niebuhr's Prophetic Role in the Twentieth Century* (Harrisburg, PA: Trinity Press, 1992), 217.

in a religiously vapid age, in which even Christians fail to penetrate to the more ultimate issues of life.[16]

Democracy is worthy of a qualified loyalty, but we have to realize what it is, 'a method of finding proximate solutions for insoluble problems'.[17] What is fatal is to think that what it offers are final solutions.

Our knowledge that there is no complete solution for the problem would save us from resting in some proximate solution under the illusion that it is an ultimate one.[18]

This means that the balances struck in a democratic society, for example between government control and individual initiatives, or between individual property and state intervention, will always be temporary and have to be re-struck in the light of new problems. So democracy is not a final solution to human problems; nevertheless, as a proximate one it contains features that are vital to the political life of every human society.

---

[16] 'Christianity and Crisis', 8 Apr. 1947, reprinted in Larry Rasmussen (ed.), *Reinhold Niebuhr, Theologian of Public Life, Selected Writings* (London: Collins, 1989), 256.
[17] *The Children of Light and the Children of Darkness*, 83.
[18] Ibid. 100.

12

Realism and Progress

Niebuhr's Thought and Contemporary Challenges

Anatol Lieven

We stand at a point in history where many of the liberal capitalist certainties of the past generation have collapsed. This applies equally to blind faith in the free market, to belief in the United States' unqualified geopolitical supremacy, and to belief in the ability of the United States and its allies to spread their version of 'democracy' to other parts of the world. At the same time, the West is facing real threats and challenges, above all from the imbalances of the world economy and from terrorism.[1]

In the longer term, climate change looms as an unprecedented danger to modern civilization as a whole. These challenges require close cooperation between the United States, the European Union, and a range of different states around the world, some with political systems alien to our own. The United States and Britain, in particular, will have to learn how to pursue ethical goals not unilaterally and by dictation, but through compromise and agreement with other great powers like China and Russia.

This makes Reinhold Niebuhr's thought of unparalleled importance today as a guide to both the understanding and the practice of international relations. His relevance lies above all in three areas: in his preaching of modesty and prudence at a time when the power of the United States and the West has been greatly reduced; in his understanding of the vital role of the state and of state interests, at a time when the importance of the state is growing due to the decline of free-market capitalism and the rise of China and other non-Western states; and finally, in the intellectual marriage he helps create between the realist and progressive traditions. This in turn is

---

[1] Some of the key ideas of this essay were previously developed by John Hulsman and myself in our book *Ethical Realism: A Vision for America's Role in the World* (Pantheon, NY, 2006) and by me in my essay 'In the Sweep of History: Where Progressives and Realists Can Meet', Boston Review, Jul./Aug. 2007.

rooted in an essentially Christian belief on the one hand in the fallen, imperfect, and imperfectible nature of man; but on the other in man's moral duty to seek the good in so far as he is able; just as a Christian is called upon to imitate Christ while knowing that he or she can never hope fully to resemble Him.[2]

PROGRESSIVES AND REALISTS

To take the last point first. The estrangement of progressive and realist thought has done terrible damage to both intellectual traditions. Despite the work of Niebuhr, and of more recent intellectual descendants like John Herz, Kenneth Thompson, and others, it has been widely and almost instinctively assumed that a progressive approach to foreign policy, animated chiefly by moral convictions and universal goals, and a realist approach, animated chiefly by national interest, are fundamentally opposed.[3]

In Sean Molloy's excellent formulation:

It is a part of IR [International Relations] folklore that realism is amoral or immoral, without any of its critics properly elucidating the reasons why this is the case. The realists certainly provided a critique of a particular form of moral thinking, but this does not necessarily make them amoral, unless one insists on the infallibility of a single ethical code, one that is liberal in origin and universal in scope. Realist ethics are in fact built on a rejection of the notion of overarching moral codes, the observance of which signifies 'good' behaviour and the contravention of which signifies bad or evil behaviour. Realism instead asserts that political ethics should not be based on the subordination of political life to absolute standards of ethical conduct that are derived from an inappropriate context. This inversion of morality over power, to a position of power over morality, does not necessitate an ethical void, however, as realists have developed a variety of ways through which to reformulate and modulate the relationship, not by the excision of ethical concerns, but rather through the accommodation of political power and ethics.[4]

---

[2] For the clearest presentation of Niebuhr's Christian ethic of realism, see his *The Children of Light and the Children of Darkness* (New York: Scribner's, 1944). Jean Bethke Elshtain has sought to develop some of Niebuhr's ideas and apply them to contemporary US policy in the 'war on terror' in her *Just War against Terror: The Burden of American Power in a Violent World* (New York: Basic Books, 2003)—but in my view, largely mistakenly.

[3] See for example Charles Beitz, *Political Theory and International Relations* (Princeton: Princeton University Press, 1979), 15.

[4] Sean Molloy, 'E. H. Carr versus Hans Morgenthau: Conflicting Conceptions of Ethics in Realism', in Duncan Bell (ed.), *Political Thought and International Relations: Variations on a Realist Theme* (Oxford: Oxford University Press, 2008); for Morgenthau's ethical vision of

The assumption that realism and progressive thought, like realism and ethics, are natural enemies, is both mistaken in itself and a significant obstacle to the creation of a progressive strategy in opposition to the imperial dreams of the US establishment.[5] By helping befuddle the Democratic intellectual establishment, it has contributed greatly to the failure of the Democratic Party in the United States to emerge as an effective force in this regard, and has had a similar effect on sections of the New Labour Party in Britain.

The progressives' hostility to realism has meant that many of their proposals for change have proved simply impracticable in the real world. As the great American realist Hans Morgenthau wrote,

The equation of political moralizing with morality and of political realism with immorality is itself untenable. The choice is not between moral principles and the national interest, devoid of moral dignity, but between one set of principles divorced from political reality and another set of principles derived from political reality.[6]

Their lack of intellectual contact with realism has also helped leave many progressives vulnerable to the seductions of liberal imperialism as practised by Bush and Blair—through their belief that the demands of morality give the West the right and equally importantly the ability to spread its versions of progress to the rest of the world, by force if necessary. This attitude has combined to fatal effect with a decadent tendency in Western academia to rely on abstract, Western-derived models for analysis of very different societies, thereby sparing the analysts the physical risk and discomfort of actually traveling there, and the moral unease of being forced to question their own assumptions.

The instinctive hostility of many realists to progressive thought has also impoverished the realist tradition.[7] A core failing of classical realists like Kenneth Waltz has been an indifference not just to ethics but to the internal

realism, see Hans Morgenthau, 'The Demands of Prudence', in his *Politics in the Twentieth Century*, iii: *The Restoration of American Politics* (Chicago: University of Chicago Press, 1962), 16, 38–9.

[5] For wider discussions of realist ethics, see for example Richard Ned Lebow, *The Tragic Vision of Politics: Ethics, Interests, and Orders* (Cambridge: Cambridge University Press, 2003); Alistair Murray, *Reconstructing Realism: Between Power Politics and Cosmopolitan Ethics* (Keele: Keele University Press, 1997); Joel Rosenthal, *Righteous Realists: Political Realism, Responsible Power, and American Culture in the Nuclear Age* (Baton Rouge: Louisiana State University Press, 1986); Jonathan Haslam, *No Virtue Like Necessity: Realist Thought in International Relations Since Machiavelli* (New Haven: Yale University Press, 2002).

[6] Hans J. Morgenthau, *In Defense of the National Interest* (Washington, DC: University Press of America, 1982), 34.

[7] See the discussion of this theme in Bernard Williams, 'Realism and Moralism in Political Theory', in his *In the Beginning was the Deed: Realism and Moralism in Political Argument*, ed. Geoffrey Hawthorn (Princeton: Princeton University Press, 2005), 1–18.

nature of states, and the impact of this on their external behaviour.[8] Indeed, Waltz sought with a depressing degree of success to strip the modern academic school of Realism of many of the features that made the work of Niebuhr and Morgenthau so rich and interesting.[9]

This has even been true to some extent of the greatest contemporary American realist thinker, John Mearsheimer, whose work *The Tragedy of Great Power Politics* was marred by a sometimes bizarre concentration on abstract national power rather than national culture.[10] This led him for example to the suggestion that Germany would re-emerge over the next generation as a great military power dominating Europe—something which does not seem likely to anyone who has studied modern German culture and society rather than simply adding up German economic statistics and the numbers of Germany's (so-called) soldiers. Realists were also particularly bad at predicting the collapse for internal reasons of the Soviet bloc.

This tendency in turn has blinded many realists like Waltz to the need for long-term progress if the international peace and order that most realists desire is to be achieved. An innate tendency to pessimism can also lead to a failure to recognize when progress is in fact possible. Finally, an obsession with states, state interests, and state power has contributed in our own time to an inadequate recognition of new global threats, and the need for global alliances and institutions to combat them.

For it is not merely that 9/11 has demonstrated that the internal decay of even a very weak country can create appalling terrorist problems for much more powerful states. Equally important is the fact that throughout much of modern history, from the French Revolution through the Russian Revolution to Nazism, radical internal developments have led in turn to catastrophic international wars. This is increasingly admitted even by 'classical' realists to have been a failure of their tradition.

The second area where realists need to learn from parts of the left refers to the threat of global warming and what to do about it, since it is increasingly evident that the extent of this development—far more than terrorism—will present the greatest menace to modern civilization over the generations to come. Of course, for a realist focused exclusively on the wellbeing of

---

[8] Kenneth Waltz, *Theory of International Politics* (New York: McGraw-Hill, 1979); 'Realist Thought and Neorealist Theory', *Journal of International Affairs*, 44 (1990), 21–38.

[9] Richard K. Ashley among others has argued strongly that Morgenthau in particular does not fit the rigid mould into which Waltz tried to fit him. See Richard K. Ashley, 'Political Realism and Human *Interests*', *International Studies Quarterly*, 25 (1981), 204–36; Ashley, 'The Poverty of Neorealism', *International Organization*, 38 (1984), 225–86.

[10] John Mearsheimer, *The Tragedy of Great Power Politics* (New York: Norton, 2001).

himself, his family, or his nation only in this generation, this need not matter very much.

But one of the great ancestors of modern Anglo-American realism, Edmund Burke, famously believed in society as a contract between the living, the dead, and those yet to be born—a statement close to the famous environmentalist maxim that 'we have only borrowed the world from our grandchildren'. Given the scientific evidence about the extent of the future threat of global warming to human civilization, a principled Burkean realist is therefore virtually compelled to action on behalf of our descendants. Or as Niebuhr wrote, 'A consistent self-interest on the part of a nation will work against its interests because it will fail to do justice to its broader and longer interests, which are involved with those of other nations.'[11]

The estrangement between progressives and realists stems ultimately in large part from different views of the nature of man, between the progressives' fundamental optimism and the realists' pessimism in this regard.[12] Niebuhr's Christian realism bridges this gap. As he memorably observed, man is a lion— a ferocious and carnivorous animal—but he is also 'a curious kind of lion who dreams of the day when the lion and the lamb will lie down together'.[13] In other words, acknowledging reality does not mean approving that reality, or abandoning the duty to try to change that reality for the better.[14]

Niebuhr therefore rejects at the same time a universalist Western idealism which can never in fact find practical implementation in the real world, like that of the Quakers; a purely, or even cynically, realist obsession with the interests of particular states, classes, or individuals, in the style of Henry Kissinger; and a ruthless pursuit of national interest cloaked in the language of morality and progress, as practiced by the neoconservatives:

It is possible for both individuals and groups [including nations] to relate concern for the other with interest and concern for the self. There are endless varieties of creativity

---

[11] Niebuhr, *Christian Realism and Political Problems* (New York: Scribner's, 1953), 137.

[12] For an interesting discussion of this issue, see Joshua Foa Dienstag, 'Pessimistic Realism and Realistic Pessimism', in Bell (ed.), *Political Thought*, 259–88.

[13] Niebuhr, 'Christianity and Communism: Social Justice', *Spectator*, 157 (6 Nov. 1936). See also Kenneth W. Thompson, 'Beyond National Interest: A Critical Evaluation of Reinhold Niebuhr's Theory of International Politics', *The Review of Politics*, 17 (April 1955); Mark L. Haas, 'Reinhold Niebuhr's "Christian Pragmatism": A Principled Alternative to Consequentialism', *The Review of Politics*, 61/4 (Autumn 1999), 605–36.

[14] For overviews of ethical realist thought, see Joel H. Rosenthal and Kenneth W. Thompson, *Righteous Realists: Political Realism, Responsible Power, and American Culture in the Nuclear Age* (Baton Rouge: Louisiana State University Press, 1991); Robin Lovin, *Reinhold Niebuhr and Christian Realism* (Cambridge: Cambridge University Press 1995); Robert C. Good, 'The National Interest and Political Realism: Niebuhr's "Debate" with Morgenthau and Kennan', *The Journal of Politics*, 22/4 (Nov. 1960), 597–619.

in community; for neither the individual nor the community can realize itself except in relation to, and in encounter with, other individuals and groups . . . A valid moral outlook for both individuals and for groups, therefore, sets no limits to the creative possibility of concern for others, but makes no claims that such creativity ever annuls the power of self-concern or removes the peril of pretension if the force of residual egotism is not acknowledged.[15]

Although Niebuhr is chiefly remembered for his championing of liberal democracy against first Nazi Germany and then the Soviet Union, and for his work in helping to consolidate liberal support for US 'containment' of Stalinism, Niebuhr began his intellectual life as a socialist and considered himself a progressive to the end of his days. For both socialist and Christian reasons, Niebuhr maintained throughout his life a strongly critical attitude to Western democratic capitalist materialism and its belief that it had found a solution to all the problems of man. Today, the nostrums of radical free-market capitalism have been shattered by the present economic crisis, and in the longer term run absolutely contrary to the vital human necessity of reducing climate change. As the report of the British Commission headed by Sir Nicholas Stern (former chief economist at the World Bank and hardly a natural leftist) has it, global warming 'is the greatest and widest-ranging market failure ever seen'.

Niebuhr was dedicated to the defence of freedom, but of capitalism only in so far as it underpinned freedom, and he was austerely hostile to the American—or modern—idea that wealth and material development equates with spiritual merit. A key challenge of the decades to come will be precisely to uphold freedom and democracy while moving away from the gross consumerism of recent decades, which, as is ever clearer, is simply incompatible in the long term with the maintenance of a civilized human existence on earth, let alone the survival of the existing natural world. We need to move back to a more austere and restrained ethic, which in the West is bound to have partly Christian roots.

MODESTY AND PRUDENCE

Closely connected to Niebuhr's scepticism concerning capitalism and materialism was his strong hostility to American triumphalism, expressed above all

---

[15] Niebuhr, *The Structure of Nations and Empires: A Study of Recurring Patterns and Problems of the Political Order in Relation to the Unique Problems of the Nuclear Age* (New York: Scribner's, 1959), 193.

in his great work *The Irony of American History*, and in his opposition to the Vietnam War. Niebuhr was a strong American patriot who regarded US power as essential to the defence of freedom and democracy against totalitarianism, but he never ceased to warn his compatriots against the assumption that American power and American virtue were synonymous, and against pursuing crude American national interests in the name of high ideals.

This combination of patriotism and national modesty should be of great importance to the America of Barack Obama as it tries to restore American influence and prestige after the debacle of the Bush years. Indeed, President Obama's inaugural address of January 2009 was infused with realist-sounding language of prudence and responsibility. Unfortunately, though, the hawkish elements of the Democratic establishment who influence Hillary Clinton are not that far behind the neoconservatives in their automatic equation of American power with absolute virtue, and in their self-delusion concerning America's ability to convince the rest of the world of this.

Niebuhr by contrast declared that 'there is only one empirically provable element in Christian theology, namely that "All have sinned and fallen short of the glory of God."' This applies as much to states as to individuals. He recalled the lessons of the Old Testament, in words which may be taken as also prefiguring the threat to modern materialist civilization as a whole from climate change:

The prophets never weary of warning both the powerful nations and Israel, the righteous nation, of the judgment which waits on human pretension. The great nation, Babylon, is warned that its confidence in the security of its power will be refuted by history...The great nation is likened unto a cedar whose boughs are higher than all other trees. This tempts it to forget 'that the waters made it great and the deep set it on high', which is to say that every human achievement avails itself of, but also obscures, forces of destiny beyond human contrivance...Israel [in the Bible] is undoubtedly a 'good' nation as compared to the nations surrounding it. But the pretensions of virtue are as offensive to God as the pretensions of power. One has the uneasy feeling that America as both a powerful nation and a 'virtuous' one is involved in ironic perils which compound the experiences of Babylon and Israel.[16]

As a realist, Niebuhr had no patience with idealists who insisted that all actions taken by states had to be moral; but he was equally critical of American nationalists who believed that American power was inherently good:

We take, and must continue to take, morally hazardous actions to preserve our civilization. We must exercise our power. But we ought neither to believe that a nation is capable of perfect disinterestedness in its exercise, nor become complacent

---

[16] Reinhold Niebuhr, *The Irony of American History* (New York: Scribner reprint, 1985), 160.

about particular degrees of interest and passion which corrupt the justice by which the exercise of power is legitimated.

Niebuhr warned that given unrestrained power, messianic American liberalism might prove capable of imitating communism in its capacity to mix up nationalism and idealism, and commit great crimes in the belief that it was serving a greater good. Hans Morgenthau wrote in the same vein that,

Political realism refuses to identify the moral aspirations of a particular nation with the moral laws that govern the universe ... The light-hearted equation between a particular nationalism and the counsels of Providence is morally indefensible, for it is the very sin of pride against which the Greek tragedians and the Biblical prophets warned rulers and ruled. The equation is also politically pernicious, for it is liable to engender the distortion in judgment which, in the blindness of crusading frenzy, destroys nations and civilizations.[17]

Niebuhr also wrote of the 'biblical paradox' that Christians have access to the truth, but also have to recognize that as mortal beings in a fallen world they can never possess it fully:

Our toleration of truths opposed to those which we confess is an expression of the spirit of forgiveness in the realm of culture. Like all forgiveness, it is only possible if we are not too sure of our own virtue. Loyalty to the truth requires confidence in the possibility of its attainment; toleration of others requires broken confidence in the finality of our own truth.[18]

So the third area where Niebuhr can help bring realists and progressives together is in opposition to the idea of Western liberal capitalist unipolarity, geopolitical, ideological, and spiritual. This opposition, as expressed by all the leading ethical and progressive realists, applies both to overweening US imperial power itself and to the ideological positions which underpin it, summed up in repeated statements by both Bush and Blair that 'freedom' is understood the same way everywhere. Speaking of the need to create an international coalition against Soviet communist totalitarianism and imperialism, and to ameliorate global poverty, Niebuhr wrote that,

Today the success of America in world politics depends upon its ability to establish community with many nations, despite the hazards created by pride of power on the one hand and the envy of the weak on the other. This success requires a modest awareness of the contingent elements in the values and ideals of our devotion, even when they appear to us to be universally valid; and a generous appreciation of the

---

[17] Hans J. Morgenthau, *Politics among Nations* (New York: McGraw Hill 2005), 10.
[18] Niebuhr, *The Nature and Destiny of Man: A Christian Interpretation, ii: Human Destiny* (New York: Charles Scribner, 1951), 243.

valid elements in the practices and institutions of other nations though they differ from our own. In other words, our success in world politics necessitates a disavowal of the pretentious elements in our original dream, and a recognition of the values and virtues which enter into history in unpredictable ways and which defy the logic which either liberal or Marxist planners had conceived for it.[19]

Morgenthau, and the other great American realist George Kennan, though not in a broader sense progressives, came together with Niebuhr in opposition to the Vietnam War and to a US imperialism justified in the name of spreading 'Democracy' and 'Freedom'. This stance stemmed in part from Niebuhr's longstanding recognition of the positive appeal of anti-colonial nationalism, and the ways in which this could flow into communism in the developing world.

With rare prescience, Niebuhr foresaw the end of the Cold War and recognized as early as 1952 that even unqualified US victory would not lead to stable US leadership in the path of peace and justice: 'The victors would also face the "imperial" problem of using power in global terms but from one particular centre of authority, so preponderant and unchallenged that its world rule would almost certainly violate basic standards of justice.'[20]

The left, with its long tradition of opposition to Western imperialism and neo-colonialism, should have an instinctive sympathy for such views. And clearly, respect for the opinions and the interests of other nations has to involve a readiness to respect their right to generate political, economic, cultural, and moral orders different from those of the West, as long as these have not been proved beyond reasonable doubt to be disastrous to their own peoples or a real threat to international peace. the left's opposition to Western unipolarity stems in large part from a scepticism about the true worth of the existing Western democratic capitalist order, especially in the radical form adopted by the United States and its more slavish imitators, and expressed in the Washington Consensus.

Julien Benda called for Western intellectuals to liberate themselves from the service of their respective nationalisms. Long before the emergence of Francis Fukuyama, the immensely powerful force of US nationalism, based on what has been called the 'American Creed', identified America absolutely with the achievement of successful modernity, and even with the 'end of history' through the achievement of a perfect and permanent model for the world. This means that for American intellectuals to liberate themselves from the

---

[19] Niebuhr, *Irony*, 79.
[20] Ibid. 2.

service of nationalism and imperialism, they also need to liberate themselves from their present slavery to time.

Like enlightened conservatives, progressives need to develop an intellectual capacity to step outside the present age, and contemplate the broader sweeps of human history; to situate themselves somewhere between Conrad's fictional British captain Marlowe, remembering that the Thames, like the Congo, was once 'one of the dark places of the earth', and Macaulay's imaginary future visitor from New Zealand to the archaeological ruins of London.[21] This is of course a terribly difficult task. It is not however an inappropriate one for the intellectual elites of a country which has defined its own role in the sweep of human history as equivalent to that of Rome, the 'Eternal City'.

The US and Western approach to democratization in other societies should therefore be governed by rigor of the intellect, and generosity of the spirit. Progressives need to learn rigor in studying the history, political culture, and social, economic, and ethnic orders of other societies in order to determine what kind of political system they can in fact support at present and in the near-to-medium term. Both realists and progressives need to learn generosity in sympathizing with the historical fates and contemporary sufferings of other countries, and giving real economic help to them—rather than preaching at them from the pedestal of our own assumed supreme national virtue and success, and expecting them to sacrifice their own interests and values at our feet.

THE ROLE OF THE STATE

This capacity for empathy and tolerance in Niebuhr is related to another lesson that he and other realists can impart to progressives, which is the vital importance of the state in human affairs, and its essential role in progress. This is something of which progressives should hardly need reminding, since in previous generations the transformation of the state for progressive ends was central to first the liberal and then the socialist programmes. However, in the 1990s a strange idea grew up among many progressives that the state was withering in importance and being replaced by a mixture of transnational economic formations and by NGOs representing international 'civil society'.

This was both ludicrously self-flattering on the part of the classes which staffed these NGOs, and a very serious misrepresentation of reality.

[21] Joseph Conrad, *Heart of Darkness* (London: Penguin, 1995), 18.

International NGOs can of course bring successful pressure to bear on governments to make changes in policy—climate change being the most important example—but it is states that have to implement the resulting policies. No serious action against climate change can be contemplated without increased state intervention in the economy. The key role of the state has been emphasized in recent years by the rise of state-led capitalism in China and Russia, and more recently by the massive economic interventions of Western states in their faltering economies.

For Realists, states are the essential element of the international system; doomed to constant competition, but also the only possible building blocs of any international order. For the left, in the developing world many states are the product of struggle against previous Western imperialism, and are essential to defend peoples against a return of that imperialism. Progressives can, and certainly should therefore, have some sympathy for the ambivalent attitude of many ordinary people in the non-Western world towards their own states: on the one hand, knowing and fearing them as oppressive, greedy, and brutal, but seeing them nonetheless as an essential defence against the brutality and exploitation of some of the dominant capitalist powers.

Moreover, strong states are essential to smash the grip of predatory elites, ensure an adequate distribution of economic benefits and social goods to the mass of the population, and in future perhaps to limit consumption of fossil fuels. To do this, of course, states have to be sufficiently strong to defeat the elites. As the nineteenth-century German-American thinker Franz Lieber put it, reflecting Hegel, 'a weak government is a negation of liberty'.[22]

Today, the liberal imperialists and a large part of the progressive or pseudo-progressive camp share a common hostility to states across much of the world. The imperialists dislike specific states, like Iran, Syria, China, and Russia, because they oppose their plans for American world domination. In a more general sense, it is in their interest to denigrate states because that means that the opinions of their governments need not be taken into account (even when they are shared by their populations), their interests can be disregarded, and in general, they can be portrayed as barbarian entities unworthy to be consulted by the civilized imperial power, and even as fit subjects for military intervention. As Martin Jacques has written concerning the work of one of the arch-liberal imperialists, Michael Ignatieff:

It has become fashionable to argue that sovereignty should no longer be regarded as sacred, that human rights, even democracy, could, under certain circumstances,

---

[22] Quoted in Eric Foner, *The Story of American Freedom* (New York: W. W. Norton, 1998), 53.

justify its subordination and breach. For the majority of nation-states, self-rule and sovereignty are a historical novelty, a product of the last half-century or so. The United States now poses a serious threat to this sovereignty, in the form of shock and awe interventions, brief occupations and hasty exits. Ignatieff's sweeping dismissal of the achievement of post-colonial states serves both to reinforce a Western hubris easily dismissive of other cultures, and to justify imperialist adventurism on a scale far wider even than that used to threaten the 'axis of evil'.[23]

The anti-imperialist tradition of the left should bring an understanding of the critical role of nationalism not just in state-formation, but also for many forms of democratic mobilization. In the past, this was true in Europe from the French Revolution on. It was self-evidently true of the colonial revolts against colonial rule. The idea that one can create democratic states in the teeth of local mass nationalism—which is the professed liberal imperialist program in Iran and much of the Muslim world—is a historical absurdity. This approach assumes a positively surreal form when it is argued that in Iran, for example, democratization can go hand in hand with submission to the will of the United States in foreign policy—when from their very origins in the 1890s, Iranian democratic politics have been associated with protest against Western domination.

In providing a bridge between the realist and progressive traditions, Niebuhr's thought therefore can help underpin a new US and Western strategy towards the rest of the world, and Eurasia in particular. Niebuhr was close to Morgenthau's notion of a 'cosmopolitan ethic' binding the representatives of different states in a common responsibility for peace and order—an idea which linked him and them in turn to the intellectual and practical architects of the various attempts at a 'concert of Europe' in the century before 1914. This 'cosmopolitan ethic' involves in turn a sense of humility in each of the participants, and a willingness not only to accommodate the legitimate interests of others where possible, but to acknowledge their right to build different kinds of state.

The approach of the past twenty years by contrast has been to try to extend US hegemony over wider and wider areas with economic help from the EU. This has worked well to date in Central Europe, where local nationalism pushes the countries concerned in a pro-Western and anti-Russian direction, and where the EU accession process, with all its immense economic benefits and transformative effects, has backed up the promise of US military protection.

[23] Martin Jacques, 'The Interregnum', *London Review of Books*, 26/3 (5 Feb. 2004).

Elsewhere, it must be obvious by now that the US-led transformation project has collapsed in the face of anti-American local nationalisms and intractable social and cultural realities. As British officials and soldiers have stressed, we will be very lucky in Afghanistan if we can leave behind minimal stability and peace—and even this will depend critically on the support of local states. In the Middle East, the Bush administration's rhetoric of democracy and freedom was accompanied—with almost Soviet hypocrisy—by an actual programme of backing a range of Sunni autocracies against Iran. In the former Soviet Union, EU enlargement has halted due to lack of will and money among existing members, and NATO enlargement has been stopped by a mixture of Russian power and the pro-Russian orientation of large parts of the population in the Caucasus, Ukraine, and Belarus.

If we are to help bring stability to these regions as a basis for economic, social, and political progress, we have to learn to do so together with, not against, local nationalism, and in alliance with, not against, powerful local states. In particular, the United States needs to seek reconciliation with Iran if it is to have any chance of developing and stabilizing Afghanistan. Better relations with Russia are part of the key to this, just as better relations with China can help bring China's ally Pakistan into a regional concert to stabilize Afghanistan, or at least contain the civil war that will probably follow eventual Western withdrawal.

The alternative—to press on with the Western campaign in Afghanistan without reaching out to the states of the region—involves a strong possibility not just of defeat and chaos in Afghanistan, but of extending the war to Pakistan as well. This would be a geopolitical catastrophe that would dwarf even what we have seen under George Bush's presidency. To avoid it, the US elites in particular need to develop a new awareness of the point of view of other peoples, and of the fact that while the US role in many parts of the world is bound to be temporary, the countries of the region will have to stay there forever, or at least as long as states themselves survive in the affairs of men.

President Obama himself may be capable of this, given his richly mixed origins and links with Africa. I have grave doubts, however, whether his subordinates like Clinton, and the intellectuals who advise them, will be capable of such an intellectual and moral leap. It would require a degree of imagination and vision that they have never demonstrated, and a capacity to distance themselves from the US nationalist mythology in which they were raised. Most are as far as can easily be imagined from 'a generous appreciation of the valid elements in the practices and institutions of other nations though they differ from our own', to repeat Niebuhr's words.

Moreover, even if they were capable of such a shift themselves, rendering it into policy would require great moral and political courage in confronting very powerful groups in the US establishment which would resist such changes in strategy to the bitter end. Since the individuals concerned have never shown such courage in the past, it seems optimistic to hope that they will do so in future. They will stand a much greater chance of achieving this intellectual and moral revolution, however, if they take the trouble to study the works of Reinhold Niebuhr.

13

Reinhold Niebuhr and the Use of Force

John D. Carlson

Near the end of his presidency in late 1992, George H. W. Bush placed an unprecedented and historically momentous call to Dick Cheney, his secretary of defense, and General Colin Powell, chairman of the Joint Chiefs of Staff. The president had been watching news coverage of the humanitarian crisis in Somalia, a famine of enormous proportion and human instigation. Warring clans were using relief supplies as a source of power. Rewarded to some, withheld from needy others, food in effect was being 'weaponized'. The gut-wrenching images of starving Somali children splashing across television screens elicited pity from around the world, including the highest corridors of power. 'Please come over to the White House', the president told his military counselors, 'I—we—can't watch this anymore. You've got to do something'.[1] Presumably, 'we' included the First Lady, who had been watching the news with him. But the president's words also reflected the compassion, urgency, and crippling sense of helplessness felt by millions of people. 'We', the world, he seemed to be saying, cannot tolerate this human suffering any longer. 'You', the US military, must do something to end it.

The vignette crystallizes the political phenomenon that was dubbed the 'CNN effect'. The force of 24-hour global news coverage to shape public consciousness and form public opinion would become (alongside the internet) an informational pillar of the era and phenomenon we now call globalization. The president's call also brings into stark relief—in ways that previous wars and military interventions often had not—the moral potential attendant upon the use of force. Like other international crises of the 1990s that followed—Rwanda, Bosnia, Kosovo—dire moral and humanitarian dimensions often took center stage. The post-Cold War context was crucial. With regional politics no longer framed by the nuclear context or a potential US–Soviet confrontation, new possibilities for using force emerged. New confusion was

---

[1] Cragg Hinnes, 'Pity, not U.S. security, motivated use of GIs in Somalia, Bush says', *Houston Chronicle*, 24 Oct. 1999, A11.

sewn as well. For how exactly did ending human suffering or preventing gross human rights abuses further the security interests of the United States or its allies?

The suffering in Somalia eventually prompted President Bush's commitment of US forces in December 1992 to help oversee the distribution of food. Far more memorable than the US's role in ending the famine was the ensuing phase when the US escalated its role from peacekeepers to peacemakers. The most vivid illustration of this heightened engagement played out when eighteen US servicemen were killed in October 1993 during a botched raid to apprehend Somali warlord Mohamed Farrah Aidid. Critics viewed the incident as the price paid for an impoverished ideal: the US willingness to commit blood and treasure on behalf of others in a place where no US interest was at stake. President Bush's admission years later that pity and compassion drove his military decision stoked new variations of an old realist critique, which, dating at least to Machiavelli, contends that politics is no place for emotional, effete—even womanish—propensities.[2] For many, the Somalia operations came to signify what happens when moral intentions run amok, hauntingly and tragically symbolized by television images of Somalis dragging the corpses of US servicemen through the dusty streets of Mogadishu. Were these not the very people whom US forces came to help? How could this be?

In Mark Bowden's bestselling *Black Hawk Down*, which meticulously chronicles the Battle of Mogadishu, the author reflects solemnly in his afterword: 'The foreign policy lesson I take from this story is like the old prayer, "Lord, grant me the strength to change the things I can, to accept the things I can't, and the wisdom to know the difference".'[3] For students of Reinhold Niebuhr, Bowden's incantation of the 'Serenity Prayer' comes as little surprise. Whether or not Bowden knew Niebuhr to be the author of this famous prayer, he speaks to a profound Niebuhrian worry about the limits of American military power. Bowden's book, like the 2001 Ridley Scott film of

---

[2] Machiavelli offered a stark account of this classical realist view, as when he lamented those religious and ethical attachments that hinder citizens and rulers from performing their civic duties or recognizing what political 'necessity' requires. More recently, Edward Luttwak castigated those willing to employ US forces for 'essentially disinterested and indeed frivolous motives, such as television audiences' revulsion at harrowing scenes of war'. Far better, he claimed, to 'resist the emotional impulse to intervene in other peoples' wars'. See 'Let Minor Wars Burn Out', *Foreign Affairs*, 78/4 (Jul./Aug. 1999), 37, 44.

[3] Mark Bowden, *Black Hawk Down: A Story of Modern War* (New York: Signet/Penguin Putnam, 1999), 427. Though an imprecise recitation of Niebuhr's words, Bowden adequately conveys the point. The evolutions and permutations of the Serenity Prayer are recounted by Niebuhr's daughter in Elisabeth Sifton, *The Serenity Prayer: Faith and Politics in Times of Peace and War* (New York: Norton, 2003).

the same name, graphically represents Niebuhr's caution that the US temptation to act—particularly for noble reasons and out of a sense of one's own innocence—can easily elide underlying political complexities and shroud moral ambiguities involving one's own interests or shortcomings. In Somalia, the United States quickly became engaged in cultural forces and civil strife that it poorly understood and was ill-prepared (if not unwilling) to confront fully. Bowden avers that 'it would have been hard for the United States not to go after Aidid, but it would have been better not to try'. When it escalated the use of force—going after the 'bad guys' withholding food from starving people—the United States displayed for the world the ambivalence and irony of this humanitarian mission, including the willingness to kill many in order to save a few. To wit, during the 3 October raid and subsequent efforts to rescue several trapped servicemen, US forces ended up killing (by many estimates) over 1,000 Somalis—again the very people whom US forces ostensibly sought to serve. Soon after the incident, President Clinton withdrew US forces from Somalia, leading to a spiral of political decay, civil war, and anarchy that continues as of 2010.

Despite the initial success of the mission to alleviate famine, the lessons of Somalia seemed to affirm classical realist reasoning that the use of force should be driven by national security interests. As Bowden concludes, not without evidence, 'The lesson our retreat taught the world's terrorists and despots is that killing a few American soldiers, even at a cost of more than five hundred of your own fighters, is enough to spook Uncle Sam.'[4] Unsurprisingly, the Somalia debacle also lowered the bar of US moral and political commitment to international crises in later years: the delayed commission of US forces in Bosnia,[5] the refusal to intervene in the Rwandan genocide that killed some 800,000 people, and NATO's delimited air campaign to stop ethnic cleansing in Kosovo.[6]

---

[4] Bowden, *Black Hawk Down*, 428. James Phillips notes that Osama bin Laden claimed to have trained and supported the Somalis who attacked American troops during the October 3 raid. In turn, 'the subsequent withdrawal of the U.S. peacekeeping forces from Somalia in 1994 was perceived as a triumph for bin Laden and probably encouraged him to launch increasingly devastating terrorist attacks against the United States to drive American forces out of Saudi Arabia', in James Phillips, 'Somalia and al-Qaeda: Implications for the War on Terrorism', *Heritage Foundation Backgrounder*, 1526 (5 April 2002), 1.

[5] See Mark Danner's penetrating review articles on the Balkan crises, particularly how NATO military action and the Dayton Accords codified many of Serbia's gains achieved in its ethnic cleansing campaigns: 'The US and the Yugoslav Catastrophe', *The New York Review of Books*, 20 Nov. 1997, 56–64, and 'Clinton, the UN, and the Bosnian Disaster', *The New York Review of Books*, 18 Dec. 1997, 65–81.

[6] The conduct of the 1999 air campaign elicited stinging critiques. Political philosopher and just war thinker Jean Bethke Elshtain decried the apparent turn to 'combatant immunity' in which protecting NATO combatant forces in the air trumped concerns about non-combatants

The events in Somalia and other crises of the 1990s were far from the political landscape Reinhold Niebuhr knew, occurring twenty or more years after he died, in the wake of the Soviet Union's demise and the Cold War that, among other world crises, shaped his outlook. It is doubtful that he could have conceived a situation in which a powerful nation would commit its military resources for purely moral purposes. Yet, he probably would not have been surprised that the anarchy and civil war consuming Somalia gave rise not only to more human suffering but also to terror cells and a growing piracy epidemic that has plagued some of the world's most vital shipping lanes. There is also deep worry over possible mergers between terrorism and piracy.[7] These more recent threats have returned to the fore the question of whether military intervention may become necessary again some day in Somalia. It is worth considering whether the moral outrages of the late twentieth century are related to emergent political threats in the early decades of the twenty-first.

A 're-globalized Niebuhrian' living in our times urges us to consider the moral-political connections of the international order.[8] Niebuhr keenly understood the deep and intricate connection between justice and order and between morality and politics that the use of force can bring into sharp relief.

(Serbian or Kosovar) on the ground. The strategy entailed excessive civilian casualties and damage to civilian infrastructure while allowing Serbian forces to operate with near impunity. See Jean Bethke Elshtain, 'Just War, Realism, and Humanitarian Intervention', in John D. Carlson and Erik C. Owens (eds.), *The Sacred and the Sovereign: Religion and International Politics* (Washington, DC: Georgetown University Press, 2003), 102–4. See also Michael Mandelbaum, 'A Perfect Failure: NATO's War against Yugoslavia', *Foreign Affairs*, 78/5 (Sept.–Oct. 1999), 2–8.

[7] A recent news story lays out such a scenario:

> 'Potentially, piracy is a platform for their [terrorist] activities', says Robert D. Kaplan, a fellow at the nonpartisan Center for a New American Security. 'There are already al-Qaida affiliates in Somalia. If they can make contact with pirate federations, then al-Qaida can use piracy as a form of terrorism.'
>
> In recent months, al-Qaida has strengthened its ties with a Somali terrorist group called al-Shabab. And experts worry that group, through clan ties or family connections, could give al-Qaida an opening to the pirates.
>
> . . . The failed state has become a breeding ground for terrorists. Terrorism experts say it is no accident that if you put a pirate and an al-Shabab fighter side by side, they are remarkably similar. Both are young, unemployed and highly impressionable. The pirates answer to warlords; the jihadists follow ideologues. The difference between them is so slight, experts worry they will start working together.

(Dina Temple-Raston, 'Experts Fear Al-Qaida May Turn To Piracy', *Morning Edition*, 14 April, 2009, <http://www.npr.org/templates/story/story.php?storyId=103064945>).

[8] Robin Lovin has offered us a bracing new vision of how Niebuhrian insight both enlarges and refines our global perspectives in the twenty-first century, in *Christian Realism and the New Realities* (New York: Cambridge University Press, 2008).

Niebuhr did not bequeath to us an elaborate theory of war or precise ethical criteria as can be found within the just war tradition, with which he is often—and, in my view, mistakenly—associated. Rather, the legacy of Niebuhr's ethical realism offers a supple and distinctive interpretative framework for understanding the coterminous yet sometimes conflicting claims of justice and order and how their relationship might guide and inform the use of military force. Thus might Niebuhr's thought illumine our understanding of war and peace in an age when humanitarian concerns and other moral dimensions of war are clearly present, frequently endangered and linked to broader security interests. In undertaking this approach, it is helpful to begin by placing some distance between Niebuhr and just war thought to give space for his insights to unfold on their own. What emerges instead is an 'ethical realist' approach that, in navigating between moralism and dark forms of realism, appreciates how military force highlights connections (or exacerbates tensions) between justice and order. Niebuhr's more expansive framework for conceiving the moral totality of war helps us fathom not only international crises of his day but new challenges of our own era such as the Iraq War and the Somalia crisis redux.

ENGAGING JUST WAR

Just war thought has become the dominant mode of ethical reflection on the use of force in the last fifty years. Reinhold Niebuhr, though, was not a just war thinker. He certainly believed in the moral justifiability of war, and his political writings perhaps helped facilitate the American recovery of just war thought in the twentieth century.[9] But Niebuhr himself was, at best, uneasy about the tradition, theory, or casuistry we today know well as 'just war'.[10] For him, it was an unequivocally Catholic permutation of medieval natural law tradition which, therefore, shared natural law's shortcomings. Niebuhr's general critique of natural law was aimed at its tendency to place 'undue confidence in human reason', since Niebuhr believed reason could not be exempted from 'the disease of sin'. Failure to acknowledge such noetic effects of sin, he claimed, has the effect of making natural law a 'vehicle of human sin'. Specifically, he worried that belief in 'unspoiled reason' gives way to the 'sanctity of a false universality'

---

[9] For a nice discussion of this, see chapter 10 of James Turner Johnson, *Just War Tradition and the Restraint of War: A Moral and Historical Inquiry* (Princeton: Princeton University Press, 1981), 325–66.

[10] I treat Niebuhr's relationship to just war at length in my 'Is There a Christian Realist Theory of War and Peace? Reinhold Niebuhr and Just War Thought', *Journal of the Society of Christian Ethics*, 28/1 (Spring/Summer 2008), 133–61.

which, in natural law's effort to transcend its finite medieval character, assumes the 'sinful pretensions of the age'.[11] Within just war thought, this critique applied to such ostensibly universal categories as legitimate authority, just cause, and the principle that just methods must be employed in war's prosecution. That Niebuhr attributes these tenets to the sixteenth-century Jesuit Francisco Suarez provides evidence for his view that such concepts are rooted in medieval political life.

For the purposes of this chapter, I set aside the precision of Niebuhr's critique of natural law as well as his only partial understanding of the just war tradition.[12] Yet, in spite of his narrow premises, trenchant insights do emerge. One significant shortcoming Niebuhr identified in just war theory's reliance on enduring moral principles and categories was an over-readiness to assume 'obvious distinctions' in a conflict: between justice and injustice, between aggression and self-defense. 'Not all wars are equally just', he maintained, 'and not all contestants are equally right. Distinctions must be made. But the judgments with which we make them are influenced by passions and interests, so that even the obvious case of aggression can be made to appear a necessity of defence.'[13] Evidence of this dynamic was on display in certain just war arguments over the 2003 invasion of Iraq. Many just war thinkers who supported the US case for war defended the policy of preemptive use of force, which putatively was necessary to defend the United States and protect its citizens against a potential act of aggression involving nuclear, biological, or chemical attack. Other just war critics—and many observers outside the United States—decried such arguments. Some even perceived the Iraq War as an instance of US aggression and construed appeals to self-defense as a deceptive pretext.[14]

I return later in the chapter to consider how Niebuhr's thought enhances our discernment of the Iraq War. Suffice it to say here that Niebuhr's apprehension about rendering definitively normative judgments, by making use of historically contingent categories, retains purchase in an era of globalization in which there is far from a consensus on the moral criteria of war (let alone the interpretation of them). What war-making body qualifies as 'legitimate

[11] Reinhold Niebuhr, *The Nature and Destiny of Man*, i: *Human Nature* (New York: Scribner's, 1941, repr. 1964), 277, 281.

[12] For example, Niebuhr does not seem to acknowledge that these principles have tendrils originating in antiquity or that, as others claim, just war has evolved significantly since the Middle Ages. Nor does Niebuhr address Protestant dimensions of just war thought as found in Luther, who is less frequently associated with natural law thinking.

[13] Niebuhr, *Human Nature*, 283.

[14] For different sides of this debate, see James Turner Johnson, *The War to Oust Saddam Hussein: Just War and the New Face of Conflict* (Lanham, MD: Rowman & Littlefield, 2005) and Richard B. Miller, 'Justifications of the Iraq War Examined', *Ethics and International Affairs*, 22/1 (Spring 2008), 43–67.

authority?' Which account of 'just cause' is authoritative? The indeterminacy of such fraught just war categories and rival just war approaches casts doubt on the ability to overcome debates within just war discourse, let alone with those who speak from outside the tradition. Given Niebuhr's well-known opposition to political pacifism, he might well have resisted those who, out of religious commitments to non-violence, appropriate just war as way to oppose any war.[15] But Niebuhr also would seem to warn against the dangers of 'just war statecraft', wherein a tradition that 'exists to serve statesmen' can dull our awareness of how political interests pervade certain claims to justice.[16] Appeals to justice must be evaluated critically, particularly when gilded by a moral discourse that claims to transcend political interest but can never operate independently of them.

For all of these reasons, justice is a provisional and partial concept in Niebuhr's thought. The political language of justice is never sufficient and must be leavened with love. 'There is no justice, even in a sinful world, which can be regarded as finally normative', he affirmed. 'The higher possibilities of love, which is at once the fulfillment and the negation of justice, always hover over every system of justice.'[17] Niebuhr did not mean that compassion and sentimental forms of love are sufficient constituents of statecraft, as the 1992 Somalia intervention perhaps illustrates. Rather, love's ability to shape and elevate the pursuit of justice, including the use of force for moral purposes, must be situated within—and inevitably compromised by—impure institutional contexts. The ability to give voice to humanitarian impulses and moral motivations depends vitally upon structures found in the political order. That nations and political institutions turn on their collectivized interests 'is not fatal to the establishment of justice'.[18] In fact, the very political bodies and authorities most tempted to misuse their power also frequently offer the best hope for the efficacious and practical defense of human dignity and freedom. But it is also the case that whatever justice is achieved will be relative to higher possibilities that simultaneously reveal the self-interested quality of institutions and the sinful and occasionally self-deceived authorities responsible for them.

For Niebuhr, just war is an attempt to achieve a moral judgment about the use of force that can transcend the historically contingent character of the moral criteria on which that judgment relies. Operating from a different starting point, Niebuhr's ethical realism presupposes the historical

---

[15] See his famous essay, 'Why the Christian Church is Not Pacifist', in Reinhold Niebuhr, *Christianity and Power Politics* (Hamden, CT: Archon, 1969 [1940]).

[16] George Weigel, 'Moral Clarity in a Time of War', *First Things*, 129 (Jan. 2003), 27.

[17] Niebuhr, *Human Nature*, 285.

[18] Reinhold Niebuhr, 'Augustine's Political Realism', in *Christian Realism and Political Problems* (New York: Scribner's, 1953), 127.

contingency of any claim to justice, which is a product of the tension between the infinite possibilities of love and the inescapably finite necessities and limitations of politics. The ultimate norm of love possesses a transcendent and enduring quality that distinguishes relative norms of justice from moral relativism more broadly. Hovering over every human and political scheme of justice, agapic or sacrificial love provides a constant spur to new forms of moral ambition that go beyond previous moral formula and formulations. As such, future moral judgments are not bound by past ones; rather, the pursuit of justice in political life evolves to accommodate the changing character of the political order. Thus might Niebuhrians today explain the recent emergence of humanitarian military interventions.

As a moral framework of war and peace, Niebuhrian ethical realism entails the commitment to translate the moral-humanitarian concerns enjoined by the love commandment into the language of justice, reconciling such concerns, however imperfectly, with the interests of nations and other institutions that constitute the political order. Ethical realism may be so called for three reasons: first, for the ability to integrate real—not simply imagined or constructed—moral concerns into the interests and dynamics of politics; second, for the realist insight that attending to moral concerns serves a polity's national interest, particularly its long-term legitimacy, strength, and viability. The point is well illustrated in Niebuhr's plea to rise above darker forms of political realism: 'the loyalty of a leavening portion of a nation's citizens to a value transcending national interest will save a "realistic" nation from defining its interests in such narrow and short range terms as to defeat the real interests of the nation'.[19] Finally, ethical realism suggests a propensity to be 'realistic' rather than idealistic about the morally limited and imperfect achievements polities generally have made, particularly when the pursuit of justice seems to conflict with their collective interests. Not all three features resonate equally among Niebuhr's followers, with some emphasizing certain aspects over others. Nonetheless, features of this ethical realist framework are evident in several discussions of war that Niebuhr himself took up.

JUSTICE AND ORDER

Niebuhr's political thought was steeped in an affinity for Augustine. He did not treat Augustine as a just war thinker as many do today. Rather, he was taken by Augustine's realist sentiments and his appreciation that

---

[19] Niebuhr, 'Augustine's Political Realism', 137.

'commonwealths are bound together by a sense of common love, or collective interest, rather than by a sense of justice; and they could not maintain themselves without the imposition of power'.[20] Augustine gleaned that politics requires thinking clearly about 'the power realities which underlie all large scale social integrations' and the coercive features that hold human communities together. Politics achieves order and militates against chaos. Without power, the moral character of social and political life cannot take form. Niebuhr contrasted such Augustinian realism with the tendencies of idealists or moralists who demur at the corrupting influences of power and who are disposed to certain 'illusions about social realities' given intense 'loyalty to moral norms and ideals, rather than self-interest'. On the other hand, unlike classical political realism, Augustine and Niebuhr's realism takes 'moral norms' seriously in the effort to prevent order from hardening into despotism. As he explains in his seminal work *The Children of Light and Children of Darkness*: 'the first task of a community is to subdue chaos and create order; but the second task is equally important and must be implicated in the first. That task is to prevent the power, by which initial unity is achieved, from becoming tyrannical.'[21] Niebuhr's ethical realism, then, navigates between two sets of poles: morally speaking, between idealism and classical political realism (sometimes depicted as a struggle between 'children of light' and 'children of darkness'); and, politically speaking, between anarchy and tyranny. These two modes of analysis converge for Niebuhr in and through the simultaneous pursuit and negotiation of order and justice, which structured his reflections on war and peace.

Niebuhr's clearest defense for the use of force emerges when the relationship between justice and order could be clearly established. Writing on the US Civil War, Niebuhr spoke of Lincoln's explicit willingness to save the union 'half slave and half free'. This is one way of saying that Lincoln was willing to put the interests of the state (i.e., to preserve the union and defeat secession) over the concern to liberate oppressed slaves.[22] Yet, Niebuhr also understood well that this was a provisional stance. Lincoln was no cynical realist but, rather, an ethical statesman who understood the necessities and limits of politics and war every bit as much as he saw the potential of politics and war to advance moral causes and end injustice. Niebuhr reflects,

---

[20] Ibid. 126.

[21] Reinhold Niebuhr, *The Children of Light and the Children of Darkness: A Vindication of Democracy and a Critique of Its Traditional Defense* (New York: Scribner's, 1944, 1960), 178.

[22] See Harry Stout's *Upon the Altar of the Nation: A Moral History of the Civil War* (New York: Viking, 2006), ch. 19, p. 184.

It was significant, however, that though Lincoln was prepared to save the union 'half slave and half free', it soon became apparent that this could not be done. The union could be saved only by abolishing slavery. This is a nice symbol of the fact that order precedes justice in the strategy of government; but that only an order which implicates justice can achieve a stable peace. An unjust order quickly invites the resentment and rebellion which lead to its undoing.[23]

Niebuhr observes that force was necessary if Lincoln hoped to 'save' the union. Politically speaking, only the resort to force could keep north and south together. But the moral meaning of this claim is that it would take a war to abolish slavery and make the union *worthy* of saving. Lincoln's ethical realism varied starkly from abolitionists whose religious opposition to slavery emanated from the same source as their opposition to war. 'William Lloyd Garrison was certain that the Christian ethic forbade the Civil War',[24] Niebuhr comments. This was an impoverished interpretation of Christian love wherein loving one's enemies entails abjuring war—such that one has no enemies. For Niebuhr, the more complex and daunting task of Christian love required discerning how to love one's opponent even (especially) when he is designated the enemy in time of war. This account of agape love Garrison seems not to have grasped. Indeed, Niebuhr implores, 'He never knew to what degree his self-righteous hatred of the South actually contributed to the inevitability of the conflict'. Another not so small irony was that when war did come, Garrison's deep moral commitments (to pacifism) undermined support for the effort that ultimately would vindicate his abolitionism.

Parallels between the moral and political dimensions of war also appear in Niebuhr's writings prior to the Second World War. Niebuhr peered deeply into the events leading up to the war, viewing the collective moral, political, and religious dimensions of the growing international crisis: 'every moral problem is political on the side of its application and religious on the side of the basic presuppositions from which the moral judgment flows'.[25] Niebuhr never separated his moral concerns from the broader political struggles of which they were a part. The crisis threatening the international order was steeped in injustice. In a famous essay, Niebuhr warned that Germany

[23] Niebuhr, *Children of Light*, 181.
[24] Reinhold Niebuhr, 'Love Your Enemies', in D. B. Robertson (ed.), *Love and Justice: Selections from the Shorter Writings of Reinhold Niebuhr* (Louisville, KY: Westminster/John Knox Press, 1957), 221. Lincoln also clashed with others whose firm anti-slavery commitments compromised his broader strategy. I explore in more detail the Civil War and the Second World War in my essay 'The Morality, Politics, and Irony of War: Recovering Reinhold Niebuhr's Ethical Realism', *Journal of Religious Ethics*, 36/4 (Dec. 2008), 619–51.
[25] Reinhold Niebuhr, 'To Prevent the Triumph of an Intolerable Tyranny', in Robertson, *Love and Justice*, 273.

intends to root out the Christian religion; that it defies all the universal standards of justice . . . that it threatens the Jewish race with annihilation and visits a maniacal fury upon these unhappy people . . . that it explicitly declares its intention of subjecting other races of Europe into slavery to the 'master' race . . . that it intends to keep them in subjection by establishing a monopoly of military violence . . . that it is already engaged in Poland and Czechoslovakia in destroying the very fabric of national existence . . . that, in short, it is engaged in a terrible effort to establish an empire upon the very negation of justice rather than upon the minimal justice which even ancient empires achieved.[26]

Niebuhr's moral and religious analysis amplified his appreciation of the growing political threat as Hitler marched through Europe. It afforded him a perspective that was prescient though very much resisted by many isolationists and pacifists in his day. For moral, religious, and political reasons combined, Niebuhr called for the use of force—war—to end the 'intolerable tyranny' of Nazism a full year before the attack upon Pearl Harbor and the US entry into war. He also recognized and expressed his concern about Hitler's plan for the Jews two years before Roosevelt publicly acknowledged the Holocaust.

Niebuhr's ethico-political grasp of the threat that extreme injustice posed to the international political order enabled him to foresee the political dangers sooner, to articulate his position with greater passion and precision, and to issue calls to action in more persuasive ways than was evidenced by the US government at the time. One wonders if Niebuhr knew of Winston Churchill's claim that the Second World War was 'an unnecessary war' that could have been prevented—or, preempted, we might say today—by attacking Germany in 1938 or 1939.[27] Many resisted such forward-leaning views and deplored the 'rush toward war'. Against such critics, though, Niebuhr shot back,

I believe that contemporary history refutes the idea that nations are drawn into war too precipitately. It proves, on the contrary, that it is the general inclination, of democratic nations at least, to hesitate so long before taking this fateful plunge that the dictator nations gain a fateful advantage over them . . .[28]

This passage reveals not only Niebuhr's view that coercion and force are necessary constituents of politics but that those who resist this reality are vulnerable to giving sanctuary to evil. This strident contention reflects the

---

[26] Ibid. 274–5.
[27] See Jeffrey Herf's succinct discussion of the 'unnecessary' Second World War in his 'Liberal Legacies, Europe's Totalitarian Era, and the Iraq War: Historical Conjunctures and Comparisons', in Thomas Cushman (ed.), *A Matter of Principle: Humanitarian Arguments for War in Iraq* (Berkeley: University of California Press, 2005), 50–3.
[28] Niebuhr, 'Intolerable Tyranny', 272.

times and contexts of Niebuhr writings, particularly his unstinting polemic against pacifist moralists.[29]

Yet it is hard to imagine him making the same kinds of assertions—about the too infrequent use of force—during the Cold War. Amidst the arms race and nuclear balance of power that ushered in an utterly different and tenuous new international order, the careless use of force risked confrontation that could result in the elimination of entire peoples and nations. So, while Niebuhr's justice–order dynamic shaped his support for the Second World War, not all questions of force found such neat overlap in the era that followed. We look now to an example that illustrates a more delicate tension between justice and order. In so doing, we see further how Niebuhr's war and peace framework differs from just war thought.

ORDER OVER JUSTICE?

A different articulation of the relationship between justice and order emerges in a 1955 statement that Niebuhr co-authored with Episcopal bishop Angus Dun. The purpose of 'God Wills Both Justice and Peace' was to aid the Christian's conscience in matters pertaining to the use of force. In the statement, Niebuhr and Dun discuss three just war positions. They specifically critique those just war views (found in Roman Catholic and other ecumenical settings) which contend that 'modern warfare, with its mass destruction, can never be an act of justice'. However, they express explicit support for the duty to participate in war that vindicates 'an essential Christian principle: to defend the victims of wanton aggression, or to secure freedom for the oppressed'—a position put forward earlier at a previous meeting known as the Oxford Conference.[30] The 'essential Christian principle' seems to provide the most succinct statement of Niebuhr's view on the moral justifiability of war. Unlike the other just war positions described, this approach allayed Niebuhr's qualms with 'elaborate formulas' that, like some forms of just war reasoning, can become overly legalistic. This articulation 'has the merit of simplicity and flexibility in the face of changing crisis', Niebuhr claims. But, he notes, 'It also has the weakness of giving little precise guidance to the conscience.'

---

[29] In addition to Niebuhr's most famous critique of pacifism, 'Why the Christian Church Is Not Pacifist', in Niebuhr, *Christianity and Power Politics*, see also part IV of *Love and Justice*.

[30] Angus Dun and Reinhold Niebuhr, 'God Wills Both Justice and Peace', *Christianity and Crisis*, 15/10 (13 Jun. 1955), 77.

In an intriguing passage from the Dun–Niebuhr statement, they gloss briefly on the justice–order dynamic as related to this 'essential Christian principle':

A war to 'defend the victims of wanton aggression,' where the demands of justice join the demands of order, is today the clearest case of a just war. But where the immediate claims of order and justice conflict, as in a war initiated 'to secure freedom for the oppressed,' the case is now much less clear. The claims of justice are no less. But because contemporary war places so many moral values in incalculable jeopardy, the immediate claims of order have become much greater.[31]

In this caveat, Niebuhr (with Dun) here suggests that lines can—and, at times, should—be drawn between defending against aggression, on the one hand, and securing freedom or liberating the oppressed, on the other. While the former entails a clear cause of justice, the latter, given the nuclear context of the Cold War and the destructive potential of a Western–communist face-off, puts justice at cross-purposes with the competing value of political order. Niebuhr makes clear, though, that it is not only a political but also a moral imperative that obliges one in the nuclear age not to initiate 'a war of incalculable consequences to end such oppression'. In this instance, a larger moral and political rationale justifies not pursuing what might otherwise be a plain instance of a just military intervention.

To consider a more contemporary example, one could have made a similar argument (and some did) that the effort to liberate Iraqis from the oppressive regime of Saddam Hussein would gravely undermine political order in Iraq and beyond. The massive destruction of Iraq's infrastructure, the barbarous insurgency, and the costly sectarian warfare following the invasion all would seem to vindicate Niebuhr's concern that a pursuit of justice to secure freedom from an oppressor can jeopardize essential moral and political foundations of order.

The deliberative effort to weigh competing goods of justice and order parallels just war calculations of proportionality (though Niebuhr makes no such mention of this longstanding tenet). Instead, Niebuhr seems to affirm 'the essential Christian principle' (and caveat) because it provides the broadest and least restrictive formulation for guiding the use of force. He even concedes it may 'breathe more of a crusading spirit' into the discourse than many Christians would find appealing. In this sense, Niebuhr moves in a different direction from many just war thinkers in his day (and our own) who often conceive the tradition as a way of limiting the occasions for war. Throughout this discussion Niebuhr also implicitly distinguishes between the general *concept* of a just war—armed conflict that is justified by the claims of justice or other moral

[31] Ibid.

values—and the specific principles and formulations of the just war *tradition*. Indeed, Niebuhr seems able to affirm even the general concept of just war because 'the essential Christian principle' (of defending against aggression and securing freedom for the oppressed) departs sufficiently from what Niebuhr understands to be just war doctrine's characteristic rigor and formulaic precision.

What is particularly noteworthy, though, is that Niebuhr actually has trouble sustaining 'the essential Christian principle' without simultaneously undercutting his earlier insights about the dangers of presuming not at all obvious distinctions between aggression and defense, between justice and injustice. The eminent just war thinker Paul Ramsey picked up on this confusion, noting that Niebuhr's embrace of, and caveat to, 'the essential Christian principle' preserves and confounds the kinds of distinctions Niebuhr earlier called into question. Ramsey observes,

> Since the Dun–Niebuhr statement, however, the Hungarian revolution has shown that sometimes the obligation to restrict action in face of more serious consequences, or the consideration of order as well as justice that was mentioned, cuts right across the distinction between defense against aggression and securing the freedom of the oppressed.[32]

Ramsey seems to question the coherence of this Niebuhr–Dun caveat which privileges order over and against justice based upon an overstated differentiation between aggression and oppression. Specifically, Niebuhr and Dun likely had in mind a distinction between using force as self-defense against an outside aggressor and using force to intervene on another's behalf to secure freedom for the oppressed. But Ramsey rightly notes that the 1956 Hungarian Revolution, in which Hungarian anti-Communists rose up against Soviet and Soviet-backed oppressors, eludes such easy classification.

More broadly, though, Ramsey seems to want to hold Niebuhr to his earlier caution about the impossibility of making obvious distinctions (for example, between justice and injustice, aggression and defense). These cautions still retain currency even in our contemporary context. For example, the Iraq War raised worries about obvious distinctions: between the justice of overthrowing a brutal tyranny and the injustice of sectarian violence that followed, or between the aggression Saddam's Iraq made against other countries and the 'preemptive self-defense' of the US, which, in overthrowing a sovereign government by force, was perceived widely as aggression. Niebuhr's framework of war prompts us to question categories and distinctions that are often assumed to be clear-cut

---

[32] Paul Ramsey, *War and the Christian Conscience: How Shall Modern War Be Conducted Justly?* (Durham, NC: Duke University Press, 1961), 89.

or absolute. Ramsey's critique reinforces this effort, while perhaps going further to question Niebuhr's own occasional distinction between justice and order.

It is not my view that Niebuhr's amendment to the essential Christian principle—his prescinding of justice and order—undermines his Christian realism or insights on war. Niebuhr amply understood the interrelationship between justice and order, their mutual interdependence, and, over time, the inability to make obvious distinctions between them. Justice without order will soon turn to anarchic injustice. Order without justice cannot sustain itself without cruelty and terror. Niebuhr's ethical realist framework of war and peace turns on the tensions and challenges of achieving and preserving a just order of politics. Niebuhr remains a helpful guide today as we seek to integrate justice into the contemporary order of global political life.

BETWEEN TYRANNY AND ANARCHY

When in 1991, President George H. W. Bush launched the Persian Gulf War, he declared the military effort to rout Saddam Hussein's regime from Kuwait to be of a piece with a 'new world order' heralded by the end of the Cold War. Indeed, following the collapse of the Soviet Union, its newly reconstituted forces joined the United States and other nations under a UN flag that many thought would be the model of legitimate authority for future wars. The Gulf War precedent hung over the president's son, George W. Bush, when as president he declared war on Iraq in 2003. The younger president announced that the effort to unseat Saddam Hussein would be made up of a coalition of the willing, cobbled together after the failed UN Security Council attempt to authorize (explicitly) the use of military force to conduct regime change. George W. Bush's challenge to the prevailing perception of the international order undermined support for his moral argument for war, including his effort to secure freedom for oppressed Iraqis. But the Iraq War also undermined the national interests of the United States, if gauged by loss of life to US servicemen and women, political instability in Iraq and the Middle East, a costly financial burden, the emboldening of other adversaries in the regional balance of power, and loss of US standing in the world. Finally, it was widely perceived that the controversial preemption defense threatened the international order by establishing a precedent by which regional actors might set off future wars. For these and other reasons, many traditional political realists opposed the war.[33]

---

[33] John J. Mearsheimer, 'Hans Morgenthau and the Iraq War: Realism versus Neo-Conservatism', <opendemocracy.com> (posted 19 May 2005).

As the war dragged on, the US administration assured the public that history would judge favorably its decision to depose Saddam Hussein in spite of countervailing costs and even in spite of the falsity of the original claims about WMD or Iraq's dangerous links to terrorists. Indeed, some contended that the moral causes were so strong that the political arguments were no longer paramount: the justice of the Iraqi liberation overrode the costs of the upheaval it caused to the international order or even the violent disorder that overwhelmed Iraqi society in the months and years after.

This line of argumentation offers a strong case for why Niebuhr's ethical realism could not be appropriated to support the US administration's case for war. But it does not follow that Niebuhr would have shared the views of many critics of the war whose arguments were steeped in a form of moralist perfectionism. Indeed, drawing out the implications of Niebuhr's justice–order dynamic and his defense of the 'essential Christian principle', an ethical realist defense for the Iraq War seems quite conceivable had it attended as concertedly to the threat Saddam Hussein posed to his own citizens as to the perceived threat he posed to the international order. In short, it seems naive to believe that a long-term solution to Iraq's efforts to circumvent UN resolutions, let alone ending Saddam's repression of Iraqis, could have been achieved without the use of force—that is, as long as one assumes (as I do) that the existing regime of sanctions and inspections remained a morally and politically suspect policy. Yet, that kind of argument also would have entailed locating the claims to justice and the appeals to securing freedom for the oppressed within a scheme that was more attentive to the semblance of international order that existed before the invasion and to the need for social order in Iraq afterwards. An ethical realist argument in support of overthrowing the tyranny of Saddam Hussein also would have shown greater prudence, patience, and humility sufficient to mitigate the US foreign policy pietism which presumed that the justice of one's cause was more important than careful and detailed planning to provide basic order and security in post-war Iraq.[34]

The Iraq War offers a lesson in how easily America can be blinded by its righteousness. Like the idealist children of light whom Niebuhr warned about, many in the United States underestimated how brazenly its interests were on display to the rest of the world during the run-up to war. These interests involved something more than simple concerns for national security, which would have been understandable enough had they been jeopardized as desperately as was contended. For the existing international order still acknowledges the right to wage war—even preemptively—when imminent

---

[34] A fuller version of this argument appears in my 'Morality, Politics, and Irony of War'.

danger lurks. Nor do the charges of empire or crusade explain the phenomenon. Rather, the American self-interest that was sublimated through moral rhetoric was nothing less than the desire to assert one's identity and ideals that is common to all nations; the aspiration to have one's values recognized and respected; and the zeal to vindicate one's innocence and goodness before the world. The irony of this messianic strain of moralism, Niebuhr gleaned, is that when we fail to recognize how our own self-interest adulterates our cause, the strength of our moral convictions becomes a liability. Virtue turns to vice: 'a too confident sense of justice always leads to injustice.'[35]

Knowledge of how the mind is impaired by sin helps guard us against using our moral pretensions to shroud or cloak our actions, particularly in times of war. Niebuhr's realism helps the mind gain 'a clearer view of the total human situation and become conscious, in some degree, of the confusion and dishonesty involved in its action ... When the self in contemplation becomes contritely aware of its guilt in action it may transmute this realization into a higher degree of honesty in subsequent human actions.'[36] A commitment to contrition and moral renewal—prior to, amidst, and following the conduct of war—must be as sturdy as the moral causes for which one undertakes war.

If the Iraq War provides a cautionary tale for confronting contemporary forms of tyranny, the crisis plaguing Somalia—with its ongoing civil war and lack of permanent government—reminds us of the other extreme of anarchy that coercive force often must resist and correct (much of which will occur from within Somalia). Like the Iraq War, a central problem posed by the 1993 Somalia operations was that costly blood and treasure were expended in ways that, according to many, impaired or were unnecessary to the national interest. While this judgment was understandable in 1993, Niebuhr's framework for war invites us to rethink the contemporary context. Specifically, we now have a much clearer sense of the dangers that anarchy and failed states pose to the international order including piracy, terrorism, and regional war. These concerns—along with a basic moral regard for the humanitarian toll anarchy has taken on Somali people—all point to the converging claims of justice and order, which together might again some day justify the use of external military force from an ethical realist stance. One small incident pointing to the combined moral–political status in Somalia is the recent rescue by the US Navy of the captain of the *Maersk Alabama,* who was taken hostage by Somali pirates. It is no small point that we remember his cargo ship was transporting humanitarian aid to Ethiopia at the time it was overtaken.

---

[35] Reinhold Niebuhr, *The Irony of American History* (New York: Scribner's, 1952), 138.
[36] Niebuhr, *Human Nature,* 259.

CONCLUSION

Ethical realism invites us to see how moral concerns are often intimately bound up in the affairs of states and their effort to bring a minimal level of order to their common life together. But this approach does not offer precise formulae or principles for employing force beyond appreciating the connections between justice and order. For that reason, much like Niebuhr warned of 'the essential Christian principle' and the effort to navigate between anarchy and tyranny in the pursuit of a just international political order, ethical realism can leave a troubling sum of latitude for the resort to war. For this reason, it is imperative to recall Niebuhr's cautions about the limits of force. I end by noting two.

First, the actual application of military power—what Niebuhr described as the 'ultima ratio' of international relations—must always be carefully circumscribed. Military force, as we have seen in Somalia and Iraq, can give way to intense violence and disorder, no matter the justice of the cause. To wield military might like a 'meat ax' rather than like a 'surgeon's tool', Niebuhr warned, not only risks excessive loss of human life and unnecessary destruction but also undermines the moral and political prestige necessary for nations such as the United States to live up to their responsibilities. In this vein, after the use of force, 'healing must follow quickly upon its wounds'.[37]

Secondly, the political situations in which military power can be justifiable and effective are also limited by the moral and political factors that inform ethical realism. Niebuhr was keenly aware of the limits of force, and his words from over fifty years ago ring true today. 'Military power is, in short, ineffective when it lacks a moral and political base. It is the fist of a hand; but the hand must be attached to an arm, and the arm to a body; and the body must be [in place] before the fist can be effective'.[38]

Niebuhr described the moral character of the body politic in an essay opposing further US military involvement in Vietnam entitled 'The Limits of Military Power'. What is striking is that Niebuhr rendered this proleptic and prudent judgment in 1955, well before the height of the war or the domestic crisis it spawned. Niebuhr, of course, was no communist apologist.[39] But he understood deeply how moralists and those who appeal to virtue to justify war—whether political officials, advisers, military leaders,

---

[37] Niebuhr, *Moral Man and Immoral Society* (New York: Touchstone, 1932, 1960), 220.
[38] Niebuhr, 'The Limits of Military Power', in *Love and Justice*, 192.
[39] One of his essays rhetorically asks 'Why Is Communism So Evil?', in Reinhold Niebuhr, *Christian Realism and Political Problems* (New York: Scribner's, 1953), 33–42.

and foreign policy makers with all the attendant sources of power available to them, or their boosters—can ironically turn their pursuit of justice to opposite effect. This occurs when they are blinded by their moralism and do not see how their efforts to vindicate their values through war will bleed through their actions for all the world to see. Thus, the prudential rules of realism, diplomacy, and statecraft must always be followed, preferably in ways that limit force and that produce moral accretions, however gradual, to the existing political order.

Here it seems prudent to give Niebuhr the last word, again from 'The Limits of Military Power':

It is well to remember that in collective, as well as individual life, the force which coerces the body but does not persuade the will can have only negative influence. It can prevent something that we abhor more than conflict, and it can enforce our will and purpose momentarily on a recalcitrant foe. But the loyalties and cohesions of the community are managed and transfigured not by force but by wise statecraft. Therefore our [US] military power cannot be as potent as we think in making our world hegemony sufferable either to our friends and allies or to ourselves. Britain learned the limits of force in Ireland and then in India. We have not had comparable lessons, which may be the reason we do not have a comparable wisdom.[40]

Since Niebuhr wrote these lines, there have been considerable occasions for such 'comparable lessons'. The question for our times is whether we will use those occasions to garner the comparable wisdom that Niebuhr commends.

---

[40] 'The Limits of Military Power', 195.

14

The Irony of American Evangelical Politics

Kevin Carnahan

American evangelical political theology is facing a crisis of self-identity. Many evangelicals have claimed that evangelical political theology has been taken captive by the Republican Party. In reaction, evangelical reformers have attempted to wrest their political theology from the grip of partisan political programs. God, they claim, is not a Republican or a Democrat. Despite agreement on this project, however, proposals in American evangelicalism have failed to provide a political theology that maintains a sense of evangelical public responsibility and a sense of God's transcendence over partisan political debates. This essay argues that Niebuhrian Christian Realism offers a theological approach that could open new avenues for political thought which might carry evangelicals past their present conundrum.

I will first shortly summarize the position of the religious right as the backdrop to the current reform movements in evangelicalism. I will then survey several of the proposals of the evangelical reformers. The deficiencies in these proposals, I will suggest, are tied to (i) their inability to move beyond a model of ethics that reads the Bible as a sourcebook for rules which can be directly applied to human history; and (ii) their unwillingness to qualify the claim that the purpose of political activity is to bring about progressive realization of the kingdom of God within history. I will go on to explore Niebuhr's critique of Billy Graham's individualism and Graham's deployment of purportedly biblical rules in efforts to win converts and order Christian lives within history. Niebuhr, I will suggest, offers a model of political ethics in which the perfect ethic at the core of the biblical narrative problematizes every effort to apply a biblical ethic directly to history, and complicates any effort to participate in a progressive realization of the kingdom of God. I will conclude by arguing that while recent proposals for reforming evangelical political theology have addressed Niebuhr's critique of individualism, they have not

I am indebted to John Sanders, J. Aaron Simmons, and Robert Zajkowski for their comments on earlier drafts of this chapter.

attended sufficiently to his arguments against the attempt to apply biblical rules to history.

A BACKDROP FOR REFORM

By the late 1970s a group of American fundamentalists were coming to reject the sectarian political quietism that had guided the last half-century of their own movement. Reacting against the removal of prayer from school and the legalization of abortion, the religious right entered the culture wars that had been stirring in America for the last decade.[1] They sought to establish the sovereignty of God over American law and culture. Curiously, however, according to the religious right, God's sovereign will almost always paralleled the policies of the Republican Party. By the turn of the millennium the relationship between the Republican Party and the religious right had become so tight that after a Republican victory, Jerry Falwell could claim that 'The Church won the 2004 election.'[2]

For many evangelicals, the politics of the religious right has raised questions about the ordering of its religious and political convictions. Challenging the political plans of the religious right is nothing new within evangelical circles. Evangelicals like Jim Wallis and Ronald Sider were arguing for alternative visions of evangelical politics even before the religious right rose to prominence. Today, however, criticism of the religious right is gaining momentum from a new generation of evangelicals who did not live through the culture wars of the last century, and are seeking a less partisan model of political thought. In this context, despite its continued prominence, many suspect that a new evangelical political movement will come to take the place of what David Gushee has called the 'graying evangelical right'.[3]

THE EVANGELICAL REFORMERS

Jim Wallis and Tony Campolo are two of the most prominent voices seeking to provide an evangelical alternative to the religious right. Wallis' *God's*

---

[1] George Marsden, *Understanding Fundamentalism and Evangelicalism* (Grand Rapids, MI: Eerdman, 1991), 98–121.
[2] David Gushee, *The Future of Faith in American Politics: The Public Witness of the Evangelical Center* (Waco: Baylor University Press, 2008), 47.
[3] Ibid. 87.

Politics (2005) quickly became a bestseller, and introduced the phrase 'God is not a Republican or a Democrat' into evangelical discourse. The problem, they claim, is that the religious right was not religious enough—it abandoned the true teachings of Jesus. 'It is almost as if the real message of Jesus has been kept a secret', Wallis writes, 'utterly disguised by prosperity pastors, television evangelists and radio talk show hosts who preach a conservative American religion across the world, giving a very different impression of Christianity than Jesus taught.'[4] The upshot of this is that the 'process of actualization' of the kingdom of God, inaugurated by the incarnation of Christ, has been stymied. The solution is to reclaim the 'broader moral vision' provided by Jesus, and thus to become 'the ultimate swing vote' in American politics.[5]

In practice this 'turn' toward 'biblical politics' leads to greater emphasis on issues of social justice, an activist stance on environmental issues, a tendency toward pacifism, and a reinterpretation of what the gospel requires on traditionally religious right issues. On abortion, for instance, Wallis and Campolo defend a consistent ethic of life, but question the effort to illegalize abortion, citing evidence that this has not been a successful strategy in lowering the number of abortions.[6] They favor economic and social reforms that would support poor mothers who would often choose to abort because of strains on their lives. Thus abortion is transformed into an issue that demands progressive social action.

This solution to the problem of evangelical politics has not been universally lauded. Nor have all of its detractors emerged from the religious right. Some have charged that Wallis and Campolo have simply embraced a new partisanship. David Gushee, locating Wallis and Campolo as representatives of the 'evangelical left', states that: 'the question can legitimately be asked whether the evangelical left has steered fully clear of becoming a bloc within the Democratic Party'.[7] Wallis and Campolo, Gushee suggests, could be seen as 'essentially drifting away' from the 'evangelical' and 'biblical view' on issues such as abortion and homosexuality.[8]

This does not lead Gushee to advocate a return to religious right politics. The true solution to the problem, Gushee concludes, is to enter politics with one's loyalty given exclusively to Jesus Christ.[9] This means *really* holding to

---

[4] Jim Wallis, 'Foreword', in Tony Campolo, *Red Letter Christians: A Citizen's Guide to Faith and Politics* (Ventura, CA: Regal, 2008), 10.

[5] Ibid. 11.

[6] Jim Wallis, *God's Politics: Why the Right Gets it Wrong and the Left Doesn't Get It* (San Francisco: Harper, 2005), 297–301; and Campolo, *Red Letter Christians*, 119–26.

[7] Gushee, *The Future of Faith in American Politics*, 84.

[8] Ibid. 80–2.

[9] Ibid. 50.

the biblical ethic, advocating a politics that is entailed by the 'specifiable, this-worldly content' of the kingdom of God.[10] In practice this means emphasizing social justice issues against the tendencies of the right, and being more activist than the evangelical left against homosexual marriage and abortion.[11] This is the position Gushee identifies with the 'emerging Evangelical Center'.

Unfortunately, Gushee's proposal does not seem to solve all the problems of evangelical political ethics. First, questions should be asked about the grounding of Gushee's charges against the evangelical left. His claim that the evangelical left 'does not signal that it takes fully seriously the sanctity of *all* human life, including those lives developing in the womb' begs the question against Wallis and Campolo who have stated their support of a consistent ethic of life and have argued that their policy proposals would bring about a decline in abortions. Like Gushee, Wallis and Campolo have claimed that their analysis is grounded on no less secure a source than the Bible. This disagreement is not about whether the Bible provides principles from which a political policy on abortion can be deduced. The disagreement is about what lies at the end of the chain of deduction. At the very least, further argument is needed to show how the participants are claiming to deduce these particular policies from the Bible.

This model for using the Bible in policy debates leads to a second oddity of Gushee's proposed reform in evangelical politics. Despite his own efforts to escape the right and the left, it seems on Gushee's account that God is *only contingently* neither a Republican nor a Democrat. If the evangelical center could convince either party to take up 'Evangelical Center' policies, or if Gushee could start an 'Evangelical Center' party, it seems that God would be a member of that party. God is a partisan politician. God is just not a partisan of the evangelical right or the evangelical left!

Given the problems in the above positions it is not surprising that some evangelicals have sought even more radical projects to extricate themselves from the problems of partisanship. Greg Boyd, an evangelical minister and theologian, has articulated yet another alternative that makes clear why Christians must stand against the forms of politics advocated by both the right and the left.[12] Christ's kingdom, he writes, is not the same as the kingdom of the world (John 18:36). The kingdom of this world is a kingdom ruled by coercion which is organized toward the realization of human ends.

---

[10] Ibid. 9.

[11] This is only a partial list of Evangelical Center issues. See ibid. 88–91.

[12] Greg Boyd, *The Myth of a Christian Nation: How the Quest for Political Power is Destroying the Church* (Grand Rapids, MI: Zondervan, 2005), 9.

Christians are members of God's kingdom on earth, and their lives should be lived as manifestations of this kingdom in imitation of Christ. As Boyd explains, according to the Bible, 'the central goal of Jesus' life was to plant the seed of this new kingdom so that, like a mustard seed, it would gradually expand.... We are to be nothing less than "the body of Christ," which means, among other things, that we are to do exactly what Jesus did.'[13] This means that, in contrast to the coercive liberal or conservative politics of the world, Christian lives must be constituted by acts self-sacrificial love. *Really, really* taking seriously the biblical ethic requires living one's life outside of the coercive political scheme. Christians, Boyd concludes, must be absolute pacifists.[14] While Boyd claims that his position does not entail that Christians withdraw from politics, he does say that participation in partisan activities— such as voting and public argument—should be radically relativized in importance while service is raised to a predominant place in the Christian life.[15]

Several questions should be asked about the consistency of Boyd's position. If God's self-sacrificial action has such radical implications when applied to defense of self, nation, and family, why does it not have the same implications when it comes to other forms of participation in coercive worldly politics? What justifies the Christian in continuing to vote, or to pay taxes that support military expenditures, or argue for particular forms of worldly politics at all?

Further, Boyd's position raises questions about the function of Christology in Christian ethics. There can be no doubt within Christianity that Christ's action provides the ideal that should be imitated to the highest degree possible by Christians. But in his emphasis on the need to imitate Christ, Boyd obscures the distinctness of Christ, and the extent to which Christ's perfect act of love is impossible to imitate. As the theologian Paul Ramsey writes:

His incarnation, his life as the God-man among us, his suffering, his death, his resurrection were unique, never to be repeated. Certainly not by us. He was THE Pattern, so as at any moment to assume an accusative role of Judge. He is the Pattern, yet also Savior. We are neither co-Creators nor co-Saviors. Hence, as the Reformers knew, we are to follow him—*from a distance.*[16]

---

[13] Greg Boyd, *The Myth of a Christian Nation: How the Quest for Political Power is Destroying the Church* (Grand Rapids, MI: Zondervan, 2005), 9.

[14] Ibid. 161–73.

[15] Ibid. 12, 127–46.

[16] Paul Ramsey and Stanley Hauerwas, *Speak Up for Just War or Pacifism: A Critique of the United Methodist Bishops' Pastoral Letter 'In Defense of Creation'* (University Park, PA: Pennsylvania State University Press, 1988), 113.

In a competition to see who can more fervently apply biblical rules to history, each evangelical reformer ends up reducing the biblical ethic to one or another historical project which falls short of transcendence and the glory of God. This is perhaps the case because the evangelical reformers have not taken their reformation far enough. Despite efforts to diverge from the religious right, the evangelical reformers have all agreed with the political theology of the religious right on two key points. First, they use language that suggests a model of moral judgment that seeks to deduce particular policies for life within history directly from biblical propositions. In the context of this model all disagreements about political policy must arise from one side failing to take the Bible sufficiently seriously, or failing to apply it consistently. This is straightforwardly the case for Gushee, Wallis, and Campolo. It is also the case for Boyd inasmuch as the truths deduced from the biblical ethic determine the form of life for the Christian, even as secular political policies are (utterly?) relativized. Second, evangelical reformers tend to maintain an image of Christian political action as aiding the progressive realization of the kingdom of God within history. Both these presuppositions must be challenged if evangelical political theology is to overcome its self-diagnosed ailment. In taking the reformation of evangelicalism to its next stage, it is useful to look back to a friendly critic of evangelicalism from the past: Reinhold Niebuhr.

NIEBUHR AND THE NEO-EVANGELICALS

The religious right was not the first movement to break away from fundamentalism. In the 1940s and 1950s the neo-evangelicals, represented by Billy Graham and the faculty of Fuller Theological Seminary, preceded the religious right. The neo-evangelicals were reclaiming the revivalist impulse in the evangelical tradition.[17] They were also rebelling against anti-intellectualism, opening themselves to a wider ecumenism, and seeking to reclaim a social activism that marked evangelicalism prior to the American fundamentalist/modernist split.

As the neo-evangelicals emerged from fundamentalism, they met theologians with significantly different theological pedigrees from their own. Reinhold Niebuhr was one of these theologians in the unique position of having enough overlap with the neo-evangelicals to prompt their attention,

---

[17] Marsden, *Understanding Fundamentalism and Evangelicalism*, 62, 68.

while remaining sufficiently distinct to sustain a rigorous prophetic critique of their positions.

As the neo-evangelicals had been contemplating their break with fundamentalism, Niebuhr had been breaking away from the extremes of liberal theology in America. Niebuhr rejected the scriptural inerrantism favored by some fundamentalists and neo-evangelicals as contrary to the best lights of the Christian tradition.[18] Still, Niebuhr's criticisms of the liberals overlapped with those offered by the fundamentalist forefathers of the neo-evangelical movement. Christian liberals had, Niebuhr claimed, abandoned the revelation of the 'absolute word of God' in favor of a message of historical human progress. 'Consequently', Niebuhr writes, 'the Christology of liberal Christianity departed from the classical and Biblical Christology.'[19] The need for Christ's unique atoning act was abandoned by liberals as they forgot about the entrenched nature of sin. This was a point on which the neo-evangelicals could find common ground with Niebuhr.[20]

Niebuhr's apologetics also resonated with some neo-evangelicals. E. J. Carnell wrote a dissertation on Niebuhr's apologetics.[21] While president of Fuller, Carnell would write that he could 'cheerfully acknowledge' his debt to Niebuhr. 'It was only as I studied Christian realism, long after I graduated from seminary', Carnell reflects, 'that I began to sense the power of pride and pretense in my own life.'[22] Carnell later used the Niebuhrian language of 'pride and pretense' when critiquing sectarian fundamentalists who thought that they could purify the Church by eradicating the sins of the modernists while ignoring their own sinfulness.[23]

---

[18] Niebuhr favored Luther's hermeneutics, which he saw as invoking 'a principle of criticism of Scripture itself in the Christ of Scripture'. See Reinhold Niebuhr, *The Nature and Destiny of Man*, 2 vols. (New York: Scribner's, 1964), ii. 202. For an account of the contrast between the early reformation view of scripture and the later 'protestant scholasticism' that grew into fundamentalism, see Gary Dorrien, *The Remaking of Evangelical Theology* (Louisville, KY: Westminster John Knox Press, 1998), 19–24.

[19] Reinhold Niebuhr, *Essays in Applied Christianity*, ed. D. B. Robertson (New York: Meridian Books, 1959), 124.

[20] Niebuhr had been impressed in his early life with the theme of God's judgment and forgiveness in the preaching of Billy Sunday. See Richard Fox, *Reinhold Niebuhr: A Biography* (Ithaca, NY: Cornell University Press, 1996), 47–8. Compare Niebuhr's claims to J. Gresham Machen's argument that liberal theology had compromised Paul's theology of the cross by transforming Christ from a divine being who atones for sin into a thin moral exemplar: J. Gresham Machen, *The Origin of Paul's Religion* (New York: Macmillan, 1921).

[21] E. J. Carnell, *The Theology of Reinhold Niebuhr* (Grand Rapids, MI: Eerdmans, 1960).

[22] E. J. Carnell, 'Can Billy Graham Slay the Giant?', *Christianity Today*, 1/16 (1957), 3–5, at 4.

[23] E. J. Carnell, *The Case for Orthodoxy* (Philadelphia: Westminster Press, 1959), 116 (for context, see Dorrien, *The Remaking of Evangelical Theology*).

Niebuhr too recognized that he shared some theological common ground with the neo-evangelicals. Niebuhr found 'some of the central themes of the Christian faith' in the work of Billy Graham.[24]

It may come as a surprise to the enlightened critics of the famed evangelist, Billy Graham, that his message is, despite its obscurantist framework ('The Bible says . . . '), or probably because of it, infinitely superior to the other popular versions of the Christian, or at least Protestant, message. Graham has preserved something of the biblical sense of a divine judgment and mercy before which all human strivings and ambitions are convicted of guilt and reduced to their proper proportions.[25]

This was not, however, enough to make Niebuhr an advocate for Graham's crusades. While Graham had recovered some central biblical themes, Graham made two mistakes when dealing with sin.[26] First, he failed to appreciate the social dimensions of sin. Second, he suggested that individual religious conversions could solve all the problems of the individual and the society within history.[27]

Niebuhr called Graham out for both errors. The liberal Social Gospel movement, represented especially by Walter Rauschenbusch, had failed to articulate a sufficiently robust account of sin and Christocentric soteriology. But Rauschenbusch and his followers, Niebuhr concluded, had been faithful to the Bible in areas where the neo-evangelicals failed. This was especially true with regard to the prophetic recognition that judgment for sin came not only against individuals, but also, and especially, against societies and social structures.[28] This made the social gospel movement 'infinitely more realistic than the pietistic individualism' manifest in Graham's revivalism.[29]

The upshot of Graham's individualism was a hobbled Christian ethic. Graham's preaching focused on personal, uncontroversial moral issues like alcoholism to bring about a change in the heart of the individual, but could not articulate a prophetic word against the sins embedded in a systematically sinful society. Graham's failure was especially visible on the question of race.

---

[24] Reinhold Niebuhr, 'Varieties of Religious Revival', *New Republic*, 132/23 (1955), 13–16.

[25] Reinhold Niebuhr, *Pious and Secular America* (New York: Scribner's, 1958), 21.

[26] Niebuhr, *Essays in Applied Christianity*, 123–31.

[27] See Graham's comments in Mark Noll, *American Evangelical Christianity: An Introduction* (Malden, MA: Blackwell, 2001), 52; and David Lockard, *The Unheard Billy Graham* (Waco, TX: Word Books, 1971), 97. Niebuhr's favorite example of Graham's naivety was Graham's claim that one could solve the problem of atomic war by converting people to Christ. See Reinhold Niebuhr, 'Billy Graham's Christianity and the World Crisis', *Christianity and Society*, 20/2 (1955), 3–4.

[28] Reinhold Niebuhr, *Faith and Politics*, ed. Ronald Stone (New York: George Braziller, 1968), 38.

[29] Niebuhr, *Essays in Applied Christianity*, 127.

Graham held personally responsible attitudes toward racial equality and even integrated his crusades, much to the chagrin of his fundamentalist critics. But Graham failed to preach extensively on the subject, or to push for social restructuring of American society.[30]

As Graham's individualism led him to be unrealistic about the mechanisms for bringing relatively greater justice, Graham's overstatement of the benefits of conversion led him to overestimate what the Christian could achieve within history. Graham spoke as if conversion could bring about total individual and social fulfillment within history. It was only possible to preach such a message, Niebuhr saw, inasmuch as Graham had reduced the demands of the Bible to maxims that were useful for drawing converts. The Bible was treated as a sourcebook for principles that, when applied, happened to parallel the ideal life of a middle-class white American family living in the 1950s. Living as an imitation of Christ was thus reduced to living as a good father, hard worker, and responsible citizen. This ideal represented a standard that most of Graham's audience failed to reach, but one which they could live up to if sufficiently motivated.

Niebuhr resisted all such reductive uses of the biblical narrative. This is because he saw that at the heart of the Bible not a rulebook for history, but a story of historic human failure and ultimate divine victory that problematized any attempt to move directly from the biblical story to a historical human ethic. Christ was not simply a good father, hard worker, or temperate person. Christ was the ideal human, through whom God 'reconciles the whole of the world to Godself', allowing for the ultimate salvation of every person.[31] Christ's death on the cross—his self-giving, opening the way to the fulfillment of the need of every neighbor in need—is the 'goodness' of Christ and the 'symbol of the fulfillment of human selfhood'.[32] This is the story of perfect love, a love that provides for all who are in need. Christ's act on the cross is the antithesis of partisanship; it is the offer of universal salvation through self-sacrifice. The ideal revealed in Jesus is as uncompromising as it is definitive.

[30] Reinhold Niebuhr, 'Differing Views on Billy Graham', *Life Magazine*, 43/1 (1957), 92; Dorrien, *The Remaking of Evangelical Theology*, 56. There is a Niebuhrian irony in that Niebuhr himself, while insulated from many social pressures that would have restrained Graham, was never as much of an activist on the issue of race as he encouraged Graham to be. See Gary Dorrien, 'Niebuhr and Graham: Modernity, Complexity, White Supremacism, Justice, Ambiguity', in Michael G. Long (ed.), *The Legacy of Billy Graham*. (Louisville, KY: Westminster John Knox Press, 2008), 141–60.

[31] Reinhold Niebuhr, *The Structure of Nations and Empires* (New York: Scribner's, 1959b), 136; and also Niebuhr, *Essays in Applied Christianity*, 126–7.

[32] Niebuhr, *The Structure of Nations and Empires*, 136.

Through this act Christ reveals both the promise and the despair of humanity. It is the despair of humanity inasmuch as it reveals that within history, as Niebuhr writes, 'the final possibilities of social virtue cannot be realized'.[33] Christ's perfect act falls outside the reach of finite human action within history. History is stained by human sin. The noetic affects of sin render humans incapable of loving consistently. But even if this were not the case, humans within sin-stained history would not be able to live up to the law of love. Because of the stain of sin, conditions are such that any simply historical action will deliver goods to some only at the expense of others. In a world marked by sin, action within social life entails partisanship. The perfect principle of self-sacrificial love is always already compromised when it is invoked within history. Efforts to argue directly from the core of the biblical narrative to an applied ethic in history will be deluded attempts to apply a perfect ethic to an imperfect world. This can only result in advocacy for an imperfect ethic with overstated claims for certainty and security of the moral analysis involved.

Conversion is not a solution to this problem. The Christian is justified but not saved within history.[34] Knowledge of God's act eases the anxieties that set the stage for sin. But more than others, Christians ought to know the dangers of deluding themselves into believing that they can apply, or participate directly in God's ultimate politics. They know of the height of God's act and the depth of the sin that has corroded history. As a measure beyond possible realization within history, God's politics of love stands as a 'principle of indiscriminate criticism', over against all standards and institutions within the sinful world.[35] God is not a partisan politician because no partisan project can offer salvation to all people, and this is ultimately what God brings about.

This does not, however, mean that the Christian ethic is irrelevant to historical politics, or that the Christian has an excuse for irresponsibility. Christians do gain moral content from the Bible. They learn of the ideal of perfect love, of the image of perfect harmony in the kingdom of God, and of the ways in which sinful humans distort judgments. Using the ideal of love as principle of 'discriminate criticism', the Christian has an obligation to enter into public discourse and contribute to the maintenance of relative justice within history.[36] In contrast to a model in which the Bible is treated as a source for first principles from which one can deduce particular political

---

[33] Ibid. 135.

[34] Niebuhr, *The Nature and Destiny of Man*, ii. 198.

[35] Reinhold Niebuhr, *The Essential Reinhold Niebuhr*, ed. Robert McAfee Brown (New Haven: Yale University Press, 1986), 113–18.

[36] Ibid. 116–18.

policies, the model of moral discernment here is one of moving from an ideal embedded in the biblical narrative to an approximation of the ideal under imperfect conditions.

It is helpful to draw an analogy. Imagine a situation in which two groups of three persons are each given the task of arranging themselves so as to create a perfect square. One group may arrange itself with one person lying on the floor while the two others take positions standing at the head and feet of the first, thus using (relatively) right angles and the lengths of their bodies to create the impression of a square while leaving one side of their representation empty. The other group may decide that having a closed geometric shape is more important than the presence of (relatively) right angles, and thus contort their bodies so as to produce a (relatively) closed, but more rounded figure. Over time the groups may discuss the criteria they employ in the process of approximating the square. Some regulative principles (such as 'being a closed shape' and 'having right angles') may become stable criteria for judging amongst approximations. The ideal square is relevant to judgments about the approximations. But criteria cannot be simply deduced from contemplation of the square, nor can one simply apply the requirements of 'being a square' to the situation. Criteria must arise from the practice of finding possible approximations. In a similar way, Christians should proceed from the ideal of perfect love in the kingdom of God to the world of history.

The Christian does this with humility, recognizing her or his own continuing temptation to sinfulness, and recognizing that while God has revealed the ideal of human life, God has not revealed the measure of an approximation of the ideal. Arguments about approximations of the ideal take place within the muddiness of historical human interaction.[37] Multiple policy combinations and forms of life may measure up equally well in approximating the ideal, even while they manifest different balances of goods. No system within history will realize all goods simultaneously. At every turn, the Christian should be expected forthrightly to acknowledge the particular costs associated with her or his proposed approximation.

This approach to the biblical narrative also makes clear why it is problematic from the Niebuhrian perspective to speak of participating in a *progression* of the kingdom of God within history. Humans, Niebuhr stresses, are not in control of history. They react to the conditions into which they have been placed, and in those conditions ought to seek to approximate the kingdom.

---

[37] Niebuhr, *The Nature and Destiny of Man,* ii.252; also Niebuhr, *The Essential Reinhold Niebuhr,* 143; and Reinhold Niebuhr, 'The Problem of a Protestant Social Ethic', *Union Seminary Quarterly Review,* 15/1 (1959), 7–11.

There is no assurance that conditions will always allow for fuller approximations of the kingdom in the next moment than in the last, and history is often
marked by ironic reversals that set back purported social progress. The
political role of the Christian is not to maintain the progress of the kingdom
of God (as if this were in her or his power), but to seek out and advocate the
best approximation of kingdom flourishing that is available at any particular
moment.

In Graham's efforts to entice people to convert, Graham had obscured the
ongoing tragedy of history into which God had come, and from which God
ultimately offered salvation to all people. Graham's emphasis on what
God *had done* in Christ led him to obscure what God *had still to do* in the
parousia, and led him to confuse justification and salvation in the moment of
conversion. As Niebuhr wrote:

This pietism, invariably coupled with perfectionist illusions, knowing nothing
about the Reformation's restoration of the part of the gospel which revealed the
moral ambiguity in the life of the redeemed, is still powerful in the evangelistic
traditions... It has come to our notice in our own day because it has a personable
and honorable exponent in the person of Billy Graham.... There are no perfectionist
solutions for the problems of an atomic age—or indeed of any age in which men have
accepted responsibility for the justice and stability of their communities and civilizations, and yet have had the grace to measure the distance between the divine holiness
and all fragmentary human righteousness.[38]

NIEBUHR, PROPHET TO THE EVANGELICALS?

Though Billy Graham later recalled that he had appreciated Niebuhr's criticisms, these criticisms did not lead Graham to adjust his evangelistic
program.[39] This is unfortunate inasmuch as it allowed the religious right to
build upon Graham's mistakes. Combining individualism and a view of the
Bible as a rule book for history in a more aggressive form than Graham had
imagined, the religious right delivered a position which was both tone deaf to
social injustices and arrogant in its efforts to deduce from the Bible a legalistic
code to uphold its understanding of the demands of individual responsibility.
Without a sense of the transcendence of perfect love above all particular
biblical commands, as Niebuhr would have predicted, the appeal to scriptural

[38] Niebuhr, *Essays in Applied Christianity*, 127–8.
[39] Billy Graham, *Just as I Am* (San Francisco: Harper San Francisco, 1997), 301.

norms 'merely resulted in one more human effort to find an absolutely secure and safe position, beyond historical ambiguities and contradictions'.[40]

The evangelical reformers have found the truth in at least part of Niebuhr's critique of Graham. While individualism remains prominent in evangelical ethics, leaders like Wallis, Campolo, Gushee, and Boyd have recognized that the Gospel has a significant social dimension. As Campolo writes: 'It has taken Evangelicals like me far too long to come around to embracing Rauschenbusch's kind of holistic gospel that not only promises eternal life to individuals but also offers hope for dramatic positive changes in our present social order.'[41]

At the same time, however, evangelical reformers have resisted recognizing the truth of Niebuhr's second critique. As Campolo continues:

It would remain for Reinhold Niebuhr and others of later decades to raise the awareness that there is something desperately wrong with all of us, and that assimilating the spirit of Christ as some kind of transforming moral influence is not enough to create the new humanity Rauschenbusch envisioned. I wish Rauschenbusch had asserted the need for personal conversion in which an individual enters into a dialogue and transforming relationship with a living Christ. We Evangelicals . . . affirm the need for a miraculous transformation of who we are into what we should be, a transformation that comes as Christ himself invades our hearts and minds and souls—as mystical as that might sound.[42]

This is an invocation of Niebuhr that ignores the force of Niebuhr's position. While acknowledging the reality of sin, Campolo stresses the impact of conversion and obscures the limitations of Christian action in a sin-stained world. The upshot is that Campolo corrects for Rauschenbush's error in obscuring the limitations brought by sin, then recreates the affect of Rauschenbush's error by obscuring the distinction between present justification and eschatological salvation.

The upshot is a new evangelicalism that in practice parallels the mistakes of the Social Gospel movement in thinking that it can, by one reading of the biblical ethic or another, simply apply God's revealed ethic to the world of sinful humanity. What follows is a game of one-upmanship in claiming that the politics *I* propose is *really* the biblical ethic as applied directly contemporary political society. Thus Wallis and Campolo claim to be 'red letter Christians' reading off the words of Jesus to determine that abortion should be combated with economic measures while Gushee complains that they have

[40] Niebuhr, *The Nature and Destiny of Man*, ii. 203.
[41] Paul Rauschenbush et al., *Christianity and the Social Crisis in the 21st Century: The Classic that Woke up the Church* (New York: Harper One, 2007), 75.
[42] Ibid. 78.

not yet understood that the *true* biblical ethic requires more aggressive action against abortion. None have fully appreciated that all efforts to implement biblical justice within history are ironic in that they entail a contradiction of that same measure of justice. The principle of the sacredness of life, for instance, is itself already a derivative of the law of love, which at times within sinful history conflicts with other principles (such as the 'sanctity' of human freedom) that would be united in a society governed by perfect love. Further, the principle of the sacredness of life itself underdetermines particular judgments within history inasmuch as at times choices must be made between sacred lives. Illegalizing abortion would protect some lives at the cost of suppressing the freedom of some, and at the cost of the lives of others. Treating abortion with economic measures would be an unstable solution inasmuch as economics is never within the control of any group, and can end up rewarding poorly chosen behaviors. Which of these lesser evils one chooses is important. But it is wrong to sully the perfection of God by identifying any of these solutions with God's ultimate politics. God is not a Republican or a Democrat, but this is not because these parties have not yet found the true biblical policy. It is because God's ultimate politics transcends the possibilities of historical politics through a love and power that dwarfs the power of any historical political platform.

On this point, at least, Boyd is right. God's kingdom is a kingdom driven by love and not by force, and God's kingdom is not of this world. Boyd, however, errs in thinking that biblical principles might still be applied unproblematically within the individual Christian life. Despite Boyd's claims to be living the 'simple, straightforward, and uncompromising' way of the kingdom, here again, we find the reduction of the perfect law of love into historically realizable maxims.[43] Christ's perfect peaceableness is only part of Christ's perfect love. Christ's act combined peaceableness with the provision of perfect justice in the kingdom. Such is not always an available action for the Christian within history.[44] Efforts to manifest peaceableness in times of conflict may allow the unjust to lord over the innocent. To allow such is certainly incompatible with Christ's example, which gave nothing over to injustice. Boyd's effort to apply the biblical ethic to history, as Niebuhr would have predicted, reduces the principle of perfect love to something less than its full form. The tension between Boyd's wish to maintain some level of political activity and his advocacy for absolute non-coercion can be read in a Niebuhrian framework as the predictable outcome of an overly simplistic biblical legalism.

---

[43] Boyd, *The Myth of a Christian Nation*, 15.
[44] Niebuhr, *The Nature and Destiny of Man*, ii. 88.

In various ways, all of these moves in contemporary evangelical political theology have emerged from attempts to apply the biblical ethic to historical existence, and to participate in the progressive realization of the kingdom of God in history. The alternative is not an abandonment of political responsibility and social activity. The alternative is a humble wrestling with the various approximations of love that are available in history. There is no final security in this process, and there can be no one Christian political program. Security is found only in what *God* has done and what *God* will do for the ultimate salvation of humanity. Until God comes again, politics is a game of responsibility without security in which the Christian is called to be an always humble prophet drawn by the standard against which we are measured and recognizing that this measure is finally beyond our grasp.

CAN EVANGELICALS BE NIEBUHRIANS?

What, then, are the prospects that Evangelicals will take up this solution to their problems? Given the diversity of evangelicalism, there is no contradiction between being a Niebuhrian and being an evangelical. Niebuhr's is a thoroughly biblically grounded ethic, even though it is an ethic that denies any simply application of the biblical ethic to human history.[45] Niebuhr's moral theology is entirely compatible with a robustly orthodox conception of the Christian faith, whether evangelical or not. Recently, many of the evangelical reformers have even taken to quoting Niebuhr in their own arguments. When criticizing American exceptionalism during the invasion of Iraq, Wallis cited Niebuhr's insight that 'every nation, political system, and politician falls short of God's justice, because we are all sinners'.[46] Ronald Sider, a famous evangelical reformer, has gone so far as to call Niebuhr 'America's greatest political theologian'.[47] Despite holding to the effort to deduce historical rules from the biblical ethic, many of the evangelical reformers have also been more open than the religious right to the possibilities of disagreements in interpreting the implications of the biblical ethic.[48] The step to a Niebuhrian realism may be a reasonable conclusion of the reformation that some

---

[45] Some evangelicals have sought alternative models to biblical legalism. See Ronald Sider, *The Scandal of Evangelical Politics* (Grand Rapids, MI: Baker Books, 2008), 49–75; and Richard Mouw, *Politics and the Biblical Drama* (Grand Rapids, MI: Eerdmans, 1976).

[46] Jim Wallis, 'Dangerous Religion: George W. Bush's Theology of Empire', *Sojourners*, 32/5 (2003), 20–6, at p. 24.

[47] Sider, *The Scandal of Evangelical Politics*, 34.

[48] See, for instance, Campolo, *Red Letter Christians*, 119–26.

evangelicals have already begun. Taking this last step requires only that the Christian find again the story of Christ's act of salvation at the center of the biblical narrative rather than a set of rules for life, and that in the light of Christ's act accepts her or his place as a penitent creature that tills the ground until God calls history home.

15

Reinhold Niebuhr and the Problem of Religious Pluralism

Wilfred M. McClay

After a lengthy period of being distinctly out of favor and fashion, the work and person of Reinhold Niebuhr seem rather suddenly to have made a serious comeback in moral, theological, and even political discourse in the anglo-phone world.[1] This is in many respects a remarkable turn of events. Niebuhr had already faded from the theological scene in the latter years of the Cold War, and until very recently stood condemned in the eyes of his many influential critics as an apologist for the Western liberal status quo—or, as in Stanley Hauerwas's famous words, a 'chaplain to power'.[2] Not only were his moral reasoning and ethical probity called into question by his critics, but even the reality and depth of his Christian commitment.[3] The cold and calculating features of 'Christian realism' seemed to betray—most disappointingly because it became most operative in crucial instances such as war and power politics—not only a Machiavellian amorality, but an utter disbelief in the radical claims and transformative power of the Christian Gospel, and an unwillingness to take seriously the central Christian claim of the Lordship of

---

[1] The political element arose in the course of the 2008 US presidential campaign, beginning with some remarks by the *New York Times* columnist David Brooks: 'Obama, Gospel and Verse', 26 Apr. 2007, A21, in which Barack Obama was quoted saying that Niebuhr was one of his 'favorite philosophers'. This led to much speculation about the extent to which Obama's political outlook was 'Niebuhrian'. See for example Liam Julian, 'Niebuhr and Obama', *Policy Review*, 154 (Apr./May 2009), found at <http://www.hoover.org/publications/policyreview/41687702.html>; and Krista Tippett et al., 'Obama's Theologian: David Brooks and E. J. Dionne on Reinhold Niebuhr and the American Present', found at <http://speakingoffaith.publicradio.org/programs/2009/obamas-theologian/video-brooksdionne.shtml>.

[2] Hauerwas has attacked Niebuhr with frequency and gusto. see especially his Gifford Lectures, *With the Grain of the Universe: The Church's Witness and Natural Theology* (Grand Rapids: Brazos Press, 2001). In a related vein, see John Milbank, 'The Poverty of Niebuhrianism', in *The Word Made Strange* (Oxford: Blackwell, 1998), 233–51; and the various works of John Howard Yoder.

[3] Hauerwas, *With the Grain of the Universe*, 87–115.

Christ, i.e., the belief that the person and teaching of Christ should, and does, reign supreme. For in this view, the claims of the Gospel, though foolishness to men, were the source of a power far beyond that offered by the world. Niebuhr, it seemed, was an apostate and a hypocrite.

This brash and unsparing critique of Niebuhr was, I believe, unfair and overblown, in the typical manner of generational academic polemics.[4] Its excesses were a reflection, and perhaps a partial cause, of the general margin-alization experienced by theology, and particularly public theology, in the years since Niebuhr's death. The attacks could be so wild because the stakes had become so small, and no one outside the seminar world cared much what theologians thought about politics. The genuine defects of Niebuhr's thought, for example in the area of ecclesiology, were and are just as visible in the thought of Hauerwas, whose idiosyncratic blend of Catholic and Mennonite perspectives lurches toward a kind of sectless sectarianism, offering little practical direction and less help in thinking through the question of religious pluralism.[5] Yet discourse abhors a vacuum, and it was inevitable that an author of Niebuhr's undeniable substance, a first-rate theological mind that could produce a masterwork like *The Nature and Destiny of Man*, would eventually once again command a thoughtful and sympathetic readership.[6]

But the immediate reasons for Niebuhr's return, at least in the United States, have mainly to do with the fresh and troubling problems of war and international conflict that have emerged in the post-9/11 era. The peculiarly brutal and terrifying means used by the radical jihadists of al-Qaeda and other militant Islamist groups, and the fierce and radical totality of their animus toward the West, seemed to slam the door on a brief interlude of meliorist hopefulness, and indicated the need for a more robust theological doctrine of evil, as well as a view of human affairs that took into account the reality of intractable human conflict. More generally, the concerns stirred up by the controversial work of the late Samuel Huntington reflected an effort to understand whether the post-Cold War world order would be the product of hardwired 'civilizational' conflict, or some other organizing principle; and the events of 9/11 only gave added impetus to such concerns and debates.[7]

The introduction of Niebuhr brought to such discussions a moral com-plexity, an awareness that while the West surely needed to defend itself, and needed to do so in ways that were realistic about the nature of power in the

---

[4] Gabriel Fackre, 'Was Reinhold Niebuhr a Christian?', *First Things*, 126 (Oct. 2002), 25–7.

[5] See the insightful analysis in Jeffrey Stout, *Democracy and Tradition* (Princeton: Princeton University Press, 2004), esp. 149.

[6] Reinhold Niebuhr, *The Nature and Destiny of Man*, 2 vols. (New York: Scribner's, 1941–3).

[7] Samuel P. Huntington, *The Clash of Civilizations and the Remaking of World Order* (New York: Simon and Schuster, 1996).

world, it also needed to do so in ways that recognized its own flaws, its own blindnesses, and its own susceptibility to corruption and power-seeking, not to mention the moral dangers inherent in any struggle in which one is tempted to place all virtue on one side and all vice on the other. Niebuhr seemed to many writers at the time, myself among them, to provide resources for striking that near-impossible balance, of defending oneself effectively while recognizing the enemy's humanity, and owning up to one's own all-too-human faults.[8]

Clearly, whatever the value of Huntington's specific arguments about the shape of the twenty-first-century world, he was surely right in pointing out what is painfully obvious, that the element of religious conflict is never far absent from the world's most dangerous chronic flashpoints. Whether religious ideology is itself a generative source of conflict, or a proxy for other political, cultural, and social factors, whether its presence imparts a particular inflection to conflicts, making them either more or less intractable, or whether its influence manifests itself in other and subtler ways, these are questions that need not detain us here. The point is that religious conflict is a continuing reality which we are very far from having put behind us, and we are unlikely to succeed in doing so in any readily foreseeable future. The dream of a comprehensively secularized world order, so immensely plausible as to seem inevitable to so many Westerners just a few decades ago, seems literally incredible today.[9]

There are, as James Madison famously argued in *The Federalist Papers*, two ways to deal with the problem of faction in human affairs.[10] One can seek to eliminate the causes of faction. That, however, is precisely the option that has failed, since it would mean the reduction of all religions to one religion, or one post-religion. Or one can seek, not to swallow up all factions, but to accept their multifarious existence as a feature of the human condition, and indeed an expression of the most fundamental of all human liberties, and one should therefore restrict one's efforts to the management of the factions' effects.

The latter option remains the only sensible and humane one open to us, particularly in the religiously vibrant and diverse world we actually inhabit. Such respectful accommodation to the reality of deep religious faction is precisely the goal of all doctrines of religious pluralism, which seeks to balance

[8] Wilfred M. McClay, 'The Continuing Irony of American History', in *First Things*, 120 (Feb. 2002), 20–5.

[9] Two of many works offering this theme are John Micklethwait and Ardian Wooldridge, *God is Back: How the Global Revival of Faith is Changing the World* (New York: Penguin Press, 2009); and Peter L. Berger (ed.), *The Desecularization of the World: Resurgent Religion and World Politics* (Grand Rapids, MI: Eerdmans, 1999).

[10] I refer here especially to Madison's celebrated analysis in Federalist #10.

strong adherence to particular faith traditions in strong communities of faith, but insists upon room for tolerance of difference in the interactions between and among such communities and faiths.

*   *   *   *   *

Is Reinhold Niebuhr's body of work useful in addressing this problem? At first glance, one would most definitely think so. During his heyday, Niebuhr was admired not only by his liberal Protestant brethren, but also by many other mainline Protestants, Catholics, Jews, and notably by secularists such as the historians Perry Miller and Arthur M. Schlesinger, Jr., whose enthusiasm for Niebuhr gave rise to the quip (often attributed to the Harvard philosopher, Dewey admirer, and Niebuhr non-admirer, Morton G. White) that there ought to be an organization called 'Atheists for Niebuhr'.[11] These men and women of widely different intellectual and theological stripes shared a belief that Niebuhr provided a way of understanding moral responsibility that was at once vigorous and reflective, and that guarded against the epistemological immodesty of thinking that any human being could be fully in possession of the truth.

In addition, Niebuhr now and then put forward elements in a doctrine of religious pluralism that seem remarkably prescient, and remarkably applicable to present-day circumstances. Consider, for example, this passage from his 1944 work, *The Children of Light and the Children of Darkness*, where he explores the possibility of a 'religious solution of the problem of religious diversity':

> This solution makes religious and cultural diversity possible within the presuppositions of a free society, without destroying the religious depth of culture. The solution requires a very high form of religious commitment. It demands that each religion, or each version of a single faith, seeks to proclaim its highest insights while yet preserving an humble and contrite recognition of the fact that all actual expressions of religious faith are subject to historical contingency and relativity...Religious toleration through religiously inspired humility is always a difficult achievement. It requires that religious convictions be sincerely and devoutly held while yet the sinful and finite corruptions of these convictions be humbly acknowledged; and the actual fruits of other faiths be generously estimated.[12]

It is hard to imagine a deeper and more morally serious effort to limn such a pluralist order, and imagine what kinds of hearts and minds it would require (and presumably produce). And let it be noted that Niebuhr is not merely

---

[11] Donald Meyer, *The Protestant Search for Political Realism: 1919–1941*, 2nd edn. (Middletown, CT: Wesleyan University Press, 1988), p. xx.

[12] Reinhold Niebuhr, *The Children of Light and the Children of Darkness: A Vindication of Democracy and a Critique of Its Traditional Defense* (New York: Scribner's, 1944), 134–8.

arguing for religious pluralism as a *political* doctrine, as a way of managing inevitable conflict for the more general benefit of a peaceable polity. He is doing something far more ambitious. He is envisioning the cultivation of religious toleration not merely as a process of bracketing one's own religious beliefs in the encounter with others, but as itself the product of redoubled *religious* intensity, as a kind of ascetic spiritual discipline leading to an ever-higher form of religious commitment. Nor, interestingly, does toleration for him involve the believer in a sympathetic engagement with the traditions of the other, so much as it does a penetrating self-critical gaze directed inwardly by each individual believer. It is, so to speak, a largely self-regarding rather than other-directed discipline.

Yet for all its initial moral appeal, such an approach may in the end have less to offer than it might seem, as a generalizable defense of religious pluralism. As I will attempt to show in what follows, Niebuhr's outlook was grounded in, crucially dependent upon, and inseparable from certain distinctive features of the Christian cultural and intellectual tradition. These features can be reduced to two: first, a robust concept of original sin, a concept that for him means something far more than just the recognition of human limitation and fallibility; and second, a belief in the idea of progress, grounded in doctrines that are, and remain, uniquely Christian. To grasp how this is the case, and how Niebuhr's grounding in these two fundamentally Christian assumptions makes him an uncertain guide to a more neutral form of pluralism (if such neutrality is possible, a legitimate question that I hope can also be raised by this essay), I think it will be useful to follow some of the key steps in Niebuhr's development.

*   *   *   *   *

Born in 1891 in rural Missouri, he was the son of a German immigrant pastor affiliated with a tiny Protestant denomination known as the German Evangelical Synod.[13] He inherited from his father not only a strong sense of theological vocation, but a keen interest in social and political concerns. As a consequence of that influence, as well as his two years at Yale Divinity School, Niebuhr began his pastoral career as a devotee of the Social Gospel: the movement within liberal Protestantism that located the Gospel's meaning in its promise as a blueprint for progressive social reform, rather than in its assertions about the nature of supernatural reality. Social Gospelers were modernists who played down the authority of the Bible and the historical creeds, insisting that the heart of the Christian gospel should be understood

[13] For biographical details, I rely upon Richard Wightman Fox, *Reinhold Niebuhr: A Biography* (Ithaca, NY: Cornell University Press), 1985.

symbolically, and expressed in the language and practice of social reform. In Walter Rauschenbusch's words, 'we have the possibility of so directing religious energy by scientific knowledge that a comprehensive and continuous reconstruction of social life in the name of God is within the bounds of human possibility'. The Kingdom of God was not reserved for the beyond, but could be created in the here and now, by social scientists and ministers working hand in hand.[14]

Of course, it is well known that Niebuhr soon grew impatient with what he saw as the willful innocence of the Social Gospel, and spent much of the rest of his career deriding it. He found the progressive optimism undergirding the Social Gospel to be naive about the intractable fallenness of human nature, and therefore inadequate to the task of explaining the nature of power relations in the real world. What Christianity called 'sin' was not merely a byproduct of bad but correctible social institutions. 'Sin' identified something inherent in the human condition, some deep and uncorrectable disorder in the structure of the human soul, something social institutions could never completely reform. The doctrine of original sin was at bottom empirically valid, he frequently argued, simply because it reflected the observable truth about human behavior as it actually was, and did so far better than any of the alternatives on offer. It required an enormous leap of faith to conclude that men are perfectible, while it requires only open eyes to conclude that they are perverse.

Nor did Niebuhr accept the belief of so many American progressives that the individual was improved and morally uplifted by being 'socialized', by being incorporated into the moral solidarity of social groups and thereby lifted out of the moral anomie of individual self-seeking. In *Moral Man and Immoral Society* (1932), written in the depths of the Depression, at a time when many American intellectuals were supporting the Communist Party candidates for President, Niebuhr turned the Social Gospelers' emphasis on its head, arguing that there was an inescapable disjuncture between the morality of individuals and the morality of groups, and that the latter was generally *inferior* to the former. Individuals could transcend their self-interest only rarely, but groups of individuals, especially groups as large as nation-states, almost never.[15]

In a word, he argued that groups generally made individuals morally worse, rather than better, for the real glue that held human groups together was something more complicated than shared ideals. The larger the group, the greater the hypocrisy, the less genuine the altruism, and the less humane the moral outlook. This became particularly complicated in questions of the

---

[14] Walter Rauschenbusch, *Christianity and the Social Crisis* (New York: Macmillan, 1907).
[15] Reinhold Niebuhr, *Moral Man and Immoral Society* (New York: Scribner's, 1932).

nation, where some of the most admirable sentiments may feed the most unworthy goals. 'Patriotism', he observed, 'transmutes individual unselfishness into national egoism', and grants the nation moral *carte blanche* to do as it wishes. 'The unselfishness of individuals', he mused, 'makes for the selfishness of nations.' That is why the idea of solving the social problems of the world 'merely by extending the social sympathies of individuals' was so completely vain.[16]

Thus, Niebuhr dismissed as mere sentimentality the progressive hope that the sources of individual sin could be overcome through intelligent social reform, and that America could be transformed in time into a loving fellowship of like-minded comrades, holding hands beside the national campfire. Such a dismissive view of his progressive contemporaries was, to be sure, something of a caricature and unfair exaggeration, made for polemical effect. And, more importantly for our present purposes, it concealed the extent to which Niebuhr's criticism of progressives reflected his acceptance of a shared set of assumptions. But it served to provide an effective contrast to Niebuhr's own approach, which insisted relentlessly upon facing up to the harsh and inescapable facts of fallen life.

These harsh facts, however, did not mean that Niebuhr gave up on the possibility of social reform and the possibility of progress. On the contrary, Christians were obliged to work actively for progressive causes and for the realization of social ideals of justice and righteousness. Fatalism and complacency were not allowed. But in doing so they had to abandon their illusions, not least in the way they thought about themselves. The pursuit of good ends in the arena of national and international politics had to take full and realistic account of the unloveliness of human nature, and the unlovely nature of power. Christians who claimed to want to do good in those arenas could count on getting their hands soiled, for the pursuit of social righteousness would inexorably involve them in acts of sin and imperfection. Not because the end justifies the means, but because the fallenness of the world militates against the moral purity of any purposive action. Even the most surgical action creates collateral damage, the responsibility for which cannot be waved away.

But the Christian faith just as inexorably called its adherents to a life of perfect righteousness, a calling that gives no ultimate moral quarter to dirty hands. The result would seem to be a stark contradiction, a call to do the impossible. Niebuhr insisted, though, that the Christian understanding of life embraced both parts of that formulation. Man is a sinner in his deepest nature. But man is also a splendidly endowed creature formed in God's image, still capable of acts of wisdom, generosity, and truth, and still able to advance the cause of social improvement. All these assertions were true, in his

---

[16] Reinhold Niebuhr, *Moral Man and Immoral Society* (New York: Scribner's, 1932), 91.

view. All had an equivalent claim on the Christian mind and heart. In insisting upon such a tense, complex formulation, Niebuhr was correcting the idea of progress, but he was by no means abandoning it.

*   *   *   *   *

These ideas would continue to be developed in subsequent years. In his own Gifford Lectures of 1939, later published as *The Nature and Destiny of Man* (1943), Niebuhr offered a magisterial *tour d'horizon* of the entirely intellectual and spiritual history of the West, and in the process addressed himself more directly to the idea of progress itself.[17] His vision there incorporated fresh insights, but enmeshed them in his characteristically tense and self-critical view.

As Niebuhr saw it, the Christian worldview had had always understood history to be meaningful, but with its meaning sometimes discovered inside the crosscurrents of history and sometimes entirely outside them, a fact that, for him, made the interpretation of history a hazardous but necessary undertaking. The secularized idea of progress, however, had as its guiding principle belief in an immanent *Logos*, which was no longer regarded as transcendent but was thought of as operating in history, bringing its disorder gradually under the dominion of reason, making chaos into 'cosmos'. Like his contemporary Christopher Dawson, he understood this idea of progress as something that had originated under the wing of Christian theology and eschatology; the very language was the biblical language of creation, in Genesis and in the Gospel according to John. But the idea had been transformed and 'liberated' during the Renaissance by two crucial post-Christian innovations, each of which discloses the emergence of a characteristic Niebuhrian theme.

First, this new understanding of progress presumed that 'the fulfillment of life' could occur without the supernatural interventions of 'grace', and that the laws of reason and nature would serve as 'surrogates for providence', giving 'meaning to all of history'. As for the questions of power that were at the heart of *Moral Man and Immoral Society*, the new view simply did not take those questions to be very important, precisely because it assumed that the *Logos* would 'inevitably bring the vitalities of history under its dominion'. Over against the foundational Christian idea that the Fall had rendered all of reality, and particularly human reality, out of joint with itself and beyond the reach of natural or human rescue, the new understanding sought to render all of reality as one potentially harmonizable continuum.[18]

A second and related point was that the thinkers of the Renaissance, while coming to regard history as dynamic, failed to see that the dynamism of

---

[17] Reinhold Niebuhr, *The Nature and Destiny of Man*, 2 vols. (New York: Scribner's, 1941–3).
[18] Ibid. 165–6.

history was *twofold* in character, and double-edged. It assumed, Niebuhr wrote, that 'all development means the advancement of the good'. But in so assuming, it failed to recognize that 'every heightened potency of human existence may also represent a possibility of evil'.

Every heightened potency of human existence may also represent a possibility of evil. This quintessentially Niebuhrian formulation captures very well the extent to which his skepticism about progress is unthinkable without his belief in progress, and vice versa. Even a very great progressive advance may contain within itself the potential for bringing about an equally great calamity. As Niebuhr explained it, everything that has its being within history is 'involved, on every level of achievement, in contradiction to the eternal'. This contradiction reflects the inevitable tendency of every comprehensive understanding of the meaning of history 'to complete the system of meaning falsely', in a way that makes either the individual or the group 'the premature centre, source, or end of the system'.[19]

*   *   *   *   *

All modern interpretations of history, Niebuhr thought, show this tendency; and here his words are strongly reminiscent of Herbert Butterfield's roughly contemporaneous argument in *The Whig Interpretation of History* (1931): 'They identity their own age or culture, or even their own philosophy, with the final fulfillment of life and truth and history. This is the very error which they have not taken into account or discounted in their basic principle of interpretation.' But Niebuhr then goes on to add his characteristic reflexive dimension:

It is not possible for any philosophy to escape this error completely. But it is possible to have a philosophy, or at least a theology, grounded in faith, which understands that the error will be committed and that it is analogous to all those presumptions of history which defy the majesty of God.[20]

In short, for Niebuhr modern interpretations of historical progress have been right in conceiving history dynamically, and taking a broader and more generous view of history's fertile and various possibilities. In a word, their belief in progress is in no wise simply *false*. But they have conceived the dynamic aspects of history too *simply*. 'They hope for an ever increasing dominance of 'form' and 'order' over all historical vitalities', he charged, 'and refuse to acknowledge that history cannot move forward towards increasing cosmos without developing possibilities of chaos by the very potencies which

[19] Reinhold Niebuhr, *The Nature and Destiny of Man*, 2 vols. (New York: Scribner's, 1941–3), 166–7.
[20] Ibid. 167.

have enhanced cosmos.'[21] In other words, we are never clear of the reciprocal relationship of two, and indeed that relationship may become ever more intense, so that the danger only increases as we progress. Man's capacity for evil advances apace with his progress toward the good; hence the greater the progress, the greater the need for vigilance, and the greater the need for some metaphysical check upon human pride.

*　　*　　*　　*　　*

Niebuhr continued along the same line of analysis in *The Irony of American History* (1952), exploring how this same tension manifested itself in a consideration of America's role in the world.[22] Published at the height of the Cold War, *The Irony of American History* was a stinging attack on communism— and at the same time, a stinging indictment of American moral complacency, and a warning against the moral failings to which that complacency made America vulnerable. It is a book that has found a following in the wake of the Iraq War, indeed among proponents and opponents alike. Yet his arguments are in no way topical or time-bound, or tied to issues relating exclusively to the history of the United States.

Once again, Niebuhr was fighting on two fronts at once. Indeed, despite his passionate and unyielding opposition to the communist cause, Niebuhr also believed that the United States resembled its antagonist more than it cared to imagine, and much of the book is devoted to making that case. Americans rightly complained of the communists' dogmatic commitment to 'philosophical materialism', the notion that mind is the fruit of matter, and culture the fruit of economics. But, as Niebuhr pointed out, Americans could be said to be equally committed to materialism in practice: 'Despite the constant emphasis upon "the dignity of man" in our own liberal culture', he contended, 'its predominant naturalistic bias frequently results in views of human nature in which the dignity of man is not very clear.'[23]

So, he believed, the nation needed to be more rigorously self-critical in its exercise of its power. But he added that America also had to act in the world, and do so effectively. Indeed, it had no choice but to do so. One could not retreat. Just as the sinful and imperfect Christian is obliged to work intently for the cause of good, despite his incapacities and imperfections, so a morally imperfect America was and is obliged to employ its power in the world. Opting-out is not an option; or rather, it is an option that is just as morally perilous as the alternatives it would avoid. Niebuhr puts it this way:

---

[21] Ibid. 168–9.
[22] Reinhold Niebuhr, *The Irony of American History* (New York: Scribner's, 1952).
[23] Ibid. 6.

Our culture knows little of the use and abuse of power; but we [now] have to use power in global terms. Our idealists are divided between those who would renounce the responsibilities of power for the sake of preserving the purity of our soul and those who are ready to cover every ambiguity of good and evil in our actions by the frantic insistence that any measure taken in a good cause must be unequivocally virtuous.[24]

Needless to say, Niebuhr rejected either of these options, which correspond roughly to attitudes of moralistic isolationism and amoral *Realpolitik*. He continued thus:

We take, and must continue to take, morally hazardous actions to preserve our civilization. We must exercise our power. But we ought neither to believe that a nation is capable of perfect disinterestedness in its exercise, nor become complacent about particular degrees of interest and passion which corrupt the justice whereby the exercise of power is legitimatized.[25]

Niebuhr concluded *The Irony of American History* by invoking the example of Abraham Lincoln, whose Second Inaugural Address near the end of the Civil War exemplifies the doubleness of vision for which a Niebuhrian statesman should strive. Lincoln's great speech was notable for its unwillingness to demonize or diminish the soon-to-be-defeated enemy, and for its tempering of moral resoluteness by a broadly religious sense of a larger, imponderable dimension to the struggle. 'Both sides', Lincoln famously declared, 'read the same Bible, and pray to the same God. . . . The prayers of both could not be answered; that of neither has been answered fully. The Almighty has His own purposes.' The vantage point of a God who loves all his creatures was vastly greater than that envisioned by any fallible human cause.[26]

   Again, one is reminded of the *humanitas* and humble restraint underlying the historiographical stance of Herbert Butterfield. But it is also important to recognize that nothing in Lincoln's words suggested even a hint of faltering in the ultimate goal of destroying the Confederacy and reuniting the nation. Lincoln's awareness of the broader perspective invoked in his speech did not prevent him from taking strong action in the world, based on his own ideas of what constituted progress. And yet, the speech suggests not only Lincoln's great charity for the enemy, but also his keen awareness of the arrogance, blindness, or triumphalism to which his own side was susceptible, flaws that might beget precisely the ironic effects that Niebuhr feared and deplored. This reflexiveness carries a price. Lincoln himself may not have been entirely

[24] Reinhold Niebuhr, *The Irony of American History* (New York: Scribner's, 1952), 5.
[25] Ibid.
[26] Ibid. 171.

innocent of such flaws, and the fact that his conduct of the war necessarily involved him in inflicting wounds that would be painfully slow to heal only underscores the truth of his words.

The combination of moral resoluteness about the immediate issues with a religious awareness of another dimension of meaning and judgment must be regarded as almost a perfect model of the difficult but not impossible task of remaining loyal and responsible toward the moral treasures of a free civilization on the one hand while yet having some religious vantage point over the struggle.[27]

There was no better example, Niebuhr thought, of the 'dual aspect' to history's dynamism than the United States, where so many manifest strengths could also become dangerous weaknesses. America's 'quest for happiness', he wrote, is suffused in irony, precisely because it has been so triumphant. The United States 'succeeded more obviously than any other nation in making life "comfortable"'. But it has 'tried too simply to make sense out of life, striving for harmonies between man and nature and man and society and man and his ultimate destiny, which have provisional but no ultimate validity'. This has had an ironic result. 'Our very success in this enterprise', he observed, 'has hastened the exposure of its final limits.'[28] The 'naturalistic bias' which has produced a condition in which even the very genetic foundations of human personhood are increasingly viewed as malleable on the deepest level has indeed led to a view of human nature 'in which the dignity of man is not very clear'.

Niebuhr understood the doctrine of original sin—which he insisted upon as the core of the Christian understanding of human nature, with its dualities and tensions—as central to American democracy. As he often said, in various places and ways, man's capacity for goodness and justice makes democracy possible—and his susceptibility to sin and injustice makes democracy necessary. The tension between the two should be regarded as perpetual, and mutually necessary, a perfect embodiment of the tense and necessary relationship between an optimistic idea of progress and a pessimistic view of human nature. The doctrine of original sin, while surely an enemy of any utopian understanding of progress, is the best guarantor of the possibility of the marginal improvement of the human race, i.e., progress rightly understood, since it offers us a truthful and realistic view of the crooked timber of humanity, and prepares us rightly to live with a disjunction between the idea and the act, with the fact that we must strive, however imperfectly, for objectives whose fulfillment we may never see. 'Nothing which is true or beautiful or good makes complete sense in any immediate context of history',

[27] Ibid. 172.
[28] Ibid. 63.

wrote Niebuhr, in *The Irony of American History*, 'therefore we must be saved by faith.'[29]

*   *   *   *   *

One could cite other examples drawn from Niebuhr's oeuvre. But perhaps we now have accumulated enough analysis that we can step back and consider what this series of examples may enable us to conclude about the narrower question of Niebuhr's value to a twenty-first-century doctrine of religious pluralism. And it seems clear from what has come before that, although Niebuhr's view does not require conversion to Christianity, it requires that the Christian view of the human condition and of human nature be taken as the fundamental model for ways of thinking about the fallibility of the human person, and the proper way of regarding progress in human history. The fact that he himself does not treat the doctrine of original sin as a question of the historicity of the events related in the opening chapters of the book of Genesis makes little difference in this regard. The important point is that without a robustly Christian understanding of sin as a central feature of human nature—sin not just as incorrigible limitation or fallibility but sin as a deeply ingrained perversity of the will, a propensity for living at odds with what we were made to be—Niebuhr's work becomes unintelligible, a collection of strange mental tics and reflexive moral compulsions that lack a plausible basis in psychological reality.

What original sin was for the individual, the 'duality of history's dynamic' is for the idea of progress in history; the second is merely the amplification of the first. What the nineteenth century had lacked was a sense of the perilousness of progress. The twentieth century made up for that. We now understand the peril. We have 'progressed' this far, to such a level of self-understanding. But what Niebuhr sought was not a rejection of the idea of progress, but a chastened and strengthened understanding of the idea of progress, and of the possibility of genuine human altruism, that has the capacity to hold together a strong sense of both the promise and the peril that our efforts in the world inevitably entail.

Such an understanding rejects the reductive modernist myths of human plasticity, and begins with a subtler sense of what sorts of beings we are. It should affirm that we humans are creatures of enormous creativity and capacity for love and rational discernment—and yet acknowledge that we are creatures harboring depths of perversity and wanton destructiveness, the kind of creatures who are capable of appallingly hard-hearted deafness to the

---

[29] Reinhold Niebuhr, *The Irony of American History* (New York: Scribner's, 1952).

anguish of others, and who will spray-paint graffiti on masterpieces and anonymously vandalize the computers of people we will never meet, just for the sheer fun of it. It recognizes that both are always present possibilities. And, while it affirms the nobility of the modern impulse toward the universal and the comprehensive, it accepts the inevitable particularities and limitations that attend to our social and bodily existence.

*   *   *   *   *

Those of us raised in the context of a liberal post-Christian culture are likely to admire this analysis, and find it probing and insightful and subtle. The problem, however, is that it presumes that certain qualities of mind and soul, such as the value of introspective self-criticism and systemic doubt, qualities that Niebuhr consistently admires and strongly advocates, are sustainable outside of cultural premises, ultimately derived from key assumptions of Western Christianity, that Westerners generally share. There is no reason to presume that this is the case.

Niebuhr was the great teacher of self-examination and epistemological modesty, albeit combining that vocation with an imperative belief in the need for action, such that the commission of sin and the accumulation of guilt became a near-unavoidable feature of moral life. The trouble for pluralism is that Niebuhr's epistemological modesty was grounded in the doctrine of original sin, which is why his approach to religious pluralism seemed to require that all religions in their 'highest' form be self-reflexive, in the same way that his was. In other words, his approach was anything but radically pluralistic, in the end. Its fundamental algebra was, and remained, Western Christian to the core.

He was one of the great modern American critics of liberalism and progress. He was also very much an intellectual counterpuncher, who disclosed what he believed most readily and vividly in the process of attacking the things he thought were false or misleading. But he was able to perform that role so well precisely because he himself believed so passionately in the fundamental rightness of liberalism and progress. He was a critic of liberalism entirely from within, and a critic of progressivism and the Social Gospel from a stance which accepted the justice and validity of fundamental progressive goals as a foregone conclusion. He has often been embraced by conservatives, and accused of conservatism, but he was no conservative himself, unless one defined the conservation of progressivism as his credo.

Furthermore, he could be a confident counterpuncher because he could count on the cultural ubiquity of the same liberal and progressive tradition. He could be critical of liberalism from within because he knew that liberalism was strong enough and durable enough to withstand the critique and benefit from it and retain its cultural dominance. As a consequence, though, it is near-impossible to imagine him operating in anything other than a modern Western liberal environment, an intellectual and cultural milieu suffused with a deep commitment to a Western idea of progress. Niebuhr speaks with less authority or relevance to the religious conflicts of South Asia or the Middle East or Sub-Saharan Africa. The issues he struggled with were quintessentially related to the problems of advanced modernity, in a society that was poised on the cusp of secularism. He was in that sense very much a creature of his times, of a moment that seems now to have passed, and it is hard to imagine what he would have had to say to a desecularizing world. I imagine, though I cannot prove, that he would have found it disconcerting, even alarming. He was geared to the challenge of secularism, not the challenging recrudescence of vibrant, energetic, supernaturalist, and missionary faith.

*   *   *   *   *

The question of Niebuhr's usefulness in formulating a doctrine of religious pluralism for the twenty-first century then brings us up against two very different, but equally fundamental, clusters of questions. First, does a Niebuhrian perspective require that one operate within intellectual and cultural premises that are unavoidably Western and Christian—or, more precisely, that only have deep moral resonance for those who have been habituated to Western Christian forms of moral reflection?[30] Is the kind of self-critical, self-ironizing reflex that Niebuhr asks of us a reflex that is too culturally particular to admit of wider transmission? If so, what does this mean with regard to pluralism? One thinks again of the passage quoted above from *The Children of Light and the Children of Darkness*, and the logic by which he arrives at his support for pluralism.

And second, and perhaps more challenging to contemplate: is the very ideal of religious pluralism—i.e., a steady and peaceable state of religious diversity within a functional and reasonably harmonious political unity—an ideal that requires constituent religions to refashion themselves in ways that may represent profound alterations in doctrine, worship, and social practices? Is such pluralism in fact a form of toleration that is no toleration at all, a 'repressive toleration' that requires religions to conform to a standard external to themselves? What would be the fate of a religion with a different view of God and a different anthropology, one that sees no virtue in the development of the same rigorously self-critical apparatus that Niebuhr praised as the foundation of religious toleration, or sees no substantive virtue in the ethos of religious liberty

---

[30] I stress Western Christianity here, mindful of the fact that Eastern Orthodoxy is largely free of the Augustinian stress on original sin.

and individualism that are sacrosanct in the West? Does such a religion thereby forfeit a place in the respectable community of world religions? Or, in making such adaptations as admission to the pluralistic order may require, does such a religion betray itself utterly, and show the claims of pluralism to be a sham?

These questions are, of course, not the least bit hypothetical in our time. They also are recognizably the same questions that arise in critical considerations of modern liberalism, i.e., whether liberalism is a neutral container of diverse moral cultures or a moral culture itself, one that, far from being neutral, only accepts those cultures that conform to its dictates. Given the fact that these questions do not admit of easy answer, one way or the other, they are likely to be with us for a very long time to come.

As all historians know, there are limits to what ideas can accomplish as historical agents. Often they are lagging indicators of changes that have already occurred for other reasons entirely. The American experience with the history of religious toleration suggests that religious tolerance may have to be worked out in practice before it is worked out in theory. This may be equally true of a global-scale pluralism, to the extent that it is capable of being realized, and that fact may be reason enough to make no judgment at this time about the eventual value of Niebuhr for the resolution of these matters. The answer, if there is one, is likely to come incrementally.

But Niebuhr does posit one thing that goes against the conventional wisdom, and for that reason alone is worth considering. If he is right, it will be by going more deeply into our own respective traditions, not by diluting them with extraneous elements, or by the pursuit of ersatz forms of syncretism and blending, that we will find our way to a common ground. That prospect perhaps sounds counterintuitive. But it is not entirely implausible either. The Christian tradition has, and not least in the example of Niebuhr, shown that it is possible to do both things, and perhaps to become more deeply Christian in the act of openness to the other. What is less clear is how widely this can be done, and how much that characteristic owes to the particular moral and anthropological assumptions undergirding the Christian tradition.

Conclusion

Realism Revisited

Stephen Platten

In the late 1970s, the BBC in London produced a radio programme on the legacy and influence of Reinhold Niebuhr. Even taking into account the cultural changes within the past two generations, there was something remarkable about this. Theologians are not normally the regular focus of radio and television, even within the public service broadcasting sector. Echoing Richard Harries' reflections in his introduction, the first startling fact was the breadth of influence of Niebuhr on politicians and statesmen on both sides of the Atlantic. Professor Ronald Preston, a friend of Niebuhr's who embraced a similar ethic of Christian realism, noted just a few of those who recognized their indebtedness to Niebuhr. They included Jimmy Carter and Adlai Stevenson amongst American politicians and Denis Healey and Tony Benn in Britain; indeed Benn was himself interviewed on the programme. Preston argued that Niebuhr had also influenced a Bow Group Tory, Rab Butler, and that Niebuhrian influences are detectable within the 1944 Education Act, of which Butler was the architect, and which established for the first time in Britain universal secondary education up to the age of fifteen.

Equally remarkable within the programme were the brief extracts from Niebuhr's lectures at Union Seminary in New York City and elsewhere. Still to this day, even in a recording, something of his electrifying and prophetic style emerges. His delivery catches and holds one's attention. This, together with the breadth of his theological horizons, produced an excitement hardly to be expected of a middle- to high-brow radio programme on the life, teaching, and influence of one American Protestant theologian. Protestant undoubtedly Niebuhr was, although he was influenced significantly by Anglicanism—partly through being married to Ursula Keppel Compton, she being a lifelong member of the Church of England and having taken a first in theology at Cambridge. Niebuhr was himself the son of a German émigré Lutheran pastor, Gustav Niebuhr. Gustav came from the liberal Protestant tradition and Reinhold was first formed within that theological culture. His own formative work was as Pastor at the Bethel Evangelical Church in Detroit where he remained for thirteen years and where his ministry took him into the great automobile factories within that city. It was here that he wrote his *Leaves from the Notebook of a Tamed Cynic*[1] and it was during this time too that he was influenced by Marxist thought. He was furthermore influenced to some extent by the neo-Orthodox movement without ever becoming a disciple of Karl Barth, of whose thought he was critical. Indeed he criticizes both Barth and Schleiermacher whom he believes, in quite different ways, allowed religion and morality to be separated in a manner which was not so in that tradition which stems from Aquinas. In terms of neo-Orthodoxy his sympathies were nearer to those of Emil Brunner.

Niebuhr's early political and social engagement also featured in that same BBC radio programme. His work both with southern 'share-croppers' and with the workers in the Detroit car plants was featured. This was all set in the context of the 'great depression', with the 1930s tones of 'Buddy can you spare a dime' repeating itself as a leitmotif throughout the programme. This brief snapshot of Niebuhr in an unexpected medium may help us to set the context of this collection of essays. Although this collection is born of a very different culture with many contrasting and variant concerns and challenges, nevertheless we face issues which require an effective response from the Christian theologian and moralist.

Robin Lovin captures both the continuities and discontinuities sharply in his chapter (Chapter 1, this volume). He notes of criticisms of Niebuhr:

The terms in which Niebuhr is criticized sound curiously like his own judgments on Protestant liberalism. Indeed, from this new perspective, Niebuhr tends to disappear into the liberal background . . . In the hands of these critics, Niebuhr's work is not so much discarded as it is rendered obsolete by its entanglements with secular values that no longer claim the attention of serious Christians.[2]

Whilst accepting their positive insights, Lovin nevertheless engages with these critics and argues for the continuing relevance of Niebuhr for a very different age.

Nonetheless, it is crystal clear that there have been very significant cultural changes. This means that, at the very least, Niebuhr's theology and his social ethical critique must be revisited in the light of these shifts. The fall of the Berlin Wall and the collapse of Soviet communism render our situation

[1] Reinhold Niebuhr, *Leaves From the Notebook of a Tamed Cynic* (San Francisco: Harper and Row, 1929, 1956, 1980).
[2] Lovin, this volume, p. 7.

drastically changed. Although Niebuhr was never a fully paid up Marxist, he took seriously the Marxist sociological critique classically in *Moral Man and Immoral Society*. He writes: 'We can no longer buy the highest satisfactions of the individual life at the expense of social injustice. We cannot build our individual ladders to heaven and leave the total human enterprise unredeemed of its excesses and corruptions.'[3] Something of this rhetoric surfaced in the clips from his lectures in that radio programme. Where does the collapse of Soviet hegemony leave Niebuhr's Marxist critique? Undoubtedly the collapse of institutionalized state Marx-Leninism has blunted the social and political hopes and ambitions of Marxism and, indeed, of the left in general in the West. Even so, the recent events in the banking industry worldwide suggest that Niebuhr's critique, influenced by this Marxist sociological and political analysis, may not be totally untargeted or out of focus. Ian Markham suggests as much in his essay (Chapter 9). Of course, such a critique is rooted ultimately as much in Niebuhr's theological anthropology, to which we shall return.

Other developments within our society and culture have also flowered since Niebuhr's death. One crucial area, for example, is the development of feminist theology. This is of particular significance in reviewing Niebuhr remembering the essential part that anthropology plays in his work. What does this say about our understanding of human nature? Jean Elshtain (Chapter 3) focuses directly upon this, noting that talk of 'human nature' is often proscribed now within the academy and replaced with fairly loose concepts about the social construction of reality. Nonetheless, despite these caveats, Niebuhr's anthropological reflection pre-dated the sophisticated and positive contributions which feminist theology has contributed.[4] There must be a case to be answered here. Much of this returns us once again to Niebuhr's anthropology, upon which we shall focus in our first major reflection.

Before moving on to some specific themes in Niebuhr, it should be noted that both that radio programme of a generation ago and also reflection upon Niebuhr's work since his death make apparent the extraordinary compass and panoramic nature of his work. It is unrealistic to focus purely on his contribution to social ethics or indeed upon his theological anthropology since, as Kenneth Durkin indicates in an earlier analysis of Niebuhr's method, critics and commentators are not at one even in agreeing the key focus or starting

---

[3] *Moral Man and Immoral Society: A Study in Ethics and Politics* (New York: Charles Scribner's, 1932), 277.

[4] See Janet Martin Soskice, *The Kindness of God* (Oxford: Oxford University Press, 2007), 104. In passing Soskice notes: 'most importantly, this is *not only* [her italics] when the texts in question say depressing things about women, but even when the texts are, like those of Niebuhr and Nygren, ostensibly neutral—in theory speaking for "everyman".'

point for Niebuhr's theological vision.[5] It was Paul Tillich who first focused on Creation, Fall, Atonement, and Parousia as the key elements within Niebuhr's scheme. The general conclusion then followed that Atonement lay at the centre. Paul Lehmann, however, argued for a more generalized Christological key and suggested that: 'Starting from the *Christus in nobis*, Niebuhr discovers the *Christus pro nobis*. Then he insists that the *Christus pro nobis* can be correctly stated only with reference to the *Christus in nobis*' (his italics).[6] Lehmann criticizes Niebuhr for not expanding this into a full Trinitarian Christology. But, nevertheless, in the face of some of Niebuhr's later critics, who argue still more sharply over his inadequacies, here Lehmann points to this clear Christological centre, to the breadth of Niebuhr's work—and the controversies and disputes it still produces. It is, then, against this wider horizon that the present collection of essays should be placed. The essays themselves focus on a number of key themes, but here we only have space to pick up just four, which are raised in different contexts throughout this book. Those themes are: Niebuhr's theological anthropology; some key issues relating to ecclesiology; Niebuhr's role as a *public theologian*; and finally a focus on democracy and the implications of this for his 'Christian Realism'.

*   *   *   *   *

Alongside the key strand of the Marxist critique in Niebuhr's thought already noted, at the heart of his Christian Realism lies his recognition of the nature of human fallenness and the 'stranglehold of sin'. Martyn Percy alludes to this and broadens the point, noting what he describes as sin's 'absence in public space and some of the consequences of that absenteeism'.[7] It is, however, this apparent obsession with the *stranglehold of sin* for which others take Niebuhr to task.

This critique is focused with particular sharpness in the work of Stanley Hauerwas and—using a rather different critique—by John Milbank and the Radically Orthodox analysis of modernity and post-modernity. One could argue that these critiques operate at the 'foundational level'. They pose questions about Niebuhr's starting point: is his realism about human fall-enness too much directed by his Marxist critique? Does this emphasis under-mine the essentially theological critique and lead in the direction of a *human* rather than *divine* directed critique? Hauerwas detects what he believes to be an anthropological rather than a theological account. Hauerwas's

---

[5] Kenneth Durkin, *Reinhold Niebuhr* (London: Geoffrey Chapman, 1989), 175 ff.

[6] Paul Lehmann in Charles W. Kegley and Robert W. Bretall (eds.), *Reinhold Niebuhr: His Religious, Social, and Political Thought* (New York: Macmillan, 1956), 35–44.

[7] Cf. Percy, this volume, p. 116.

and Milbank's critiques are respectively cogent and need to be addressed. They are represented here in the revised critiques offered by Sam Wells and Ben Quash. Some reflection upon them may help develop a more sophisticated and 'revisionist' Niebuhrian Christian Realism.

So, Sam Wells, in a multi-fronted assault on Niebuhr following up on earlier critical analysis,[8] is particularly troubled by Niebuhr's account of human nature and humanity's destiny in the face of evil. He brings this critique to a head in his use of George Hunsinger's account of Niebuhr.[9] Hunsinger contrasts Niebuhr with Barth, of whom as we have already noted, Niebuhr was critical. Niebuhr contrasts realism and idealism, Barth uses the categories of reality and unreality. Placing on one side the opposition of some key areas of Barth's and Niebuhr's thought, there may be some sense of parody in Hunsinger's critique of Niebuhr. The implication is of an ignoring of Jesus' incarnation, crucifixion, resurrection, and ascension. Paul Lehmann, however, is clear about the significance of Christology for Niebuhr while accepting that Jesus' resurrection is given too little attention in Niebuhr's overall method.

Wells is still more critical, however, of what he would see as Niebuhr's flawed account of theology: 'The problem with Niebuhr's reasoning is his unwillingness to take seriously (note the word again) the full humanity and divinity of Christ.'[10] Niebuhr's treatment of the 'parable of the wheat and the tares' is another sign of this failure, argues Wells. Effectively he attacks Niebuhr for ignoring the eschatological conclusion of the parable; he notes later: 'My argument has been that Niebuhr's account of realism rests on the rejection of what turns out to be an inadequate account of pacifism—inadequate, because it identifies Jesus with perfectionist ethics rather than Chalcedonian doctrine.'[11] Interestingly Wells' criticisms of Niebuhr often suggest a lack of perfectionism to be a key failing. In other words, the resultant ethic is insufficiently challenging. But what of the *incarnational* critique of which Wells' is but one example in recent years? This is there implicitly too in Ben Quash's essay which, in a subtle and not uncritical manner, draws on John Milbank's own critique.

One of the key issues here is contingency and the contingent. Indeed this is also referred to in Wells' chapter. Quash notes: '[Niebuhr] claims a *necessity* for what may only be *contingencies* in historical experience (even if exceptionless or nearly exceptionless contingencies), and to do this, he makes a claim

---

[8] See, for example, Samuel Wells, *Transforming Fate into Destiny* (Carlisle: Paternoster, 1998), chs 1 and 2 and passim.

[9] Wells, this volume, pp. 76–7.

[10] Wells, *Transferring Fate into Destiny*, 4.

[11] Wells, this volume, p. 83.

that is itself a- or supra- historical. He makes a claim about "nature" ... and the "nature" of original sin' (Quash's italics).[12]

At this point we should allow Niebuhr to speak for himself. In his Gifford Lectures, whose focus is precisely upon theological anthropology, he writes:

It is important to recognize how basic the Christian doctrine of the good of creation is for a conception of man in which human finiteness is emphasized but not deprecated. In the biblical view the contrast between the created world and the Creator, between its dependent and insufficient existence and His freedom and self-sufficiency, is absolute. But this contrast never means that the created world is evil by reason of the particularization and individualization of its various types of existence.[13]

This takes us to the heart of the wider critiques of Niebuhr issuing from Hauerwas and Radical Orthodoxy. So, the Radical Orthodox see creation as good but tragically fallen and charge Niebuhr with failing to attend to original goodness and the ontology that this entails. This debate also takes us to the crux of Niebuhr's argument and effectively to the heart of philosophical theological understandings of the incarnation. For, Niebuhr is aware of the tragic contingency of all this, but this realism causes him to focus on the consequences of sin. Indeed, it is the very issue of necessity and contingency which stands behind the paradox of the incarnation in its Chalcedonian form. The Chalcedonian definition affirms simultaneously the true humanity and the true divinity of Christ. This is paradoxical. It underpins classical under-standings of God which affirm both God's necessity and at the same time equally affirm the fact of human contingency which also stands at the heart of the doctrine of creation and about which Niebuhr is a realist. This is well illustrated by Alexander Pope in his *Essay on Man*:

> Know then thyself, presume not God to scan,
> The proper study of mankind is man.
> Placed on this isthmus of a middle state,
> A being darkly wise, and rudely great
>
> . . . . . .
>
> He hangs between; in doubt to act or rest;
> In doubt to deem himself a god, or beast
>
> . . . . . .
>
> Created half to rise, and half to fall;
> Great lord of all things, yet a prey to all;
> Sole judge of truth, in endless error hurled;
> The glory, jest and riddle of the world.[14]

---

[12] Quash, this volume, p. 60.
[13] Reinhold Niebuhr, *The Nature and Destiny of Man*, i: *Human Nature* (London: Nisbet, 1941), 181.
[14] Alexander Pope, *An Essay on Man*, Ep. II, lines. 1ff.

Here, then, is encapsulated Niebuhr's understanding of humanity and the
reality of sin; here too are set the roots of his realism which rules out neither
eschatology nor human aspiration. The mediation of contingency and necessity is paradoxically foregrounded in the incarnation, in Jesus Christ, the
God-man, who manifests both the eternal and necessary in the temporal and
contingent. Niebuhr's realism sets these conclusions in the context of the
'ultimate', to use Bonhoeffer's term as very helpfully cited by Quash in his
essay. Moreover, the setting of such realism derives precisely from that
contingency which stands at the heart of the Incarnation and makes clear
the paradox. It is a paradox with which we must needs live. Nevertheless, even
towards the conclusion of his critique of individual and social ethics, Niebuhr
retains a clear sense of human aspiration. So, for example, reflecting on his
arguments about non-violent resistance, he notes:

The discovery of elements of common human frailty in the foe and, concomitantly,
the appreciation of all human life as possessing transcendent worth, creates attitudes
which transcend social conflict and thus mitigate its cruelties. It binds human beings
together by reminding them of the common roots and similar character of both their
vices and their virtues.[15]

This emphasis on the transcendent worth of human life adverts both to the
divine Creator and also to the hope to which we are called, but it does so in the
clear knowledge and acceptance of the contingency which is part of the defining
nature of our existence in relation to the God who creates and redeems us. Since
the incarnation is related to the nature of the Church, indeed some would even
argue that the Church is an extension of the incarnation, it is at this point that
Niebuhr's lack of an ecclesiology begins to exercise the theologian.

*   *   *   *   *

This lack of doctrine of the Church emerges in a twofold manner. First, it is
clear in an apparent lack of concern for ecclesiological argument; for most of
the time the nature of the Church is not a key focus within Niebuhr's
landscape. This point is made very cogently in Wendy Dackson's chapter
(Chapter 6, this volume). But, secondly, there is an incipient anti-Romanism
which surfaces quite clearly on occasions. In my chapter I advert to this and
notably in reference to 'magic'.[16] Later in that same quotation about Catholicism and Protestantism, which I noted, Niebuhr is sharper still:

To read the arguments of the sacerdotalists is enough to drive one into the arms of the
unrepentant rationalists who regard all religion as dangerous.

---

[15] *Moral Man*, 255.
[16] Platten, this volume, p. 112.

The weaknesses of Catholicism ought not to prompt one to disregard all the finer spiritual and moral values which still live in this ancient church. But there can be no final unity between an institution which reduces religion to magic and a fellowship of the spirit which tries to subdue the chaos of life under the ideal faith.[17]

Niebuhr's attitude to Roman Catholicism did admittedly mellow later in his life, but he remained suspicious of a sacramental church.[18] It is also, of course, easy to forget the extraordinary ecumenical progress of the past half-century and thus also to forget the prejudices and stereotypes which Roman Catholics and Protestants often held about each other. There is no reason to expect Niebuhr to have been immune to this. Nonetheless, that quotation does point to something of a theological distinction. Niebuhr contrasts 'an *institution* which reduces religion to magic with a *fellowship* of the spirit'. This seems to imply what we might describe as an ecclesiological distancing. Niebuhr is distancing himself from what he sees as Roman Catholicism's errant self-understanding. Dackson describes Niebuhr's understanding of the Church as an 'outsider' view, which tries to understand how the Church will be understood and perceived by external observers. Implicitly Dackson argues that amongst other things Niebuhr's critique of the Church may help the institution to have a more realistic sense of its own failings.

Here we tread on sensitive ground. The four marks of the Church include *holiness* amongst their number and this is part of an essential catholic doctrine of the Church. There is a sacramental element in the Church's being which is there to model Christ to the world. It is this that Hauerwas and the Radical Orthodox have rightly brought to the fore. Nevertheless, as F. D. Maurice indicated so clearly in the nineteenth century, *Church* and *Kingdom* are not coterminous. The 'ecclesiological self-criticisms' outlined by Niebuhr are important, but only if they stand alongside a clear and structured doctrine of the Church.

It is Stanley Hauerwas who has arguably been Niebuhr's most trenchant and consistent critic in ecclesiological terms. At root Hauerwas argues that Niebuhr's appropriation of social critiques derived from the secular world blunts his Christian theological perspective. Only by encouraging the Church to be the Church and to live out the teaching and life of Jesus Christ can the gospel have its proper impact. If theologians are to contribute to morality then they will do so exactly to the extent that they can capture the significance of the Church for determining the nature and content of Christian

---

[17] *Leaves*, 156–7.
[18] See Richard Wightman Fox, 'Reinhold Niebuhr: The Living of Christian Realism', in *Reinhold Niebuhr and the Issues of Our Time* (London: Mowbray. 1986), 20–1.

ethical reflection.[19] Kenneth Durkin points out that, for Hauerwas, the proof
of Niebuhr's ethic not being 'Christian' is made clear through the fact that
many of his contemporaries were attracted to his account of the human
condition without sharing his theological convictions.[20] A good example of
this is the British politician Denis Healey, to whom Richard Harries refers in
the Introduction.

This argument, however, feels altogether specious. Certainly it runs totally
contrary to much that has been valued in Roman Catholic moral theology.
Hauerwas may be cautious or even rejecting of, some of the moral theological
foundations in Catholic thought. So, for example, his pacifism would see 'Just
War Theory' as issuing from pagan, and then later, secular philosophical
roots. He may be suspicious too of elements of the 'natural law tradition'
for similar reasons, although he would recognize the contribution of revelation rooted in what Aquinas describes as *divine law* which contributes to
Catholic moral theology in an essential and foundational manner. But, looking to more obvious parallels with Niebuhr's work, would Hauerwas reject the
entire corpus of Roman Catholic social ethics from *Rerum Novarum* onwards?
For example, in 1997, the Conference of Roman Catholic Bishops for England
and Wales produced an excellent and prophetically challenging document,
The Common Good,[21] which grounded itself in the broader Catholic tradition
of teaching on 'the common good'. It was a document that was hailed by a
great variety of Christians from outside the Roman Catholic Church and also
by many who had no religious allegiance. The argument that non-Christian
affirmation of aspects of Christian moral teaching thereby compromises it
seems perverse.

There is no doubt that Niebuhr's thought would be further strengthened by
a clearer attempt to root his theological method more effectively within an
ecclesiological matrix. Indeed, remembering the developments manifested by
the ecumenical movement both in theology and praxis, it is possible that
Niebuhr himself might well have been persuaded to revisit his view of the
Church and engage his moral theological method within some form of
revised ecclesiological outlook. Undoubtedly such a revisiting of ecclesiology
by Niebuhr's disciples and constructive critics is a key part in allowing his
crucial social ethical and theological critique to have its impact on the politics

[19] Stanley Hauerwas, *Against the Nations* (Minneapolis: Winston Press, 1985), 31 ff.
[20] Durkin, *Reinhold Niebuhr*, 182.
[21] Catholic Bishops Conference for England and Wales, *The Common Good and the Catholic
Church's Social Teaching* (London: The Catholic Bishops Conference for England and Wales,
1996).

of our contemporary world. Indeed, the significant role of *public theology* has perhaps never been greater.

*   *   *   *   *

Ironically it is the ecclesiological edges of *public theology* that may be the crucial starting point here. Kevin Carnahan's engagement of Niebuhr with evangelicalism in the United States begins effectively on the margins of ecclesiology. Many evangelicals in the United States would stand aside from Niebuhr's brand of Protestantism with some possibly even abhorring the notion of any form of developed ecclesiology. Indeed, there is a popular understanding of American politics which sees an almost seamless alliance of the new right/the neoconservatives with evangelicalism. Many would argue that this was the vehicle that both Ronald Reagan and George W. Bush requisitioned to make their journey towards power and to park themselves there for two eight-year terms respectively. Carnahan criticizes this identification on precise Niebuhrian lines. First, evangelicals read off moral certainties too directly from the Bible. Secondly, there is an assumption that the Kingdom of God can be fully established in this world. However, Carnahan notes shifts in the evangelical landscape. He refers to Jim Wallis's quoting of Niebuhr that 'every nation, political system, and politician falls short of God's justice, because we are all sinners.'[22] This brings us directly into the realm of one of Niebuhr's most significant contributions, issuing from his realism—his insistence on taking *power* seriously.

Within the world of politics power never lies far below the surface. Niebuhr even describes social peace as a *Pax Romana* hiding its will-to-power under the veil of its will-to-peace. He argues that middle-class opposition to violence forgets the power which lies there nascent, holding that class in its social position; this is a power frequently unavailable to the proletariat. Here we encounter a pre-figuring of the talk of structural injustice, as in the work of liberation theologians in the 1970s and 1980s. Niebuhr continues by seeing the will-to-live within groups becoming the will-to-power. This is then extended into international relations when the will-to-power of competing national groups becomes the cause of international anarchy, which the moral sense of humankind has so far vainly striven to overcome.

It is precisely these issues which surface in the chapters by Lieven (Chapter 12), Carlson (Chapter 13), and McCorkle (Chapter 2). Each of these in different ways and with reference to different theatres of human striving and conflict recognizes the potency of Niebuhr's critique. Niebuhr reminds us that: 'It was a dictum of George Washington that nations were not to be trusted

---

[22] Carnahan, this volume, p. 216.

beyond their own interest.'[23] Niebuhr also develops his arguments about the relationship of individual to social ethics within nations to cover the relationships between nations. In *Moral Man and Immoral Society* and in *An Interpretation of Christian Ethics*, Niebuhr refers to the work of the League of Nations. In the earlier book, he has not given up hope entirely on the efficacy of such a body, so he writes: 'A society of nations has not really proved itself until it is able to grant justice to those who have been worsted in battle without requiring them to engage in new wars to redress their wrongs.'[24]

By 1936, however, when the second book was published, he had no illusions and wrote:

It must be admitted, of course, that international conflicts are arbitrated and mitigated to a certain degree by the force of the international community. But the League of Nations, which was expected to provide the inchoate international community with genuine organs of international cohesion, is significantly disintegrating, because its organs of cohesion were nothing more than the wills of the strong nations which compose it; and none of these nations are [sic] capable of an international perspective transcending their own interests.[25]

Very similar arguments could be stated now in relation to the United Nations. Only a generation ago, it was the Soviet Union and its satellites which were regularly castigated by the Western alliance for ignoring elements of the UN Charter. In the past decade, it has been the United States, aided and abetted by Britain, which has ignored the structures of international law as set out in the UN Charter. Here Lieven is clear that Niebuhr speaks directly to our condition:

Niebuhr was a strong American patriot who regarded US power as essential to the defence of freedom and democracy against totalitarianism, but he never ceased to warn his compatriots against the assumption that American power and American virtue were synonymous, and against pursuing crude American national interests in the name of high ideals.[26]

Lieven sees Niebuhr's realism as a key ingredient in persuading Americans to develop a new awareness of how they are perceived by others and indeed of the needs and desires of other nations and peoples. McCorkle is clear that Niebuhr himself changed in his judgements over the decades and argues that it is the bringing together of the role and responsibility of the statesman and that of the prophet, both of which Niebuhr recognized, which is essential to

[23] *Moral Man*, 84.
[24] Ibid. 111.
[25] Reinhold Niebuhr, *An Interpretation of Christian Ethics* (London: SCM Press, 1936), 139.
[26] Lieven, this volume, p. 175.

politics and international relations. McCorkle's critique resonates with one of the criticisms discussed by Robin Lovin—that is, Niebuhr's inability to see the world through the eyes of the oppressed. Niebuhr did, however, support Martin Luther King and he became increasingly critical of American engagement in Vietnam. It is worth asking whether his realism with regard to the wielding of power was at this point as much a weakness as it was a strength. The *oppressed* and those who work prophetically alongside them are, of course, often diametrical opposites to *realists*. They are clear that the world needs to change but they are not realists. Often they will not be clear about how the political structures can be engaged to affect this, but Mahatma Gandhi appears to stand as one example who does not fulfil this generalization. Niebuhr engages with Gandhi's non-violent policy but even there his realism is not far in the background. Does Gandhi ultimately imply that if non-violence is ineffective then other patterns will necessarily develop? Niebuhr reflects:

The advantages of non-violent methods are very great but they must be pragmatically considered in the light of circumstances. Even Mr Gandhi introduces the note of expediency again and again, and suggests that they are peculiarly adapted to the needs and limitations of a group which has more power arranged against it than it is able to command.[27]

Niebuhr's realism about power, then, remains germinal to his political thought but at the same time it is directly implicated in his theology. It remains an essential strand if we are to understand how theology can influence public policy within a democracy.

*   *   *   *   *

In his chapter, Richard Harries[28] is clear that Niebuhr's argument for democracy is most firmly rooted in theological realism and is a reaction against an over-optimistic view of human nature, hence the second phrase in his balanced aphorism 'man's inclination to injustice makes democracy necessary'.[29] Harries' concern is to give theological rooting to the first and more optimistic phrase in the aphorism. It is worth noting in passing here a certain irony in relation to some of Niebuhr's more recent and determined critics. For many of these critiques would derive from a so-called 'post-modern' standpoint which is itself sceptical of some of the key elements within the Enlightenment project, not least an optimism borne of the Enlightenment's

---

[27] *Moral Man*, 252.
[28] Harries, this volume, p. 156.
[29] Cf. Reinhold Niebuhr, *The Children of Light and the Children of Darkness* (London: Nisbet, 1945), p. vi.

over-confidence in a particular understanding of human rationality. In other words, those who are suspicious of Enlightenment optimism are equally critical of Niebuhr's pessimism.

It would be an exaggeration to see Niebuhr's argument for the necessity of democracy to be purely negative or rooted in pessimism. Niebuhr's realism, whilst rooted in a clear acceptance of human fallibility, is also derived from a proper sense of the empirical. This was an emphasis taken up by John C. Bennett, Ronald Preston, and others who were either disciples or co-workers with Niebuhr. Democracy, in other words, is not simply the product of one single ideology, deriving clearly from the models of ancient Athens or the philosophy of Aristotle. This point has been made eloquently in a recent monograph on the slow and haphazard development of democracy in Britain. So, David Marquand, in his historical analysis of the development of democracy in Britain in the twentieth century, is content to title the first main part of his book 'Ambling to Democracy'.[30]

Setting apart the historical contingencies which he describes, Marquand is keen to indicate that the democracy which has so far manifested itself (and it is not pure democracy, if such a category could exist—*pace* the continued presence of one hundred hereditary peers in the House of Lords) is the result of the contributions of at least four different traditions which are themselves encapsulated in particular historical narratives. These he describes as 'whig imperialism', 'Tory nationalism', 'democratic collectivist', and 'democratic republican'. Two of these are Marquand's own coinage. The other two have a longer pedigree, *democratic collectivism* being the coinage of the early Fabian Sidney Webb, whilst *whig imperialism* has a longer and more complex pedigree whose classical exemplar (and perhaps also pioneer) was Edmund Burke. None of these describes a political party; often these traditions cut sharply across party lines. Nor do these represent conscious ideologies, although some exemplars of any particular approach may be more conscious than others of standing within a particular tradition.[31]

Marquand's point is that the slow emergence of democracy in Britain has been the fruit of an engagement and sometimes the temporal triumph of one or more of these traditions. Within each of them in different ways and to different extents the Christian religion has played its part. The abrasion of the empirical, the religious, the historical, the ideological, and the sociological has been fairly haphazard. It may be possible to extrapolate a parallel analysis of American politics and the development of democracy on the western side of

---

[30] David Marquand, *Britain since 1918: The Strange Career of British Democracy* (London: Weidenfeld & Nicolson, 2008). See pp. 9–75.
[31] Ibid. 44.

the Atlantic south of the forty-ninth parallel. Here there has been a much clearer sense of a developing constitution and, of course, to some extent a reaction to that which the earliest colonists and immigrants were escaping in the 'old world'. Nonetheless, the early history of the union, notably including the engagement between John Adams and Thomas Jefferson, and then the later formal emergence of the Democratic and Republican parties—each tells its own tale. The most recent election with Barack Obama calling Hillary Clinton to be his Secretary of State itself brings together two rather contrasting traditions within the Democratic Party itself. Party politics, on both sides of the Atlantic, has not defined the emergence of democracy as it exists at present in each culture.

None of this would have surprised Niebuhr. Indeed, it could almost be seen as a sub-text of his theological-political ethics. The subtle interplay of religion and the empirical at the heart of all this was also played out in Niebuhr's understanding of social ethics. Christian doctrine could not be applied directly to the political process but, equally, the ignoring of 'theological insight' Niebuhr believed has been a weakness of that same process, as much of the argument in the foregoing essays indicates. So, the justice which should be part of the outflow of democracy is not simply a matter of prescribing what love requires. There is instead a mediating process which cannot result in precision about justice as derived from love. Picking up the argument about democracy set out above we find Niebuhr arguing: 'Rules of justice do not follow in a "necessary manner" from some basic proposition of justice. They are the fruit of a rational survey of the whole field of human interests, of the structure of human life and of the causal sequences in human relations.'[32]

Hence the engagement of the empirical and the theological is made very plain. With regard to the practicalities of social ethics, the Oxford Conferences on Church, Community and State in 1937 provoked talk of 'middle axioms'. This approach was worked out by John C. Bennett at Union Seminary,[33] and also by Ronald Preston in Britain,[34] both disciples of Niebuhr. William Temple similarly applauded such an approach.[35] Niebuhr admired the work of Bennett and others but did not use insights behind such an approach to engage history, theology, and an empirical approach to ethics.

---

[32] Reinhold Niebuhr, *Faith and History: A Comparison of Christian and Modern Views of History* (New York: Scribner's, 1949), 193.

[33] Cf. John C. Bennett, *Christian Ethics and Social Policy* (New York: Scribner's, 1946). See esp. pp. 59, 76–7.

[34] Ronald Preston, 'Middle Axioms in Christian Social Ethics', *Crucible* (Jan./Feb. 1971), 9–15; and later in *Explorations in Theology* 9 (London: SCM Press, 1981), 37–44.

[35] William Temple, *Christianity and Social Order* (Harmondsworth: Penguin Books, 1942). See for example the principles set out on pp. 98 ff.

Still running through this discussion, then, are they key strands of Niebuhr's theological anthropology and his sociological analysis. His views on democracy were, as ever, rooted in realism but inspired by the vision of the Christian Gospel and notably in the redemption promised in Jesus Christ.

Some of the more recent critiques of Niebuhr's work have helped put him into historical perspective and allowed us to see where his weaknesses and lacunae lay. They do not, however, always engage with the full spectrum of his thought and by failing to do so easily parody some of his sharper prophetic reflections. They fail to see the immediate Christian roots of his social ethical analysis. It may be fitting, in conclusion, to repeat the final sentences of Robin Lovin's chapter, themselves a classic reflection of Christian realism:

The final meaning of history lies beyond the narratives of triumph, tragedy, and irony by which we make sense of it for ourselves. Christian faith tells us that, but it does not provide a theological alternative to deciding between the concrete possibilities available to us. In historical perspective, Reinhold Niebuhr appears to be someone who was increasingly aware of the dignity and misery of that distinctly human task. He did not always get it right, but he saw enough of the possibilities and limits to help us find our way through our own difficult and very different choices.[36]

The implications of Lovin's comment and of this conclusion, then, is that a revised Niebuhrian critique is not only a possible but a necessary component within a developed social ethic. It is a critique which can be applied across the board to economic and political ethics and to the ethics of war and peace. Criticisms of Niebuhr do not undermine but instead refine his argument: *Christian Realism* is an essential part of a developed moral theology but it should heed the warnings encountered in these essays and benefit from the revisions implied.

[36] Lovin, this volume, p. 17.

Select Bibliography

Major Works and Collections by Reinhold Niebuhr

Reinhold Niebuhr, *Leaves from the Notebook of a Tamed Cynic* (San Francisco: Harper and Row, 1929).

——*Moral Man and Immoral Society: A Study in Ethics and Politics* (Louisville: Westminster John Knox Press, 2001) [originally published 1933].

——*An Interpretation of Christian Ethics* (New York: Seabury Press, 1979) [originally published 1935].

——*Christianity and Power Politics* (Hamden, CT: Archon, 1969) [originally published 1940].

——*Beyond Tragedy* (New York: Scribner Book Company, 1979) [originally published 1938].

——*The Nature and Destiny of Man* (Louisville: Westminster John Knox Press, 1996) [originally published 1941, 1943].

——*The Children of Light and the Children of Darkness: A Vindication of Democracy and a Critique of Its Traditional Defence* (London: Nisbet and Co., 1945).

——*Faith and History: A Comparison of Christian and Modern Views of History* (New York: Scribner's, 1949).

——*The Irony of American History* (Chicago: University of Chicago Press, 2008) [originally published 1952].

——*Christian Realism and Political Problems* (New York: Scribner's, 1953).

——*The Self and the Dramas of History* (New York: Scribner's, 1955).

——*Love and Justice: Selections from the Shorter Writings of Reinhold Niebuhr*, ed. D. B. Robertson (Louisville: Westminster John Knox Press, 1992) [originally published, 1957].

——*The Godly and the Ungodly* (London: Faber & Faber, 1959) [published in the US as *Pious and Secular America*].

——*Essays in Applied Christianity*, ed. D. B. Robertson (Cleveland: The World Publishing Co., 1959).

——*The Structure of Nations and Empires: A Study of Recurring Patterns and Problems of the Political Order in Relation to the Unique Problems of the Nuclear Age* (New York: Scribner's, 1959).

——*Faith and Politics*, ed. Ronald Stone (New York: George Braziller, 1968).

——*Justice and Mercy*, ed. Ursula M. Niebuhr (New York: Harper and Row, 1974).

Niebuhr, Ursula (ed.), *Remembering Reinhold Niebuhr: Letters of Reinhold and Ursula M. Niebuhr* (New York: HarperCollins, 1991).

Secondary Sources on Reinhold Niebuhr

Bingham, June, *Courage to Change: An Introduction to the Life and Thought of Reinhold Niebuhr* (New York: Scribner's, 1961).

Brown, Charles C., *Niebuhr and His Age: Reinhold Niebuhr's Prophetic Role and Legacy*, new edn. (Harrisburg: Trinity Press International, 2002).

Brown, Robert McAfee (ed.), *The Essential Reinhold Niebuhr: Selected Essays and Addresses* (New Haven: Yale University Press, 1986).

Clark, Henry B., *Serenity, Courage, and Wisdom: The Enduring Legacy of Reinhold Niebuhr* (Cleveland: Pilgrim Press, 1994).

Durkin, Kenneth, *Reinhold Niebuhr* (London: Cassell, 1989; Harrisburg, PA: Morehead, 1989).

Fox, Richard Wightman, *Reinhold Niebuhr: A Biography* (New York: Pantheon Books, 1985).

Fackre, Gabriel, 'Was Reinhold Niebuhr a Christian?' *First Things*, 126 (Oct. 2002), 25–7.

Gilkey, Langdon, 'Reinhold Niebuhr's Theology of History', *Journal of Religion*, 54 (Oct. 1974), 360–86.

——— *On Niebuhr: A Theological Study* (Chicago: University of Chicago Press, 2001).

Halliwell, Martin, *The Constant Dialogue: Reinhold Niebuhr and American Intellectual Culture* (Lanham, MD: Rowman & Littlefield, 2005).

Harland, Gordon, *The Thought of Reinhold Niebuhr* (New York: Oxford University Press, 1960).

Harries, Richard (ed.), *Reinhold Niebuhr and the Issues of Our Time* (London: Mowbray, 1986).

Kamergrauzis, Normunds, *The Persistence of Christian Realism: A Study in the Social Ethics of Ronald H. Preston* (Uppsala: Acta Universitatis Upsaliensis, 2001).

Kegley, Charles W. and Robert W. Bretall (eds.), *Reinhold Niebuhr: His Religious, Social, and Political Thought* (New York: Macmillan, 1956).

Lindbeck, George, 'Revelation, Natural Law, and the Thought of Reinhold Niebuhr', *Natural Law Forum*, 4 (1959), 146–51.

Lovatt, Mark F. W., *Confronting the Will-to-Power: A Reconsideration of the Theology of Reinhold Niebuhr* (Carlisle: Paternoster Press, 2001).

Lovin, Robin, *Reinhold Niebuhr and Christian Realism* (Cambridge: Cambridge University Press, 1995).

——— *Christian Realism and the New Realities* (Cambridge: Cambridge University Press, 2008).

Macgregor, G. H. C., *The Relevance of the Impossible: A Reply to Reinhold Niebuhr* (London: The Fellowship of Reconciliation, 1941).

Marty, Martin, 'Reinhold Niebuhr: Public Theology and the American Experience', *Journal of Religion*, 54 (Oct. 1974), 332–59.

McCann, Dennis, *Christian Realism and Liberation Theology: Practical Theologies in Creative Conflict* (Mary Knoll, NY: Orbis Books, 1981).

McKeogh, Colm, *The Political Realism of Reinhold Niebuhr: A Pragmatic Approach to Just War* (New York: St. Martin's Press, 1997).

Ramsey, Paul, 'Reinhold Niebuhr: Christian Love and Natural Law', in *Nine Modern Moralists* (Englewood Cliffs: Prentice Hall, Inc., 1962), 111–47.

Rasmussen, Larry (ed.), *Reinhold Niebuhr: Theologian of Public Life* (London: Harper & Row, 1988) [contains commentary with excerpts from Niebuhr's writings].

Rice, Daniel F., *Reinhold Niebuhr and John Dewey: An American Odyssey* (Albany: SUNY Press, 1993).

Scott, Nathan A. (ed.), *The Legacy of Reinhold Niebuhr* (Chicago: University of Chicago Press, 1975).

Sifton, Elisabeth, *The Serenity Prayer: Faith and Politics in Times of Peace and War* (New York: Norton, 2003).

Stone, Ronald H., *Professor Reinhold Niebuhr: A Mentor to the Twentieth Century* (Louisville: Westminster John Knox Press, 1992).

Warren, Heather A., *Theologians of a New World Order: Reinhold Niebuhr and the Christian Realists 1920–1948* (New York: Oxford University Press, 1997).

Other Resources and Studies of Christian Realism

Bennett, John C., *Christian Realism* (London: Student Christian Movement Press, 1941).

Dorrien, Gary, *Soul and Society: The Making and Renewing of Social Christianity* (Minneapolis: Fortress Press, 1995).

——*Idealism, Realism, and Modernity, 1900–1950,* ii: *The Making of American Liberal Theology* (Louisville: Westminster John Knox Press, 2003).

Hauerwas, Stanley, *With the Grain of the Universe: The Church's Witness and Natural Theology* (Grand Rapids, MI: Brazos Press, 2001).

Horton, Walter Marshall, *Realistic Theology* (New York: Harper, 1934).

Macintosh, Douglas Clyde, *Religious Realism* (New York: Macmillan, 1931).

Meyer, Donald B., *The Protestant Search for Political Realism, 1919–1941* (Los Angeles: University of California Press, 1960).

Ottati, Douglas, *Hopeful Realism* (Cleveland: Pilgrim Press, 1989).

West, Charles C., *Communism and the Theologians: Study of an Encounter* (London: SCM Press, 1958).

West, Cornel, *The American Evasion of Philosophy: A Genealogy of Pragmatism* (Madison: University of Wisconsin, 1989).

——*Democracy Matters* (New York: The Penguin Press, 2004).

Bibliographical Resources

Robertson, D. B., *Reinhold Niebuhr's Works: A Bibliography* (Lanham, MD: University Press of America, 1983) [Robertson provides the definitive bibliography of Reinhold Niebuhr's works, with significant secondary sources through 1983].

Kegley, Charles W. (ed.), *Reinhold Niebuhr: His Religious, Social, and Political Thought*, 2nd edn. (New York: The Pilgrim Press, 1984) [the Bibliography provides an accessible and extensive selection from Niebuhr's writings].

Brown, Charles C., *Niebuhr and His Age: Reinhold Niebuhr's Prophetic Role and Legacy*, new edn. (Harrisburg, PA: Trinity Press International, 2002) [this new edition has a significant bibliography (pp. 311–16), including new publications of Niebuhr's works and new secondary sources].

Halliwell, Martin, *The Constant Dialogue: Reinhold Niebuhr and American Intellectual Culture*. (Lanham, MD: Rowman and Littlefield Publishers, 2005) [the Bibliography contains an extensive selection of writings from and about Niebuhr].

On-line Resources

'Moral Man and Immoral Society: The Public Theology of Reinhold Niebuhr— Links and Resources', <http://speakingoffaith.publicradio.org/programs/niebuhr-rediscovered/links.shtml>.

The Niebuhr Society, 'Links', <http://www.niebuhrsociety.org/links.htm>.

Reinhold Niebuhr: *A Register of His Papers in the Library of Congress* (1984), <http://www.loc.gov//rr/mss/text/niebuhr.html>.

Index